Feminist Parenting

edited by

Lynn Comerford, Heather Jackson,
and Kandee Kosior

DEMETER

DEMETER PRESS

Funded by the Government of Canada
Financé par la gouvernement du Canada | Canada

Demeter Press
140 Holland Street West
P. O. Box 13022
Bradford, ON L3Z 2Y5
Tel: (905) 775-9089
Email: info@demeterpress.org
Website: www.demeterpress.org

FSC www.fsc.org MIX Paper from responsible sources FSC® C004071

Demeter Press logo based on the sculpture "Demeter" by Maria-Luise Bodirsky <www.keramik-atelier.bodirsky.de>

Printed and Bound in Canada

Front cover artwork: Lucy Hare, "Body," 2015, acrylic, 16 inches x 20inches. Website: @lhareart on Facebook or Lucy V Hare.

Library and Archives Canada Cataloguing in Publication

Feminist parenting / edited by Lynn Comerford, Heather Jackson, and Kandee Kosior.

Includes bibliographical references.
ISBN 978-1-77258-019-8 (paperback)

1. Parenting. 2. Feminism. 3. Mothers. 4. Motherhood. 5. Sex role. I. Jackson, Heather, 1982–, author, editor II. Comerford, Lynn, 1962–, author, editor III. Kosior, Kandee, 1967–, editor

HQ755.8.F44 2016 649'.1 C2016-904530-7

For Eleanor

—L. C.

Becoming a mother made me more aware of the world.
For Lyric, who made me want to create a better world for her,
me, and everyone else.

—H. J.

For Jim, who adventures beside me daily,
with love.

—K. K.

Table of Contents

Acknowledgements

This book would not exist without our team of generous, enthusiastic, and like-minded supporters. We wish to warmly thank Andrea O'Reilly, founder and senior editor of Demeter Press, for providing us the opportunity to put together this edited collection. We thank Angie Deveau, whose administrative and marketing support have been essential to the project. We are especially grateful to our copyeditor, Jesse O'Reilly-Conlin, and to our helpful reviewers, who provided immense clarity, insight, and inspiration.

We benefited greatly from our authors. Thank you for responding to our call and for sharing with us your academic inquiries, personal narratives, professional observations, and artistic creations. Thank you to the feminist parents who shared their stories with us. Your words inspire us to search for ways to bring feminism into our daily lives.

We sincerely thank our colleagues, partners, and friends, who listened, advised, encouraged, and otherwise kept us sane as we went through the book editing process: Barbara Lee, Carol Jones, Linn Baron, Leeann Debert, Sydney Bell, Mike da Cruz, Crystal Michels, and Chantal Tape.

Mostly, we would like to express our heartfelt gratitude to our families, who inspire us to practice feminism at a most intimate and personally satisfying level: Emily, Clayton, and Benen Powers; Michael and Eleanor Huspek; Lyric Langill; and Jasmine Sakak and Zack Sakak.

Introduction

LYNN COMERFORD, HEATHER JACKSON, AND KANDEE KOSIOR

This edited collection sheds light on feminist parenting, describes parents who identify as feminists, and offers insight on intersectional feminist family values. Feminist parenting affects the political, economic, emotional, symbolic, and physical conditions of women's and men's lives. To be a feminist parent is to confront and correct systemic gender inequalities and injustices associated with parenting children. Feminist scholars studying intimate relationships argue that gender stratification, as a lens, is helpful to expose families as gendered institutions (Hill). The contributors to this collection, with wit and wisdom, expose families as gendered and unequal institutions. Readers will be interested in our essays, academic summaries, and poems because they offer reflections on and strategies for those committed to gender equality in the family.

Feminist Parenting combines scholarly, creative, and activist responses to the topic in poetry, first-person personal essays, research, and scholarly analyses. These chapters offer sociological, queer, intergenerational, interracial, and international perspectives on the challenges and rewards of being a feminist parent. The contributors to the collection provide perspectives on feminist parenting from the fields of psychology, sociology, women's studies, social work, and literature; and they add to the current literature on feminism, parenting, gender, and family life.

The topic of feminist parenting is important because it focuses on reducing and eliminating sexism in the family. Feminists argue that gender is a system of stratification that is reproduced and socially constructed (Risman). Because the family is a system in which gender inequality is often enacted and reproduced, it is important to study how parenting contributes to this dynamic. The twenty-three contributors to this book inspire readers to consciously parent from a feminist perspective, by which respecting individual rights and opposing acts of domination and oppression is fundamental. Feminism has encouraged women to make their own choices rather than having their choices made for them by individuals and powerful social forces. For women to be free, they must be free from the demands of compulsory motherhood, must have access to birth control and abortion, and must choose to become a parent (as opposed to it being a biological or cultural mandate). Parenthood, from a feminist perspective, must be a free choice for all women: young women, poor women, women of colour, LGBTQ women, transgender women, and more.

This collection about feminist parenting is important at this time because the family is undergoing enormous change in many parts of the world. Changes in household economics, family composition, and family formation affect the balance of power in families and parenting behaviour. Feminist parents believe that women should have equal rights with men including economic, political, social and personal rights in private and public life. In the private realm, feminist parents are particularly sensitive to the issues of inequality, dominance, subordination, and oppression in the family and are committed to eradicating inequality.

There is a need for a volume on feminist parenting. Feminist perspectives are often missing from family studies (Allen). An assessment of the amount of feminist research in the journals *Journal of Marriage and Family, Journal of Family Issues,* and *Family Relations* finds that although feminist perspectives grew between the years 1972 to 1992; but after 1992, they stalled because feminist researchers feared being labelled as activists rather than as scholars (Wills and Risman). Feminism is not just a perspective through which to analyze family behaviour. It is also a philosophy that advocates for social justice.

The book is divided into four parts. The first part defines and introduces the topic feminist parenting; the second part describes the ways in which feminist parenting is resisted (both from within and from outside the family); the third part emphasizes the ways in which power and inequality necessitate feminist parenting; and the final section of the book examines feminist parenting from international perspectives. Each theme introduces readers to the topic and provides a scholarly framework for the following themes and chapters. Poems were selected as a way to introduce and transition readers into each of the book's four themes.

A good place to begin a discussion of feminist parenting is with Simone de Beauvoir's oft-quoted line "One is not born, but becomes a woman," as feminist parenting focuses on cultural norms and social expectations (rather than biology) to explain parenting behaviour. Beauvoir shatters the notions that people have a procreative drive or possess a maternal drive to reproduce and rear children. In addition, work by Nancy Chodorow in *The Reproduction of Mothering*, Dorothy Dinnerstein in *The Mermaid and the Minotaur*, and Juliet Mitchell in *Psychoanalysis and Feminism* examine the ways in which family gender dynamics, and not biology, explain differences between maternal and paternal behaviour. Legal theorists—such as Martha Fineman in *Mothers in Law* and Carol Smart in *Feminism and the Power of Law*—wanting to protect the maternal argue that law should elevate a "morality of relationship" (gender equity) over a "morality of rights" (gender equality). This scholarship reflects the social experiences of the households that they studied, which were made up of heterosexual, white, middle-class, and married parents.

Recent scholarship on the family, in contrast, emphasizes the social construction of sexuality and intimate arrangements and the enormous range and diversity of family life. It also examines power. Kath Weston's book *Families We Choose: Lesbians, Gays, Kinship,* Kathryn Edin and Marla Kefalas's study *Promises I Can Keep: Why Poor Women Put Motherhood Before Marriage,* and Chandra Talpade Mohanty's pivotal article "Under Western Eyes: Feminist Scholarship and Colonial Discourses," for example, expand notions of the family and the ways in which scholars study them. Recent scholarship encourages us to include postcolonial and transnational examinations of the family through an intersectional analysis of gender, race, ethnicity, sexuality, nation, and colonialism. The authors in this collection offer a remarkable array of essays from intersectional and transnational perspectives and captivate the reader with their observations on family diversity, the possibilities for equality in the family, and the personal triumphs and disappointments in feminist parenting.

PART ONE: WHAT IS FEMINIST PARENTING?

The 1950s Parsonian model of the heterosexual nuclear family as the bedrock of society, in which women play the "emotional" role and men play the "instrumental" role, was argued to be the optimal place to socialize children and a place to meet the psychological needs of parents (Parsons and Bales). Propelled by the civil rights movement, the women's movement, and the LBGT movement, a profound shift towards egalitarianism in family life has transpired since the 1950s. Feminists have challenged the inequality and heteronormative assumptions embedded in the Parsonian model of the family. By the 1970s, feminists had exposed and rejected the sexism in organized religion, which claims motherhood is a "divine command" for all women, as well as the bans on contraception use. Since the 1970s, many feminists have also challenged the latent ethnocentrism found in a lot of white feminist theory on mothering (Lugones; DiQuinzio; Bailey).

Since the 1950s, when 15 percent of marriages ended in divorce and less than 20 percent of women with children at home were engaged in full- or part-time paid work, a dramatic shift in parenting has happened in the United States. Today, approximately half of all marriages end in divorce; over 80 percent of custodial parents are women; and over 70 percent of these mothers are employed. Times have changed. These changes have ignited new feminist understandings of parenting and the family.

The idea that feminist parenting does not perpetuate patriarchal power dynamics is explored by Elizabeth Ann Bartlett in her chapter "Feminist Parenting as the Practice of Non-domination: Lessons from Adrienne Rich, Audre Lorde, Sara Ruddick, and Iris Marion Young." Bartlett compares and contrasts Iris Marion Young's philosophy of non-oppression and non-domination, Audre Lorde's writings on the value of authenticity, Adrienne Rich's requirements of an honourable relationship, and Sara Ruddick's philosophy of maternal thinking to the practice of feminist parenting. Bartlett examines how feminist parenting challenges those who enforce authority over children and mandate gender norms, and argues that a basic tenant of feminist parenting is to not oppress or dominate others.

Andrea O'Reilly, in her chapter "Feminist Mothering," stresses the need for women to be empowered by their choice to mother. She explores the term "feminist mothering" as an issue of individual freedom and describes an oppositional discourse of motherhood that is empowering to women. O'Reilly finds that feminist mothering is courageous and signifies maternal practices that resist and refuse patriarchal motherhood. Feminist parents reject patriarchal and pronatalist beliefs that having children is how one becomes "a real woman," "fulfilled," "a valued citizen," or an "adult." Instead, feminist parents believe that becoming a parent is an issue of individual freedom.

The idea that women are able to make their own choices is fundamental to feminist parenting, yet feminist parents wrestle with notions of formal equality, autonomy, and the liberal concept of choice. In her chapter "The Potential for Feminist Parenting," Lynn Comerford examines the terms "mother" and "father" in the context of child custody law in the United States between the years 1800 and 2000 and asks: have mothers and fathers been trapped in a gendered hierarchical binary for centuries? Or have the meanings of the terms "mother" and "father" shifted over time in a feminist direction? Comerford traces how custody law has evolved from granting fathers custody in the nineteenth century, to granting mothers custody in the twentieth century, and to eliminating gender as a variable in custody decisions in California today. She finds, however, that gender-neutral and equal physical and legal co-custody parenting after divorce is feminist if there was gender-neutral, equal feminist parenting in the family prior to the divorce or separation.

PART TWO: RESISTANCE TO FEMINIST PARENTING

Authors in this section examine the ways in which resistance dynamics construct experiences of "doing feminist parenting." Feminist parents challenge gender norms and often face discrimination from those threatened by challenges to traditional notions of motherhood and fatherhood. Many authors draw from ideas first elaborated in Adrienne Rich's essay "Compulsory Heterosexuality and Lesbian Existence" and Judith Butler's book *Gender Trouble*, in which presumptions about sexuality, household composition, and parenting are challenged. Heather Jackson challenges non-normative parenting approaches in her chapter "Mothering on Their Own Terms: How Single, Queer, and Feminist Mothering Deconstruct Patriarchy, Gender, and the Nuclear Family." Jackson examines parenting "appropriateness," and how it has been ascribed to mothers. In her interviews with young, poor, single mothers who do not fit into the traditional notion of who a "mother" should be, she reveals how they queer the world around them by resisting heteronormativity, binary gender identities, and rigid family structures. Jackson gives voice to the small revolutionary daily acts committed by women mothering on their own terms, which challenge heterosexual privilege, gender hierarchy, and the nuclear family.

Feminist parents argue that one's gender, sexual orientation, marital status, or biological relationship does not determine parenting ability, and they resist arguments that each could. At the same time, feminist parents understand that all parents struggle to raise their children in a world stratified by gender, race, class, nationality, sexuality, ability as well as by many other identity markers. In "Wild, Child: Reflections at the Intersection of Nature, Gender, Race, and Parenthood," Kate Parsons focuses on how race, gender, and ecological binaries shape her young daughter's worldview in ways that she cannot control. Parsons wants her daughter, her wild child, to run with abandon, flaunt authority, and revel in getting dirty. She contrasts her desire for her daughter to act with abandon with a bunny's wildness located in its rapt attention and watchfulness, and she wonders if the bunny's wildness is superior. This kind of wildness, Parsons argues, may form the basis for deeper ecological learning and awareness. To embrace the wild, she suggests, may be to slow down and pay attention to the surrounding environment.

Feminist parents who teach countercultural messages to their children engage in a daily struggle. Transgender countercultural messages are particularly helpful for feminist parents because they resist the idea that there is a binary gender system and encourage children to understand gender as a fluid and a multiple identity. Shannon Drury in her chapter "Childhood Phobia" explores her young daughter's gender transgressions and worries about what these transgressions mean for her daughter's future. If her playful female child is transgender, Drury wonders, will she be accepted and loved? Or will she be a victim of a hate crime? Drury argues that although the LBGT civil rights movement describes gender and sexuality on fluid spectrums, anxious parents, even feminist ones, worry about the soul-killing experiences ahead for children who do not fit neatly into gender stereotypes. She describes the tension that she experiences wanting her daughter's childhood to be a time for exploration yet, at the same time, wanting her to "fit in" and know gender codes.

Feminist parenting affects the political, economic, emotional, symbolic, and physical conditions of women's and men's lives and feminist parenting resistance strategies have been around a long time. Quincie Melville revisits the 1960s when it seemed as if all the white, middle-class women whom she knew stayed home to raise a family, except for her maternal grandmother (Mamaw), paternal grandmother (Mimi), and her Aunt Jean, all of whom influenced her. Melville describes the confidence, independence, and joy that the women experienced as working mothers postdivorce in her chapter "My Grandmothers: The Real Powerholders in the Family."

Mamaw taught Melville that she did not need to depend on a man to take care of her economically and that being self-sufficient allows one to make better relationship choices. Mimi was a stay-at-home mother who took pride in her unpaid family labor. Melville describes her grandmothers as feminist icons who taught her to be strong for her adopted son who was placed with her by his birthmother. She describes how the lessons of courage, kindness, strength, and unconditional love, which she learned from her feminist pioneer elders, are being passed onto her son, for whom strong women are the norm. Melville instills feminist values in her son with the hope that the legacy of feminist parenting, begun by the generations who preceded him, will continue to resonate in future generations.

The positive feminist parenting values of strength, love, equality, and open mindedness can be challenging for parents to adopt, especially in a culture that has fairly rigid expectations about gender performance. In her chapter "The Whole of My Child," Jana Bühlmann describes the explosive anger that her young daughter exhibits, and she realizes that her daughter's behaviour encourages her to reflect critically on her own feelings and behaviour. As a feminist parent, Bühlmann worries that the world is "chipping away" at her daughter's strength and confidence and wonders if it is her job to protect her daughter from this process or allow her to be "nicked." Rather than moving in an authoritarian direction to try to control her child, Bühlmann, as a feminist parent, engages in collaborative decision making instead and feels the humility of parenthood as a process of active learning. Feminist parents, such as Bühlmann, recognize and resist patriarchy as oppressive and work to reverse gender inequality and naturalize equality in their day-to-day parenting practices.

PART THREE: STORIES OF POWER AND INEQUALITY IN THE FAMILY

It is important to understand what feminist parenting is, and what it is not. The authors in this section focus on power and inequality in the family, with a particular emphasis on male violence and masculinity. According to the "spillover hypothesis," adults in relationships in which there is stress and anger-related intimate partner violence act out on these feelings in the parent-child relationship (Krishnakumar and Buehler). There is also a substantial co-occurrence of intimate partner violence and child abuse (Jouriles et al.). Intimate partner violence has been linked to problematic child outcomes and is associated with problems in children of all ages (Kitzmann et. al.). Many of the chapters in this section focus on the opposite of feminist parenting: gendered domestic terror. It is hard to maintain gender equality in a home in which there is domestic violence and other struggles of power.

Authors Marilyn Metta and Mae are survivors of patriarchal terrorism and courageously share their experience in their chapter "Embodying Feminist Mothering: Narratives of Resilience through Patriarchal Terrorism from Both a Mother's and Child's Perspective." Feminist resistance narratives speak out against male violence, which has no place in feminist parenting. Metta and Mae weave parent and child survivor stories of gendered domestic violence to examine patriarchal terrorism, whereby men control "their" women and children through violence or threats of violence. The authors draw from their own experiences to examine the role that they had in their family and how they survived and recovered.

Metta and Mae explore how fathers manipulate their parenting status and use their children to stop women from leaving an abusive relationship or to force them back into one. The authors describe how women who flee abusive men are often forced to leave at a moment's opportunity, with no money and without their children. Metta and Mae find that children living with patriarchal terrorism are witnesses of, and exposed to, multiple aspects of violence and abuse within the family, and their mothers are often forced to choose between escaping the violence without their children to save their own lives or staying in a violent environment, in the hope that they can protect their children from it.

Rachel O'Donnell remembers the power struggles that she grew up with in her chapter "'That's Not What Boys Do': Mothering a Boy Child, Permitting Masculinity, and Coming to Terms with Manhood." O'Donnell's childhood home was characterized by a "militaristic masculinity" and a "general disrespect for women." She describes her father as a man of extremes: he was either asleep or wide awake and yelling. She remembers being pulled by her ear when she was in "his" chair as well as his loud swearing and threats. Her father created a family home that was homophobic, unemotional, and sometimes, violent. When she was a child, her father would frequently remark: "your mother is stupid." She contrasts her father's behaviour to the feminist parenting that she engages in with her partner and their daily commitment to parent their son "with kindness and without violence." Reflecting on her own childhood, O'Donnell shares the stark contrast between the parenting that she experienced as a child and the feminist parenting she and her male partner engage in with their young son.

Fortunately, power and inequality in families infrequently manifest themselves as intimate partner physical violence. Unfortunately, power and inequality in families frequently manifest themselves as inequality in childcare and housework allocation. When one sex ends up with the lion's share of childcare and housework, it indicates imbalance and often unfairness. Arlie Hochchild describes the gendered battle over housework and childcare in her book *The Second Shift.* She describes the "second shift" as the period after women leave their paid-work employment to engage in unpaid work in the family; her study is a primer on power and inequality in the heterosexual home. One may think that LGBT families would naturally be more sensitive about unpaid childcare and housework allocation; however, as Johanna Wagner describes in her chapter "I Was Ward Cleaver: An Apologia," it is not necessarily true. Wagner humorously reflects on her life as a self-described lesbian parent and feminist (sometimes referred to as "father" or "co-mother" on legal forms), and she discovers to her amazement that she has morphed into a feminist's nightmare: she has turned into the 1950s chauvinistic father figure Ward Cleaver.

In her chapter, Wagner, an American, describes meeting a younger woman from Belgium with whom she established an intimate relationship and had children. Wagner, a feminist scholar, soon found that the sexist domestic roles she had absorbed in her youth, long before feminism, were being blindly reproduced by none other than herself in her new young family. At a young age, Wagner knew "mothers" represented a kind of "feminine" that she was uninterested in, a feminine that was the bearer of children and therefore the carer of children. Since she had no intention of bearing a child, her reasoning went, she would not have to do much caring either; therefore caring was kept to a minimum. But, as her feminist consciousness recognized her internal struggle with the unequal power dynamic that she permitted in her young family, it forced her to confront her latent sexism. This distant, hands-off parenting role she had taken on was more like the patriarchal "father" of Leave it to Beaver, a character whom she despised. Wagner's descriptions of her trials and tribulations on her journey to embrace her role as a feminist parent and mother are as entertaining as they are inspiring.

Sexual identity and gender identity are paramount in any consideration of feminist parenting, as are race and social class. Dorothy Roberts argues in *Killing the Black Body* that because nonwhites disproportionately live below the poverty line, class is racialized in the United States. Race affects parenting uniquely. Moreover, Patricia Hill Collins in her book *Black Feminist Thought* describes three goals of racial-ethnic women's motherwork: 1) raise children to protect themselves physically (including how to interact with police, shopkeepers, and racists) because of their high mortality rates; 2) develop in children a positive sense of racial-ethnic identity and individual self-definition while living in a white dominant society (socializing children for acceptance into white society and simultaneously teaching them to resist white norms); and 3) centre maternal empowerment as an explicit goal for racial-ethnic mothers in order for them to achieve their child-centered maternal goals and not allow the dominant cultures' racialized views to affect either them or their children.

Lesley Bunnell examines power and inequality from the perspective of a black, queer, working-poor, single mother of a mixed-race, middle-school-aged daughter in her chapter "Gymnastics and Equality." Bunnell describes her experience navigating her way through the white, upper-middle class, heteronormative world of competitive girl's gymnastics, in which her daughter participates. She spends a lot of time with people with whom she would not ordinarily interact and makes some insightful observations. In her chapter, she highlights the material possessions, status, and wealth that her fellow "gym moms" appear to centre their lives around. Bunnell's sophisticated feminist perspective provides a vivid window into the lives of "gym moms," who live their lives in stark contrast to hers and her daughter's. Bunnell's observations show that "white, heterosexual privilege" is a mixed bag. She finds that in contrast to their lives exuding upper-middle class white privilege, she prefers her authentic life as a black, queer, working-poor, single mother because her values elevate community over consumption and soulfulness over status. Bunnell concludes that dreams for gender equity and equality are far more vital and empowering than dreams for a new kitchen.

PART FOUR: INTERNATIONAL VOICES AND PERSPECTIVES ON FEMINIST PARENTING

Feminist parenting cannot be examined without also examining the intersection of gender, race, economic status, ethnicity, religion, marital status, ability, sexuality, and nationality, among the many identities that people inhabit. Feminist parents understand that identity is located in the tensions between these social locations. Particular norms, cultures, and ideologies shape and determine how people are "recruited" into families (Hann). In the United States, for example, during early childhood, the vast majority of mothers engage in more childcare work than fathers (Pleck and Masciadrelli). However, because individuals are shaped by many social forces, it is not necessarily true that this gendered early childhood parenting work has to reproduce itself in the future. What is a "good" or a "bad" father or what is a "good" or "bad" mother depends on social context, and the answers vary historically. In this section, the contributors provide international perspectives on the challenges of raising children in a complex world from feminist intersectional perspectives.

Contributors from Canada, Pakistan, Poland, and the United States examine the topic of feminist parenting and shine a light on the ways in which nation, gender, and inequality collide in family life. Although the international perspectives on feminist parenting in this collection differ significantly from one another, patriarchy and heterosexual normativity emerge as transnational themes feminists parents confront as they contest gendered parenting practices and gender inequality. Additionally, what it means to be a feminist parent from an international perspective also emerges. Transnationally, feminists argue that parenting must be a choice and that there must be free, accessible birth control and abortion on demand. They also challenge traditional gender roles and question inequality. Furthermore, feminists around the globe urge family members to engage one another with warmth, mutual respect, and mutual consideration, in clear, age-appropriate communication. Moreover, feminist parents across nations seek state support for the family, particularly high-quality, affordable public childcare.

This section on international perspectives on feminist parenting begins with a chapter by Pamela Redela, a self-described middle-class American woman. She describes what it is like to be a feminist parent living in coastal Southern California in her chapter "Can Ecofeminism Save the World?: Eco-mommas and Their Quest to

Raise Feminist and Environmentally Conscious Children." Redela shines a light on the pressures placed on "eco-mommas" in this part of the world and describes what it is like to feel the pressure to raise perfect kids, save the planet, and always look "hot." In addition to the typical carework involved in raising a family, an "eco-momma" must "think globally and act locally," recycle, say "no" to plastic at the grocery store, rely on chemical-free cleaning products, and either grow her own vegetables or buy organic.

Redela feels these pressures acutely because she lives in a country that is the largest national contributor to global climate warming (Matthews) and is home to Monsanto, the largest and most deadly pesticide manufacturer in the world. Because the country that Redela lives in is such a polluter of the atmosphere, the water, and the soil, she, as an American feminist parent, feels she carries additional burdens and responsibilities and, thus, must embrace the subject position, "eco-momma." An "eco-momma" is a mother who is conscious of her location at the intersection of feminist parenting, concerns about climate change, fears over pesticide-laden food and water, and critiques about American consumption. Becoming an "eco-momma" is an adjustment feminist parents make in their effort to try to improve gender equality in the family, to increase health prospects for their children and future generations, and to limit unnecessary consumption.

Feminist parents around the world want to live sustainable lives. They are concerned about overpopulation and want women to be able to choose whether or when to have children and whether to enter or exit a relationship. This is easier to do in some countries than others. Pakistan is not a country that usually comes to mind when one thinks about feminist parenting; in Pakistan, women are usually the primary parent and children are generally socialized to fulfill gendered adult roles. Anwar Shaheen, in her chapter "Feminist Parenting Strategies in Pakistan," describes Pakistan as a tribal, patriarchal, pronatalist, and multiethnic society, in which motherhood is highly valued and intensive. Shaheen's chapter focuses on the contradictory life options for women in Pakistan. On the one hand, many women have access to higher education and good jobs, yet, on the other hand, women in many ethnic groups, social classes, and religious sects find their educational, employment, and even life partner prospects limited.

Shaheen discovers in her interviews with Pakistani parents that there is much ambivalence surrounding the term "feminism" in Pakistan's feudal and tribal culture. Her interviews with Pakistani parents provide insight into how parenting practices can slowly shift in a feminist direction in a traditional society. Shaheen finds that this shift hinges on feminist fathering. She describes how males have traditionally been given more authority in the family and in public life. Yet, compellingly, she discovers over and over in her interviews with Pakistani fathers that they want more life choices for their daughters. In her interviews, she finds that it is the fathers (more than the mothers) who are the essential element when families raise strong, independent, and educated daughters. Although most Pakistani girls are raised to be submissive, caring, and motherly, in contrast to their brothers, many Pakistani fathers want more opportunities for their daughters and, frequently, subtly plant the seed of gender equality in them during their childhoods. Shaheen's interviews provide a forum for Pakistani fathers to quietly and anonymously share their "closet feminism."

In *The Feminist Mystique*, Betty Friedan exposes white, suburban, middle-class, American motherhood as something for women to escape in order to find work "equal to their capacity" (usually involving higher education). Friedan's analysis, however, overlooks the mothers who were already *in* the workplace, namely working-poor mothers and mothers of colour. Marlene Pomrenke, in stark contrast to Friedan, examines "overlooked mothers" in her chapter "The Stories and Resiliency of Manitoba Aboriginal Single Mothers in University." She interviews Aboriginal mothers fighting racial and economic barriers and attending postsecondary institutions in Canada. She finds that, unlike Friedan's mothers who suffer with "the problem that has no name" (57), Manitoba Aboriginal mothers know precisely what they are up against: poverty, racism, trauma recovery, lack of childcare, abusive marriages, and deadbeat dads. Pomrenke describes how, against the odds, these strong mothers move to urban centres and connect with similarly situated Aboriginal mothers to navigate work, higher education, and childcare. Pomrenke listens closely to these pioneering feminist mothers and, with sensitivity, shares their stories and journeys of struggle and triumph as their newfound alliances between Aboriginal and non-Aboriginal communities raise their prospects and the prospects of their families for a better future.

Studying feminist mothers in Poland, Iza Desperak describes the marginalization of fatherhood in the lives of women and children in her chapter "Lone Motherhood in Poland." Desperak highlights the role that history has played in the high rates of single mothering in Poland today. In her chapter, she describes how during the partition of Poland, women were left alone to raise their children because so many men were killed in the uprisings or were sent to Siberia for life prison sentences, and others fled from the country to avoid persecution. These feminist Polish widows had little choice but to be strong, independent, and industrious in order to scrape together what income they could while raising their fatherless children. Because of so many wars and uprisings, Polish women came to be seen as mother-widows. Yet in 1945, when Catholic Poland joined the Eastern Block, single motherhood lost its taboo because, as Desperak explains, one could always pretend that their husband died during the war. The long history of women bearing sole responsibility for children in Poland, Desperak argues, is used as an excuse today by the Polish government to economically ignore them. The Polish government's family policy emerges out of a history that includes large numbers of Polish women raising fatherless children during times of war with little government support. Desperak argues that contemporary Poland manipulates the history of mother-widows in order to explain current "war time" austerity measures imposed on single mothers.

CONCLUSION

This collection is premised on the idea that increased gender-neutral parenting is a good thing and that the term "parent" is not gender specific. The central theme running throughout this collection is that family is the site in which notions of a fixed, hierarchal gender order are confronted and refuted. The contributors, in many different ways, argue that as women become more legally, politically, socially, and economically equal to men in public life, there is an increased expectation that men, in their role as parents, must necessarily share family responsibilities equally in private life.

Increased recognition of feminist parenting has brought with it an underscoring of the importance of parenting responsibilities, the uniqueness of parenting behaviour, and the potential for a more gender-neutral approach to raising children. In encountering different conceptions and practices of feminist parenting described by the authors in this book, readers are provided the opportunity to reflect on the limitations and potentials of their own approach to parenting as well as on the cultural, legal, and economic structures that frame parenting choices.

WORKS CITED

Allen, Katherine. "A Conscious and Inclusive Family Studies." *Journal of Marriage and the Family*, vol. 62, no. 1, 2000, pp. 4-17.

Bailey, Alison. "Mothering, Diversity, and Peace: Comments on Sara Ruddick's Feminist Maternal Peace Politics." *Journal of Social Philosophy*, vol. 25, no. 1, 1995, pp. 162-182.

Beauvoir, Simone. *The Second Sex*. Vintage, 1952.

Butler, Judith. *Gender Trouble*. Routledge, 1989.

Chodorow, Nancy. *The Reproduction of Mothering*. University of California Press, 1978.

Collins, Patricia Hill. *Black Feminist Thought*. Routledge, 1991.

Dinnerstein, Dorothy. *The Mermaid and the Minotaur*. Harper & Row, 1976.

DiQuinzio, Patrice. "Exclusion and Essentialism in Feminist Theory: The Problem of Mothering." *Hypatia* vol. 8, no. 3, 1993, pp. 1-20.

Edin, Kathryn, and Marla Kefalas. *Promises I Can Keep: Why Poor Women Put Motherhood Before Marriage*. University of California Press, 2005.

Friedan, Betty. *The Feminine Mystique*. W.W. Norton and Company, 1963.

Hill, Shirley. *Black Intimacies: A Gender Perspective on Families and Relationships*. AltaMira Press, 2005.

Hochchild, Arlie. *The Second Shift*. Viking Penguin, 1989.

Jouriles, E. N., et al. "Child Abuse in the Context of Domestic Violence: Prevalence, Explanations, and Practice Implications."

Violence and Victims, vol. 23, no. 2, 2008, pp. 221-235.

Kitzmann, K.M., N.K. Gaylord, A.R. Holt, and E.D. Kenny. "Child Witnesses to Domestic Physical Violence: A Meta-analytic Review." *Journal of Consulting and Clinical Psychology*, vol. 71, no. 2, 2003, pp. 339-352.

Krishnakumar, A., and C. Buehler. "Inter-Parental Conflict and Parenting Behaviors: A Meta-Analytic Review." *Family Relations*, vol. 49, no. 1, 2000, pp. 25-44.

Lugones, Maria. "On the Logic of Pluralist Feminism." *Feminist* Ethics, edited by Claudia Card, University of Kansas Press, 1991, pp. 35-44.

Matthews, Damon. "Climate Change: United States Tops Warming List." *Nature*, vol. 506, no. 7486, 2014, pp. 9.

Mitchell, Juliet. *Psychoanalysis and Feminism.* Pantheon Books, 1974.

Mohandy, Chandra Talpade. "Under Western Eyes: Feminist Scholarship and Colonial Discourses." *Feminist Review*, vol. 30, 1988, pp. 61-88.

Parsons, T., and R.F. Bales. *Family, Socialization and Interaction Process.* Free Press, 1955.

Pleck, J. H., and B. P. Masciadrelli. "Paternal Involvement by U.S. Residential Fathers: Levels, Sources, and Consequences." *The Role of the Father in Child Development*, edited by M.E. Lamb, Wiley 2004, pp. 222-271.

Rich, Adrienne. *Of Woman Born: Motherhood as Experience and Institution.* W.W. Norton, 1986.

Rich, Adrienne. "Compulsory Heterosexuality and Lesbian Existence." *Signs*, vol. 5, no. 4, 1980, pp. 631-660.

Risman, Judith. *Gender Vertigo.* Yale University Press. 1998.

Roberts, Dorothy. *Killing the Black Body: Race, Reproduction, and the Meaning of Liberty.* Vintage Books, 1997.

Ruddick, Sara. *Maternal Thinking: Towards a Politics of Peace.* Beacon Press, 1989.

Weston, Kath. *Families We Choose: Lesbians, Gays, Kinship.* Columbia University Press, 1991.

Wills, Jeremiah, and Barbara Risman. "The Visibility of Feminist Thought in Family Studies." *Journal of Marriage and Family*, vol. 68, no. 3, 2006, pp. 690-700.

1.
WHAT IS FEMINIST PARENTING?

1.
Retrospect

At first all you will think of is the menstrual celebration.
The thick, viscous embarrassment of an eleven year old girl.

You will think of your bookshelf at home.
Toni Morrison.
Eve Ensler.

You will discover the way you see the world is not normal.
The androgyny, the equality, the openness.
You will learn how to shape yourself.

You'll hate it sometimes.
You'll wonder why you are so different.
You'll censor your friends around her.
"No, definitely don't say that word."

You'll be so grateful in other times.
You'll feel safety and acceptance in their purest form.
You'll learn of great women.
She will tell you that you are one of them.

You will find that you are a feminist too.
And you'll be unsure of how much of that came from her
and how much of that was in you all along.

And it blends, truly.

You never know what is your mother and what is you.

You'll move 25,000 miles away to find yourself.
And then one day you'll be sitting in your childhood park
With the dichromatic lights of winter and licking frost.

And you'll realize every part of her is you.

The way she speaks.
The way she loves.
The little ticks.
The idiolects.

The small town Saskatchewan.
The menstrual stains.
The Vagina Monologues.

And you'll sit there, and the sticking metal will grab at your gloves
and you will want to do it all just like her.
You'll think if you could be one-eighth of the mother she was to
you, you'll
be doing just fine.

—Emily Powers

2.
Feminist Parenting as the Practice of Non-domination

Lessons from Adrienne Rich, Audre Lorde, Sara Ruddick, and Iris Marion Young

ELIZABETH ANN BARTLETT

I PRACTICE FEMINISM. For me, practicing feminism means applying the values of non-oppression and non-domination in my relationships with others. As a parent charged with guiding my child's physical, moral, emotional, and spiritual growth, with ensuring his safety, teaching him social mores, and guiding the nurturance of his own sense of self, I have found, on occasion, the exigencies of being a parent at odds with my feminist practice. Although I regarded and related to my son as an equal, I also needed to set limits and teach him how to discern right from wrong, to get along with others, to use words rather than hitting to resolve conflict, and to follow the rules of appropriate social behaviour at home and in the world at large. I feel fortunate that I have had feminism to guide me. It gave me the wisdom to navigate the potential hazards and paradoxes in cultivating a mutually respectful and egalitarian relationship, in which my son could accept my guidance, not as control and domination, but rather as a safe boundary where he could grow into his own true self.

In this chapter, I discuss the application of Iris Marion Young's philosophy of non-oppression and non-domination, Audre Lorde's writings on the value of authenticity and listening to one's own internal guides, Adrienne Rich's powerful articulation of the requirements of an honourable relationship, and Sara Ruddick's philosophy of maternal thinking to the practice of feminist parenting. I examine how each of these informs the practice of non-oppression and non-domination feminist parenting, how they elucidate and reinforce one another, and how they may at times conflict with one another. In particular, Ruddick's requisite maternal tasks of cheerfulness and training for social acceptability can be at odds with Lorde's maternal practice of authenticity and Rich's practice of honourable relationship. In exploring this conflict, I argue that although feminist parenting requires a healthy balance of each, the demand for authenticity and honourable relationships provides the means to navigate situations and structures of domination as well as times of hardship, sorrow, or needing to fit in; it enables the sustenance of a feminist parental practice of non-domination. I also examine how these feminist parenting practices are challenged by those who would seek to enforce authority over children, mandate gender norms, or otherwise straightjacket a child's spirit, and usurp parental practices of non-domination. To this, I suggest strategies of resistance.

A basic tenet of my practice of feminism is not to engage in actions that oppress or dominate others; this extends to my practice of feminist parenting. If we, as parents, do not perpetuate the power dynamics of patriarchy and our children do not perpetuate them as well, then we engage in the work of disrupting and subverting their very foundations. Committing to this mandates vigilant attention to power dynamics in parent-child relationships and a commitment to meet our children as a peer on a soul level while we recognize our parental responsibilities for their health, safety, nurturance, and care. At the same time, we require a mutual respect from them, as our children must also recognize our parental responsibilities. This plays out differently at different ages and stages but always with a mutual respect for one another's being.

The fact that parents usually have many more resources of power at their disposal makes it all the more incumbent on them not to fall into easy patterns of using that power to dominate and oppress. In considering these issues, I find it useful to adapt Young's definitions of institutional and societal oppression and domination to include individuals, specifically parents. Young defines "oppression" to be those practices that "inhibit people's ability to play and communicate with others or to express their feelings and perspective on social life" (*Justice* 38), whereas self-development, the opposite of oppression, includes practices that provide the conditions that enable those same capacities for expression in people's lives (*In-*

clusion 31-32). She defines "domination" as those practices that "inhibit or prevent people from participating in determining their actions or the conditions of their action" (*Justice* 38), whereas self-determination, the opposite of domination, consists of being able to participate in these determinations (*Inclusion* 32). How then are we to go about the tasks of maternal practice as set forth by Ruddick—preservative love, growth, and training for social acceptability—while refusing to oppress and dominate? How do we provide the conditions that foster playfulness, communication, and self-expression as well as enable children to participate in determining their actions in the world? To address these questions, my best guides have been Rich, Lorde, and Ruddick.

Long before becoming a mother, I read Rich's essay "On Women and Honor," and it offered some of the most difficult and pivotal revelations of my life—that I had censored myself and had both allowed myself to be dominated and had dominated others through lies of silence, omission, avoidance, and denial. Raised in a home where the fun, play, laughter, and conversation that I knew with my mother ended when my father came home, and where the watchwords to protect that space of love and delight were "don't tell your father," I learned early on to censor what I said and to present or fabricate only those aspects of myself that would be acceptable. These lessons quickly became habituated responses, to the point that I could no longer discern my truths from my lies. It was not until I read Rich's essay that I gained insight into the true cost of these deceptions, not only to myself but also to others. Not only had I cut myself off from my own wisdom and truths, but in lying to others I had in fact deprived them of their autonomy. By presenting only partial visions of my realities, I had sought to control people's actions and reactions. As Rich writes: "The liar lives in fear of losing control. She cannot even desire a relationship without manipulation, since to be vulnerable to another person means for her the loss of control" (187). In constructing and presenting only those versions of events and of myself that would be acceptable to others, I had effectively manipulated and dominated them. Rich goes on: "In lying to others we end up lying to ourselves. We deny the importance of an event, or a person, and thus deprive ourselves of a part of our lives. Or we use one piece of the past or present to screen out another. Thus we lose faith even with our own lives" (186-187).

The practice of feminism demanded more. To quote Rich: "Our primary obligation to each other [is] not to undermine each other's sense of reality.... Our future depends on the sanity of each of us, and we have a profound stake, beyond the personal, in the project of describing our reality as candidly and fully as we can to each other" (190). This required, first and foremost, an honest attention to my own truths—picking up the thread of a thought that needed to be explored, following a question that may raise uncomfortable truths, acknowledging contradictions that must be held in tension, and respecting the validity of each and all. This also meant living in touch with the wisdom of my body as well as of my dreams. I learned to listen to my intuitive knowledge: the internal guide that alerts me to those things that need my attention and that is so much more perceptive than my rational mind. In short, I came to know how to live, as Lorde says, "from within outward" rather than from "external directives" (58).

In terms of my relationships with others, I aspired to what Rich calls an "honorable relationship," which, she says, is the only kind of relationship people have a right to call "love" (188). She defines this as "a process, delicate, violent, often terrifying to both persons involved, a process of refining the truths they can tell each other" (188). When considering how to use feminist practices of non-domination as a parent, I chose to be in an honourable relationship with my child. I was eager for it. Here was an opportunity to be in relationship with another human being completely fresh to this world. I was excited by the possibility. I could think of no better way to foster the conditions for self-expression and self-determination. The work I did with myself laid a critical groundwork and gave the tools of self-honesty that enabled me to scrupulously assess ways that I may be using power in our relationship to oppress or dominate. Choosing honourable relationship as a model of feminist parenting, I was committed to raising and nurturing this child in my care with honesty and respect, with validation of his perceptions, and with honouring of his truths. I was committed to welcoming the wisdom of his thoughts and dreams, the expressions of his body and spirit in song and dance and play, and his sorrows and anger and joys equally with loving attention and acceptance.

As part of being in honourable relationship, it has also been important that we not deliberately speak untruths to each other. Of course, my own commitment not to speak untruths to my son was within my own capacity and choice, but it was not something I could impose on him or control and police, nor did I want to. Such acts of domination would destroy the very foundation of respect that I was seeking and destroy our capacity for an honourable relationship. I had to trust that honesty on his part would spring out of my commitment to honesty with him. I did not prepare myself for how I might handle a deliberate untruth on his part. I did not have clearly stated consequences—"If you ever lie to me, then…." Rather, I simply believed in the basic human desire for honest relationships, given an environment of honouring and respect. So the time that I caught my young son (he was probably about eight or nine) in a deliberate lie, but of minor consequence, I gave him my honest response—my eyes welled up with tears. I remember telling him that it made me so sad that watching television (for that was what the lie was about) was more important to him than our relationship. Although this may seem a bit dramatic and over the top, it was my honest reaction, and that vulnerability was the most effective and the most honest thing I could have shown him. To my knowledge, my son has not deliberately deceived me since. This is reminiscent of Rich's idea, "there is not even a question of a lying between us" (192).

Honourable relationship has also meant a commitment to answer my son's questions honestly. When, as children do, he would point out the obvious absurdities, contradictions, and hypocrisies in so many societal practices and norms with the repeated question of "Why?," I never answered with the easy "That's just the way things are," but I would engage his questions genuinely as we explored together such things as why there are gendered terms for firefighters or for the divine. As he grew older, his questions became more difficult, more probing, and more sensitive, but it was important to me to answer him as honestly and accurately as I could and to honour his questions, struggles, and joys with an authentic response.

Another commitment towards an honourable relationship has been to listen to everything that he has been willing and wanting to share with me—not in the context of my probing, because it is important to me to respect his privacy, but in those things that he has chosen to share with me. These have not always been easy to hear, but I am also honoured and grateful beyond words that he has been able to be so open with me. With parents and children, these honest conversations and explorations are not always easy. They require recognition at the very least of issues of age-appropriate information, boundaries, guidance, privacy, and space for growing autonomy. But the ground remains the same: a commitment to honouring the truths of our mutual and individual existences and "not to undermine each other's sense of reality for the sake of expediency" (Rich 190).

One of the most important elements of my commitment to an honourable relationship as a parent was never to deny my child's perceptions of me, particularly of my emotional state. I remember moments, even when my son was very young, when he would say, "Mommy, you seem sad," or angry or upset, and I would feel the strong temptation to make everything right with his world by denying those realities in me and saying, "No, no, I'm fine." I realized that denying his accurate perceptiveness and sensitivity would not make everything right with his world. It would make his world a bit crazy. To tell him I was fine when he had clearly seen that I was not would be terribly confusing. It would also cripple his capacity to read body language and inhibit his intuitive capacities. All of those realizations, however, came to me in a millisecond, thankfully, so that I could honour his sensitivity and truths as well as my own. I told him simply, "Yes, sweetie, I'm a little sad right now." I did not need to tell him why or things that were not important for him to know, but I could honour his sanity—his clear perception of reality—and sustain an honourable relationship between us.

Thus, Ruddick's contention that among the tasks of parenting is the capacity to enlist what she calls "the virtue of cheerfulness" (74) seems at odds with an honourable relation. To charge parents to remain cheerful in the face of death and disease, hardship, tragedy, grief, sorrows, poverty, racism, war, homelessness, or everyday exhaustion seems to suggest that rather than be authentic, parents need to present a false self for the sake of the their children. However, Ruddick is quite clear that the cheerfulness that she intends is not the "false cheeriness of denial" (75) but rather a resilient hopefulness: "To be cheerful is to see a child hopefully and to welcome her hopes; for children, hope is as important as breathing" (74-75). She continues that a "cheerfulness that allows a mother herself to mystify reality drains her intellectual energy and befuddles her will" (75). Thus, the cheerfulness that she calls for requires the same kind of steadfast self-honesty demanded by Rich, which enables the parent to discern when cheerfulness is a false presentation of self and when it is a genuine and hopeful choice to persevere despite hardship. It is the latter, not the former, that Ruddick calls for.

Equally, engaging with children in an honourable relationship requires that we honour their emotions, whatever they may be. Lorde tells the story of her son, who was not one to engage in fights, coming home in tears because of other boys' bullying, and her initial response was to scold his tears. She stopped herself as she realized that she was about to reinforce "age-old distortions of what strength and bravery really are" out of a desire to protect and to ease her own pain (75-76). Lorde's partner suggested that instead she share with her son that she, too, had been afraid of bullies. A critical piece of establishing an honest, open, trusting relationship is to meet children at their feeling level first. The lesson, if any is to be had, can come later. Thus, children learn both that being in touch with their emotions is valued and that the truths that they find there are valid. To demand that children stop their crying, get tough, stuff their anger, or hide their fear is to deny their emotions and the truths that they reveal. As Ruddick says, to demand a "cheerfulness that encourages children to deny their sadness and anger or that protects them from truths they will have to acknowledge only confuses and inhibits them" (75). It is critical that children feel accepted and acknowledged no matter what emotions rise to the surface. The far more important lesson is how to access and move from the wisdom of their inner voice.

Though necessary, an honourable relationship is not sufficient for parental practices of non-domination. Other exigencies of parenting have the potential for creating conditions of domination and oppression. Ruddick's third task of maternal practice—training for social acceptability—in particular carries latent possibilities for domination. Suggesting conformation to the dominant culture, gender, race, class, or sexuality can squash a child's spirit. "Training for social acceptability" smacks of the "external directives," to which Lorde refers (58), which take us away from our "erotic guides" and make us puppets of a patriarchal system. Defining the erotic as "an assertion of the lifeforce ... the *yes* within ourselves" (55, 57), and "a true knowledge" (56), Lorde reclaims the term from the way it has been "misnamed by men" and confused with the pornographic (54). To elaborate further, Lorde writes:

> When we live outside ourselves, and by that I mean on external directives only rather than from our internal knowledge and needs, when we live away from those erotic guides from within ourselves, then our lives are limited by external and alien forms, and we conform to the needs of a structure that is not based on human need, let alone an individual's. But when we begin to live from within outward, in touch with the power of the erotic within ourselves, and allowing that power to inform and illuminate our actions upon the world around us, then we begin to be responsible to ourselves in the deepest sense. (58)

I have greater appreciation for Ruddick's point in her elaboration that, "Mothers want their children to grow into people whom they themselves and those closest to them can delightedly appreciate" (21). Thus, training for social acceptability need not be at odds with a parental role of enabling children's self-development; it can be a vital part of that role in fostering the full expression of a child's spirit in a way that others can hear and appreciate. As part of their development, children need to learn basic life skills—how to brush their teeth, choose healthy food, tie their shoes; as well as social skills—when to use inside voices, how to use their words rather than hit, to share their toys, to win and lose graciously, and to express greetings and gratitude. Parents nurture and guide their children by providing tools and techniques that will enable them to better to express their gifts and talents. Certain disciplines—scales on the piano, soccer drills, writing half an hour each day, stretching at the barre—enable children better to express themselves. In order to foster a child's societal appreciation and acceptance, parents also need to teach and impart, to a greater or lesser degree, societal and cultural norms and values, which range from virtues such as honesty, trustworthiness, care, and compassion to religious beliefs and practices, and to norms of behaviour and comportment based on gender, race, culture, and class. To a certain extent, one must learn how "to go along to get along." But where does one draw the line between the need to fit in in order to be heard and self-betrayal? If becoming acceptable to others means disloyalty to self to the point of denial and loss of self, then such training serves no self-developmental purpose. Yet children who do not behave according to social norms may find themselves the subject of cruelty, ridicule, scorn, and ostracism or worse, especially by peers. The dilemma of training for social acceptability is that it may compromise the task of fostering growth, yet not to do so may compromise the task of preservative love.

The harsh reality is that no matter how much a parent raises a child without oppression and domination, forces of domination, nevertheless, exist outside the home in the form of other adults—whether family, friend, or stranger, coaches, teachers in school or out, directors, group home managers, principals, ministers, rabbis, and priests, employers—as well as older and bigger children in the neighbourhood, the bus, the playground, and peers. As Ruddick says, mothers want power to keep their children healthy and prevail over people who frighten or demean them (37), but they quickly learn that their power with respect to their child is limited (34). Being powerless over the wellbeing of one's children in the world can be devastating.

An aspect of such training that may be especially challenging for feminist parenting is the decision whether and how much to inscribe culturally defined gender norms. Much of this is out of one's hands. Gender-specific sections of clothing stores and toy stores, media representations of gender, and comments from family and friends all act to enforce rigid expressions of gender, but none reify gender norms more so than the children's peers. It is the children in the daycare, not the teacher, who enforce the rules: "You can't wear pink—you're a boy; you can't play football—you're a girl." It was the girls in my son's second grade class who teased him so mercilessly about his participation in ballet that he quit a pursuit in which he found an avenue of self-expression and delight. The gender enforcement also came from the boys in his high school class who decided one day to cut his hair and dress him according to their culturally defined male-appropriate standards rather than his own. In trying to find my way through the morass of the oppressive power of peer approval, I once again found honourable relationship between parent and child to be of great help. Ongoing, open conversation allows children to express their thoughts and emotions about their struggles, choices, and realities of the world and of what feels right to them. This is vital in navigating the tension between social acceptability and self-expression.

More difficult to navigate are those situations and instances in which those who have power over our children by virtue of their positions of authority—teachers, police, bosses, social workers—act in ways that demean, dominate, and inhibit our children's expressive capacities, and restrain their ability to participate in choosing their actions and the conditions of those actions. The authority that such actors have over children makes parents feel powerless, especially in those instances in which resistance and objection on the part of the parent result in even further negative consequences to the child under the control of those in authority. My son had a long-term substitute teacher in second grade who was determined "to whip him into shape"—no more slouching, no more working ahead of the class, no more singing. He came home in tears nearly every day and the more I raised objections, the stricter she became. Appeals to the principal only made things worse. This also reminds me of a friend whose high-functioning autistic son had been falsely accused of inappropriate sexual behaviours. These false accusations resulted in his already-limited autonomy in his group home to become even more restricted; in the end, her advocacy on his part only made the consequences for him worse. Every avenue of appeal only supported those in the system in charge of his care. In both instances, the best recourse became knowing when to let the battle go and, whenever possible, to arrange to remove our children from those oppressive situations and give them respite. It is such a difficult balance. Although we do not want our children's spirits to be crushed or their voices to be silenced, children also need to be sufficiently adaptable to and accepting of authority to have their needs for safety and nurturance met. As Ruddick points out, "Mothers can't let children continually get into trouble with people who have power to hurt them and withhold what they need" (114). It is much more pressing of an issue when raising a child of colour in, as Lorde says, "the mouth of a racist, sexist, suicidal dragon" (74), where the consequences of getting in trouble may be far more severe.

This issue surfaced several years ago in a local battered women's shelter over questions of appropriate methods of child discipline. In an effort to introduce principles of non-domination in parenting, white staff developed policies around ways mothers at the shelter could discipline their children, with "no hitting" being a central rule. However, women coming into the shelter had different understandings and beliefs about that. As the staff grappled with how to deal with these differences, the women of colour on the staff explained, "we have to discipline our children in this way because it is extremely important that they understand what they can and can't do, because when they go out there, they're much more subject to police response than your children are" (O'Keefe). Viewed through the lens of historical trauma, parental legacies of harsh and dominating discipline passed down through generations have been designed not so much to break a child's spirit as to protect it from even more severe domination (Leary 122; Smith 35-44). They were acts of preservative love to keep their children safe. This demands the question: is a non-dominating approach to discipline a white middle-class privilege? Is it fair, prudent, or simply privileged of me to suggest such an approach when the consequences for transgressing cultural norms or questioning authority for my white middle-class heterosexual son are likely to be far less severe than if he were black or queer or working class? For insight, I turn to Lorde and bell hooks, who stress the importance of breaking these legacies of dominance passed from generation to generation. Emphasizing that love and domination cannot coexist, they argue that the lesson that domination can only be resisted through domination needs to cease (hooks, *All About Love* 17-30; Lorde 75-76).

Dealing with those who have power over the lives of our children is one of the most difficult struggles of feminist parenting. When thinking about how to navigate feminist parenting in the context of dominating external authorities, I have found that application of Young's theory of non-domination to self-determination of sovereign nations and indigenous peoples to be illuminating and instructive. Speaking in terms of nation states, Young argues that the main principle supporting self-determination of sovereign nations is that of non-interference by other nation states. However, in cases where sovereign nations face the threat of domination by other nations or where groups or entities within nation states face domination from state actors—as in cultures and traditions where men dominate women or dominant majorities dominate ethnic minorities—the *prima facie* principle of non-interference may be suspended, and the actors must join a decision-making body to adjudicate claims and negotiate conflicts ("Self-Determination" 146). At the very least, those seeking to support self-determination efforts on the part of groups that are "weak or poorly resourced" and whose self-determination is under threat need to be able to provide positive support to a level that allows those groups meaningfully to pursue their way of life, autonomy, and competence to interact with other groups ("Self-Determination" 147). Applying these principles to feminist parenting can show how children vis à vis authority figures and others poised to exercise dominance over them are generally in a situation of being weaker and lacking resources of power, skill, authority, and strength. In some of these cases, avenues for appeal are possible, but more often, this is not the case or the forces are weighed so heavily on the side of the system that a fair appeals process is negligible. In such instances of dominance by external authorities, one of the best resources parents can offer to provide positive support for their children's autonomy, competence, and ability to pursue meaningful pursuits is to teach them how to be their authentic selves.

This is particular to those times when parents disagree with those who have authority over their children; they need to model authenticity by expressing their disagreement, and not stifle their voice of genuine dissension. Not to do so would only teach blind obedience to authorities. As Ruddick says, a mother acts inauthentically when she "valorizes the judgment of dominant authorities" with whom she disagrees (113). At the very least, submitting to the decisions of authorities where no successful appeal or negotiation is possible needs to be talked about openly, with both parent and child disclosing their honest thoughts and feelings—a process akin to what Ruddick calls "developing habits of conversational reflection in the training of conscience" (118). The need for such conversations also includes times when children judge parents' decisions over their lives and choices to be arbitrary and dominating. "Because I said so" is never a good enough reason. Children need to be able to voice their sense of injustice, and parents need to be able to own up to instances when they acted unjustly. Ruddick points to these conversations occurring in a climate of what she calls mutual and "proper trust," and regards proper trust to be one of the most difficult of maternal virtues (119). I argue, on the contrary, that when developed as a habit and a commitment to honourable relation from the very beginning, mutual and proper trust is as habitual and welcome as the air we breathe.

Lorde has been my greatest guide throughout my years of parenting as she provides the most important lesson in raising children to be their authentic selves:

> The strongest lesson I can teach my son is the same lesson I teach my daughter: how to be who he wishes to be. The best way I can do this is to be who I am and to hope that he will learn from this not how to become me, which is not possible, but how to become his own person. This means learning to listen to his inner voice, rather than to those raucous, persuasive, or threatening voices from outside, that will pressure him to be what the world wants him to be. (77)

Children are incredibly perceptive, especially of their parents, and learn best when parents model the behaviour they seek, so my capacity for authenticity is the greatest resource that I can provide for my child. This means that the first requisite for feminist parenting is to learn to be who I am—how to move from that voice within myself—and to live, as Audre Lorde says, "from within outward" (58). Lorde writes: "The truest direction comes from inside. I give the most strength to my children by being willing to look within myself, and by being honest with them about what I find there" (72). And so we come full circle to Rich. In developing habits of an honourable relationship, I learn to look within and be honest about what I find, which I am then able to pass along to my child by my example.

Lorde writes of how in the face of the "perilous" journey of raising a black man in America, the best tool that she can give her son for survival is to teach him how to love and resist at the same time. That requires that he be able to feel strongly—"how to feel love, how to neither discount fear nor be overwhelmed by it, how to enjoy feeling deeply" (74). Such a capacity is nurtured in the practices of authenticity and honourable relationship that honour that inner wisdom. In a patriarchal society, in which hierarchies of domination are still the norm, from schools to supervisors to the streets, raising any child is fraught with perils, though of greater and lesser severity and cost depending on one's status and privilege, or lack thereof. The best strategies for resistance to domination are to develop strength of self through honest conversation, honourable relationship, and to foster in children the ability to be themselves by being our authentic selves.

bell hooks has described how black women resisted "by making homes where all black people could strive to be subjects, not objects, where we could be affirmed in our minds and hearts despite poverty, hardship, and deprivation, where we could restore to ourselves the dignity denied us on the outside in the public world" (*Yearning* 42). She quotes Thich Nhat Hanh, who says that the purpose of resistance is "to seek the healing of yourself in order to be able to see clearly" and that communities of resistance needed to be places where "people can return to themselves" (qtd. in *Yearning* 43). Thus, the same tools of non-domination that are requisite in feminist parenting also equip children to resist structures and strictures of dominating authorities and individuals and peers outside the home. The homeplace—as a site of honourable relationship, honest conversation, and authenticity—provides that place where children of any age can return to themselves; it equips them to resist the tyrannies and "raucous, persuasive, and threatening noise" (Lorde 77) that would seek to confine, control, or stifle their spirits.

As a feminist parent, I choose not to engage in actions that would dominate or oppress my child, in the hope that from that he would learn not only his own true self but also how to honour the same in others. Witnessing him now as a grown man who refuses actions that perpetuate domination and who prioritizes honourable relationship in his life gives me hope that a feminist future is possible.

WORKS CITED

hooks, bell. *All About Love: New Visions.* William Morrow and Co., Inc., 2000.

hooks, bell. *Yearning: Race, Gender, and Cultural Politics.* South End Press, 1990.

Leary, Joy Degruy. *Post Traumatic Slave Syndrome: America's Legacy of Enduring Injury and Healing.* Uptone Press, 2005.

Lorde, Audre. *Sister Outsider: Essays and Speeches by Audre Lorde.* The Crossing Press, 1984.

O'Keefe, Trisha. Personal interview. 13 Nov. 2014.

Rich, Adrienne. *On Lies, Secrets, and Silence: Selected Prose: 1966-1978.* W.W. Norton & Co., 1979.

Ruddick, Sara. *Maternal Thinking: Toward a Politics of Peace.* Ballantine Books, 1989.

Smith, Andrea. *Conquest: Sexual Violence and American Indian Genocide.* South End Press, 2005.

Young, Iris Marion. *Inclusion and Democracy.* Oxford University Press, 2000.

Young, Iris Marion. *Justice and the Politics of Difference.* Princeton University Press, 1990.

Young, Iris Marion. "Self-Determination as Non-Domination: Ideals Applied to Palestine/Israel." *Ethnicities*, vol. 5, no. 2, 2005, pp. 139-159. *Sage Journals*, doi: 10.1177/1468796805052112.

3.
Feminist Mothering

ANDREA O'REILLY

We were conspirators, outlaws from the institution of motherhood; I felt enormously in charge of my life.
—Adrienne Rich, *Of Woman Born* (194-195)

THIS CHAPTER, drawn from my writings on motherhood over the last decade, reflects on what it means to be a feminist mother and to practice feminist mothering. This chapter, a revised version of my chapter on feminist mothering that was published in my edited volume *Maternal Theory: Essential Readings* in 2007, provides an overview of the central issues, questions, and concerns of feminist mothering, and explores feminist mothering from the perspective of both mothers and children. The chapter is divided into four sections: "'This Is What a Feminist Mother Looks Like': Towards a Theory and Practice of Feminist Mothering"; "Possibilities: Empowering Mothers and their Children"; "Challenges: The Paradox of Feminist Mothering and the Promise of a Feminist Maternal Practice" and "Where do we go from here?: Feminist Mothering in/for the Future."

"THIS IS WHAT A FEMINIST MOTHER LOOKS LIKE!" TOWARDS A THEORY AND PRACTICE OF FEMINIST MOTHERING

Mothering and Motherhood

In *Of Woman Born*, Adrienne Rich, when discussing a vacation without her husband one summer, describes herself and her sons as "conspirators, outlaws from the institution of motherhood" (195). She writes:

> I remember one summer, living in a friend's house in Vermont. My husband was working abroad for several weeks and my three sons—nine, seven, and five years old—and I dwelt for most of that time by ourselves. Without a male adult in the house, without any reason for schedules, naps, regular mealtimes, or early bedtimes so the two parents could talk, we fell into what I felt to be a delicious and sinful rhythm.... [W]e lived like castaways on some island of mothers and children. At night they fell asleep without murmur and I stayed up reading and writing as I had when a student, till the early morning hours. I remember thinking: This is what living with children could be—without school hours, fixed routines, naps, the conflict of being both mother and wife with no room for being simply, myself. Driving home once after midnight from a late drive-in movie... with three sleeping children in the back of the car, I felt wide awake, elated; we had broken together all the rules of bedtime, the night rules, rules I myself thought I had to observe in the city or become a "bad mother." We were conspirators, outlaws from the institution of motherhood; I felt enormously in charge of my life. (194-195)

However, upon Rich's return to the city, the institution, in her words, "closed down on us again, and my own mistrust of myself as a 'good mother' returned, along with my resentment of the archetype" (195).

Rich's reflections on being an outlaw from the institution of motherhood and the references that she makes to being a "good" and "bad" mother are drawn from the distinction she develops at the beginning of *Of Woman Born* between motherhood and mothering. Central to *Of Woman Born* and developed by subsequent motherhood scholars is the key distinction Rich makes between two meanings of motherhood, one superimposed on the other: "the *potential* relationship of any woman to her powers of reproduction and to children"; and "the *institution*, which aims at ensuring that potential—and all women—shall remain under male control" (13). The term "motherhood" refers to the patriarchal institution of motherhood, which is male-defined and controlled and is deeply oppressive to women, whereas the word "mothering" refers to women's experiences of mothering, which are female defined and centred and potentially empowering to women. The reality of patriarchal motherhood, thus, must be distinguished from the possibility or potentiality of feminist mothering. To critique the institution of motherhood, therefore, "is not an attack on the family or on mothering *except as defined and restricted under patriarchy*" (Rich 14). In other words, although motherhood as an institution is a male-defined site of oppression, women's own experiences of mothering can, nonetheless, be a source of power.

It has long been recognized among scholars of motherhood that Rich's distinction between mothering and motherhood allowed feminists to recognize that motherhood is not naturally, necessarily, or inevitably oppressive, a view held by some second-wave feminists. Rather, mothering, freed from motherhood, could be experienced as a site of empowerment—a location of social change if, to use Rich's words, women became "outlaws from the institution of motherhood." However, as *Of Woman Born* interrupted the patriarchal narrative of motherhood and cleared a space for the development of maternal counter-narratives, it did not develop a theory of feminist mothering. Indeed, even though much has been published on patriarchal motherhood since Rich's inaugural text—documenting why and how patriarchal motherhood is harmful, indeed unnatural, to mother and children alike—little has been written on the possibility or potentiality of feminist mothering. "Still largely missing from the increasing dialogue and publication around motherhood," as Fiona Green writes, "is a discussion of Rich's monumental contention that even when restrained by patriarchy, motherhood can be a site of empowerment and political activism" ("Feminist Mothers" 31).

This dearth of feminist research on motherhood is indeed perplexing. A review of feminist scholarship on motherhood reveals that although the topics of motherhood, feminism, and maternal activism have been well studied (Kinser; MacDonald Strong; O'Reilly, *The Twenty-First-Century Motherhood Movement*; Rhine) only a handful of books look specifically at the topic of feminist mothering: the Maureen Reddy et al.'s edited collection *Mother Journeys: Feminists Write About Mothering* (1994); Tuula Gordon's book, *Feminist Mothers* (1990); Rose L. Glickman's *Daughters of Feminists* (1993); and Fiona Green's *Practicing Feminist Mothering* (2011). The journals *off our backs* (2006) and *Journal of the Association for Research on Mothering* (2006) include articles on feminist mothering in their issues on "Mothering and Feminism." Likewise, two of my edited volumes—*Mother Outlaws: Theories and Practices of Empowered Mothering* (2004) and *From Motherhood to Mothering: The Legacy of Adrienne Rich's Of Woman Born* (2004)—incorporate sections on feminist mothering. As well, in 2008, I edited a volume specifically on the subject on feminist mothering, *Feminist Mothering*, and my monograph *Rocking the Cradle: Thoughts on Motherhood, Feminism, and the Possibility of Empowered Mothering*, published in 2006, examines the topic of feminist mothering.

WHAT IS IN A NAME? DEFINING FEMINIST MOTHERING

The introduction to my edited volume *Feminist Mothering* (2008) begins with a review of recent publications on motherhood in the mainstream media. These books suggest that the selfless and doting mother of yesteryear has, like the eighteen-hour bra, fallen out of fashion. These authors, particularly those that write in the self-help genre, call for a new style of mothering, one that advocates balance and admonishes guilt. Bria Simpson for example, asserts in *The Balanced Mom: Raising Your Kids without Losing Your Self* that "We need to continue, rather than deny, the development of ourselves to be fulfilled" (2). Likewise, Amy Tiemann, in *Mojo Mom: Nurturing Your Self While Raising a Family*, claims that "all women need to continue to grow as individuals, not just as Moms" (xvi). Overcoming the guilt of motherhood is the focus of many recent books, as with the bestselling, and appropriately titled, book *Mommy Guilt: Learn to Worry Less, Focus on What Matters Most, and Raise Happier Kids.* Other writers challenge the excessive child centredness of contemporary parenting practices and call for a more "children should be seen and not heard" philosophy of childrearing. In *How to Avoid the Mommy Trap: A Roadmap for Sharing Parenting and Making it Work*, Julie Shields argues that "*the best alternative to parenting by mother is parenting by father*" (17). She continues:

> Since fathers can parent, too, we should not start from the assumption that mothers, and mothers alone, must choose whether to work, cut back, or hire a replacement caregiver. Instead, we can change our approach to seeking ways to provide babies the best start in life, at the same time, giving mothers *and* fathers the best opportunity for happiness, individually and together. (19)

Whether the emphasis is maternal autonomy or shared parenting, less guilt and more balance, these writers challenge traditional or, in academic parlance, patriarchal motherhood practices. Similar to Betty Friedan, who exposed "the problem that has no name" more than fifty years ago, these writers insist that women must achieve and sustain a selfhood outside of and beyond motherhood. And similar to Adrienne Rich—who attributes mothers' exhaustion and guilt to the isolation of patriarchal motherhood and its impossible standards of perfection—these writers also recognize that mothers require more support and less judgment if they are to obtain satisfaction in motherhood.

However, although these authors do challenge patriarchal motherhood, they do not use the word "feminist" in this critique, nor do they call their new mother-positive mode of mothering a feminist practice. Given this, can these new models of mothering be called feminist mothering? Does the mother have to identify as a feminist for her mothering to qualify as a feminist practice? Or more pointedly, can we have a practice of feminist mothering without a politic of feminism? And who decides and determines this?

I open my book *Feminist Mothering* with such questions to illustrate the difficulty of defining a feminist practice and theory of mothering. In this chapter, I seek to define the term "feminist mothering" and develop a theory of this maternal practice. I understand and use the term feminist mothering to refer to an oppositional discourse of motherhood—one that is constructed as a negation of patriarchal motherhood and seeks to interrupt the master narrative of motherhood and to imagine and implement a view of mothering that is empowering to women. Therefore, feminist mothering is often determined more by what it is not (i.e., patriarchal motherhood) rather than by what it is. Feminist mothering may refer to any practice of mothering that seeks to challenge and change various aspects of patriarchal motherhood that cause mothering to be limiting or oppressive to women. Rich uses the word "courageous" to define a nonpatriarchal practice of mothering, while Baba Copper calls such a practice "radical mothering." Susan Douglas and Meredith Micheals, in *The Mommy Myth*, use the word "rebellious" to describe outlaw mothering, whereas "hip" is Ariel Gore's term for transgressive mothering. For this chapter, the term "feminist" is used—though with a proviso as explained below—to signify maternal practices that resist and refuse patriarchal motherhood to create a mode of mothering that is empowering for mothers. Or, to use Rich's terminology, a feminist maternal practice marks a movement from motherhood to mothering, and makes possible a mothering against motherhood.

EMPOWERED MOTHERING VERSUS FEMINIST MOTHERING

In her book *Feminist Mothers*, the first book-length study of the subject matter, Tuula Gordon in her concluding chapter "What is a Feminist Mother?" observes, "[I]t seems impossible to conclude by explaining what a feminist mother is, or to answer the underlying question of how people conduct their lives according to alternative ideologies, in this case feminism" (148). However, Gordon does say that her study of feminist mothers reveals some "particular factors." They are the following:

> The way in which [mothers] challenge and criticise myths of motherhood; the way in which they consider it their right to work: the anti-sexist (and anti-racist) way in which they try to bring up their children; the way in which they expect the fathers of the children to participate in joint everyday lives; and the way in which many of them are politically active. (149)

Gordon goes on to conclude:

> Feminism emphasizes that women are strong, that women have rights as women, and they can support each other as women. Thus "feminist mothers" have been able to develop critical orientations towards societal structures and cultures, stereotypical expectations and myths of motherhood. They do that in the context of exploring how the personal is political, and with the support of the networks of women, which place them beyond "collective isolation." (150)

Rose L. Glickman in her book *Daughters of Feminists* likewise emphasizes that feminist mothering must be understood as lived resistance to the normative (i.e., stereotypical) expectations of both motherhood and womanhood. She writes: "[For these feminist mothers] there is no 'apart from their feminism' and no matter how ordinary their lives seem from the outside to the casual observer, *their feminism was a profound defiance of convention*.... Flying in the face of tradition, feminist mothers expected their daughters to do the same" (22, emphasis added). "The mothers' struggle," Glickman continues, "to shake off the dust of tradition was the basic dynamic of the daughters' formative years" (21).

In my work on feminist mothering, I define feminist mothering as a practice that seeks to grant mothers agency, authority, authenticity, autonomy, and advocacy-activism denied to them in patriarchal motherhood. Maternal agency, as Lynn O'Brien-Hallstein explains, refers to "the ability to influence one's life, to have power to control one's life" (698). A theory of and for maternal agency is concerned with, as O'Brien-Hallstein continues, "mothering practices that facilitate women's authority and power and is revealed in mothers' efforts to challenge and act against aspects of institutionalized motherhood that constrain and limit women's lives and power as mothers" (698). Authenticity, in turn, as Elizabeth Butterfield explains, "is an ethical term that denotes being true to oneself, as in making decisions that are consistent with one's own beliefs and values" (790). In contrast, inauthenticity is generally understood to be an abdication of one's own authority and a loss of integrity. In the context of empowered mothering, "maternal authenticity," as Butterfield continues, "draws upon Ruddick's concept of the "conscientious mother," and my own model of the "authentic feminist mother," which refers to "independence of mind and the courage to stand up to dominant values" and to "being truthful about motherhood and remaining true to oneself in motherhood" (O'Reilly, *Rocking the Cradle*). Similarly, maternal authority and autonomy refer to confidence and conviction in oneself, holding power in the household, and the ability to define and determine one's life and practices of mothering; in Ruddick's words, it is the refusal to "relinquish or repudiate one's own perceptions and values" (112; see also O'Reilly, *Rocking the Cradle* 22). Maternal advocacy-activism, in turn, recognizes the potential political and social dimension of motherwork, whether such is expressed in antisexist childrearing or maternal activism. Thus, the agency, authority, authenticity, autonomy, and advocacy-activism of empowered mothering stand in sharp contrast to the mandates of patriarchal motherhood. Such makes the obliteration of the institution of motherhood possible, which in turn creates space for the emancipatory potential of mothering to be realized.

Whether it manifests itself in combining motherhood with paid employment, insisting that fathers be involved in childcare, engaging in activism, or creating a life outside of motherhood, these studies reveal that feminist mothering has developed in response to the mother's dissatisfaction with and dislike of traditional motherhood. Commenting on Gordon's study, Ericka Horwitz in her thesis "Mothers' Resistance to the Western Dominant Discourse on Mothering" observes: "[Gordon's] findings suggest that mothers can hold beliefs that are not in agreement with those promoted by the dominant discourses on motherhood. Gordon alerts us to the possibility that *the process of resistance entails making different choices about how one wants to practice mothering*" (58, emphasis added). Both Gordon and Glickman look specifically at mothers who identify as feminists, whereas Horwitz in the above thesis and her later chapter "Resistance as a Site of Empowerment: The Journey Away from Maternal Sacrifice" is interested in "the experiences of women who believe they were resisting the dominant discourse of mothering ... [but] who may or may not see themselves as feminist" (44-45). Empowered mothering, thus, signifies a general resistance to patriarchal motherhood, whereas feminist mothering refers to a particular style of empowered mothering in which this resistance is developed from and expressed through a feminist identification or consciousness. Although the two seem similar, there are significant differences that warrant further elaboration. To this discussion, I now turn.

In her chapter, "Resistance as Empowerment," Erika Horwitz argues that although resistant, empowered mothering is characterized by many themes, they all centre on a challenge to patriarchal motherhood. These themes include the following: the importance of mothers meeting their own needs; being a mother not fulfilling all of women's needs; involving others in their children's upbringing; actively questioning the expectations placed on mothers by society; challenging mainstream parenting practices; not believing that mothers are solely responsible for how children turn out; and challenging the idea that the only emotion mothers ever feel towards their children is love. In an earlier collection, *Mother Outlaws*, I explore how empowered mothering begins with the recognition that both mothers and children benefit when the mother lives her life and practices mothering from a position of agency, authority, authenticity, and autonomy. As well, in emphasizing maternal authority and in ascribing agency to mothers and value to motherwork, this perspective defines motherhood as a political site, wherein mothers can create social change through the socialization of children and the world at large through political and social activism. Empowered mothering calls into question the dictates of patriarchal motherhood. Empowered mothers do not regard childcare as the sole responsibility of the biological mother nor do they regard 24/7 mothering as necessary for children. They look to friends, family, and their partners to assist with childcare and often raise their children with an involved community of what may be termed "co-mothers" or "othermothers." As well, in most instances, these mothers combine mothering with paid employment, studies, and/or activism, so these mothers do not practice the full-time intensive mothering demanded in patriarchal motherhood. Moreover, many of these mothers call into question the belief that mothering requires excessive time, money, and energy;

they practice a mode of mothering that is more compatible with paid employment. As well, they see the development of a mother's selfhood as beneficial to mothering and not antithetical to it, as is assumed in patriarchal motherhood. Consequently, empowered mothers do not always put their children's needs before their own, nor do they only look to motherhood to define and realize their identity. Rather, their selfhood is fulfilled and expressed in various ways: work, activism, friendships, relationships, hobbies, and motherhood, to name a few. These mothers insist on their own authority as mothers and refuse the relinquishment of their power as mandated in the patriarchal institution of motherhood. Finally, as noted above, empowered mothers regard motherhood as a site of power, wherein mothers can facilitate social change, both in the home through feminist childrearing and outside the home through maternal activism. Motherhood, in the dominant patriarchal ideology, is seen simply as a private and an apolitical enterprise. In contrast, mothering for these mothers is understood to have cultural significance and political purpose. Building on the work of Sara Ruddick, these mothers redefine motherwork as a socially engaged enterprise, which seeks to effect cultural change through new modes of gender socialization and interactions with daughters and sons.

Feminist mothering differs from empowered mothering in so far as the mother identifies as a feminist and practices mothering from a feminist perspective or consciousness. A feminist mother, in other words, is a person whose mothering, in theory and practice, is shaped and influenced by feminism. Thus, although there is much overlap between empowered and feminist mothering, the latter is informed by a particular philosophy and politic, namely feminism. In Horwitz's study, the women's demands that their husbands be more involved and that they need time off from motherhood do not derive from a larger challenge to gender inequity. For example, one woman in the study remarks "If I was going to love that baby, have any quality of time with that baby, I had to get away from that baby [and] I had to meet my own needs" ("Resistance as a Site of Empowerment" 48); and another mother "chose to paint her nails while her baby cried in her crib because 'she has needs and wants'" (47). These women resist patriarchal motherhood, in one woman's words "to have a higher quality of life" or, in the words of another, "to [become] a better mother for [her] children" (52). The reasons for their resistance are more personal than political and, as a consequence, are not developed from an awareness of how motherhood functions as a cultural and ideological institution to oppress women in patriarchal society. These mothers resist patriarchal motherhood simply to make the experience of mothering more rewarding for themselves and their children. In so far as this aim challenges the patriarchal mandate of maternal selflessness, sacrifice, and martyrdom, these mothers resist through their insistence on more time for themselves and support from others. However, these demands do not originate from a feminist desire to dismantle a patriarchal institution. In contrast, feminist mothers resist because they recognize that gender inequity, in particular male privilege and power, is produced, maintained, and perpetuated in patriarchal motherhood. As feminists, feminist mothers reject an institution founded on gender inequity, and as mothers, they refuse to raise children in such a sexist environment. Thus, although in practice the two seem similar—in demanding more involvement from fathers and in insisting on a life outside of motherhood—only with feminist mothering does this involve a larger awareness of, and challenge to, the gender (among other) inequities of patriarchal culture.

While the above discussion helps to distinguish between empowered and feminist mothering, it begs the larger question of how to define feminism itself. Feminism, as scholars of women's studies are well aware, is composed of many perspectives and positions: socialist, liberal, radical, womanist, and third wave, to name but a few. In my work on feminist mothering, I rely on a very open-ended definition of feminism: the recognition that most if not all cultures are patriarchal and that they give prominence, power, and privilege to men and the masculine; they depend on the oppression, if not disparagement, of women and the feminine. Feminists are committed to challenging and transforming this gender inequity in all of its manifestations: cultural, economic, political, philosophical, social, ideological, sexual, and so forth. As well, most feminisms (including my own) seek to dismantle other hierarchical binary systems, such as race, (racism), sexuality (heterosexism), economics (classism), and ability (ableism). In the context of this definition of feminism, a feminist mother challenges male privilege and power in her own life and the life of her children. In her own life, then, a feminist mother insists on gender equality in the home and on a life and identity outside of motherhood. As well, feminist mothering would ensure that the important work of mothering would be culturally valued and supported and that mothers, likewise, would perform this motherwork from a place of agency and authority. In the context of children, feminist mothering means dismantling traditional gender socialization practices that privilege boys as preferable and superior to girls and that socialize boys to be masculine and girls feminine. Feminist mothering, thus, seeks to transform both the patriarchal role of motherhood and that of childrearing

However, the word "feminism" remains troubled. In her book on feminist daughters, Glickman writes:

> I ruled out daughters whose mothers' lives can surely be described as feminist, but who reject the label. Once, in my search for Latina daughters, I spoke with the head of a Latino women's health collective. She said she couldn't help me because "although we have the consciousness, in our culture we don't use the word." The consciousness without the word is not what I'm looking for. (xv-xvi)

However, the insistence on the word "feminist," inevitably, as the above incidence demonstrates, excludes the mothering experiences of women of colour. Feminism, as African American scholars Patricia Hill Collins and bell hooks among others have argued, is understood to be a white term for many black women. As one daughter, a woman of colour, in Glickman's study comments: "[Feminism] has overwhelmingly, statistically, benefited white women disproportionately to women of colour" (168). And another daughter remarks: "Here you are reading all these feminist writers who are telling you to bust out of the kitchen and get into the work force. What does that have to do with the majority of women of colour who have always been in the kitchen *and* the work force at the same time?" (169). Indeed, as the mothers of colour in Gordon's study emphasize, "black women are critical of feminism dominated by white women for ideological, political and strategic reasons" (140). The question thus remains: how do you develop a specific study of feminist mothering without excluding the many women—women of colour and working-class women—who eschew or disavow the word feminism? Although I do not believe there are easy answers to such questions, I see a broader understanding of feminism to include womanist, antiracist, and global feminist perspectives as a way to begin talking about women of colour and their specific theory and practice of feminist mothering.

POSSIBILITIES: EMPOWERING MOTHERS AND THEIR CHILDREN

Maternal Empowerment

Feminist mothering, as discussed above, functions as a counter practice that seeks to challenge and change the many ways that patriarchal motherhood is oppressive to women. In an earlier volume, *Mother Outlaws*, I organize these themes under eight interrelated "rules" of "good" motherhood as dictated by contemporary patriarchal ideology. They are the following: 1) children can only be properly cared for by the biological mother; 2) this mothering must be provided 24/7; 3) the mother must always put children's needs before her own; 4) mothers must turn to the experts for instruction; 5) the mother must be fully satisfied, fulfilled, completed, and composed in motherhood; 6) the mother must lavish excessive amounts of time, energy, and money in the rearing of their children; 7) the mother has full responsibility but no power from which to mother; and 8) motherwork and childrearing are regarded as personal and private undertakings with no political import. The patriarchal ideology of motherhood causes mothering to be oppressive because it requires the repression or denial of the mother's own selfhood; as well, it assigns mothers all the responsibility for mothering but gives them no real power from which to mother. Such "powerless responsibility," to use Rich's term, denies a mother the authority and agency to determine her own experiences of mothering. Moreover, in defining mothering as private and nonpolitical work, patriarchal motherhood restricts the way mothers can and do affect social change through feminist child rearing and maternal activism.

In *Of Woman Born*, Rich writes: "We do not think of the power stolen from us and the power withheld from us in the name of the institution of motherhood" (275). "The idea of maternal power has been domesticated," Rich continues, "in transfiguring and enslaving woman, the womb—the ultimate source of the power—has historically been turned against us and itself made into a source of powerlessness" (68). The central aim of feminist mothering is to reclaim that power for mothers. Feminist mothering, thus, refers to a particular style of empowered mothering in which resistance is developed from and expressed through a feminist identification or consciousness. A feminist mother, as discussed above, seeks the eradication of motherhood, as she recognizes that such is a patriarchal institution in which gender inequality, or more specifically the oppression of women, is enforced, maintained, and perpetuated. Feminist mothering is primarily concerned with the empowerment of mothers. Thus a theory of feminist mothering begins with recognition that mothers must live their life and practice mothering from a position of agency, authority, authenticity, and autonomy. A feminist standpoint on mothering affords a woman a life, a purpose, and an identity outside and beyond motherhood; as well, it does not limit childrearing to the biological mother. Likewise, from this standpoint, a woman's race, age, sexuality, or marital status does not determine her capacity to mother. A feminist theory on motherhood also foregrounds maternal power and confers value to mothering. Mothering from a feminist perspective and practice redefines motherwork as a social and political act. In contrast to patriarchal motherhood, which limits mothering to privatized care undertaken in the domestic sphere, feminist mothering, more so than empowered mothering, regards such as explicitly and profoundly political and social.

Feminist mothering is equally concerned with feminist practices of gender socialization and models of mother-child relations in order to raise a new generation of empowered daughters and empathetic sons. However, a theory of feminist mothering insists that the latter—antisexist childrearing—depends on the former—the eradication of patriarchal motherhood. Feminist mothering first seeks to dismantle motherhood for mothers themselves so that they may achieve empowerment in mothering. That is reason enough to abolish motherhood. However, in so doing, feminist mothering also invests mothers with the needed agency, autonomy, authenticity, authority, and activism-advocacy to create the feminist childrearing that they desire. Feminist mothers recognize that the changes they pursue in childrearing are made possible only through changes in mothering.

Feminist Mothers are Better Mothers

In affirming maternal agency, authority, autonomy, authenticity and activism-advocacy, feminist mothering makes motherhood more rewarding, fulfilling, and satisfying for women. Such mothering allows women a selfhood outside of motherhood and affords them power within motherhood. As well, the practice of othermothering, or co-mothering, the ability to combine motherhood with work (paid employment and/or activism), and limiting the time, energy, money spent on children all relieve women of much of the isolation, dependency, boredom, and exhaustion experienced in patriarchal motherhood. It is evident that feminist mothering is better for mothers, and such mothering is also better for children. Mothers content with and fulfilled by their lives are better mothers. Likewise, children raised by depressed mothers are at risk. I want to suggest as well that feminist mothers are more effective mothers. Anyone who has been in a plane knows the routine if oxygen masks are required: put on your mask and then assist children with theirs. This instruction initially seems to defy common sense—children should be helped first. However, the instruction recognizes that parents must be masked first because only then are they able to provide real and continued assistance to the child: unmasked, they run they risk of becoming disoriented, ill, or unconscious because of a lack of oxygen, which would make them of no use to the child. I see this instruction as a suitable metaphor for feminist mothering: empowered mothers are able to better care for and protect their children.

In her book *A Potent Spell: Mother Love and the Power of Fear*, Janna Malamud Smith references the myth of Demeter and Persephone to illustrate the theme that children are better served by empowered mothers. Demeter, Smith argues "is able to save her daughter because she is a powerful goddess who can make winter permanent and destroy humankind" (59). "Demeter," she continues, "possesses the very qualities that mothers so often have lacked—adequate resources and strength to protect their children, particularly daughters" (59). Therefore, and contrary to patriarchal or more accepted wisdom of what a child needs most in the world, Smith argues "is a *free and happy* mother" (167, emphasis added). Smith explains further:

> [W]hat a child needs most is a free mother, one who feels that she is in fact living *her* life, and has adequate food, sleep, wages, education, safety, opportunity, institutional support, health care, child care, and loving relationships. "Adequate" means enough to allow her to participate in the world—and in mothering ... A child needs a mother who has resources to enable her to make real choices, but also to create a feeling of adequate control—a state of mind that encourages a sense of agency, thus a good basis of maternal well-being, and a good foundation on which to stand while raising a child. Surely, childcare prospers in this soil as well as, if not better than in any other. What is more, such a mother can imagine a life of possibility and hope, and can so offer this perspective to a child. [Finally] a child needs a mother who lives and works within a context that respects her labour, and that realistically supports it without rationalizing oppression in the name of safety, or substituting idealization or sentimentality for resources. (Smith 167)

Ann Crittenden, who is cited by Smith, elaborates: "Studies conducted on five continents have found that children are distinctly better off when the mother possess enough income and authority in the family to make investing in children a priority" (qtd. in Smith 120). Ann Crittenden continues: "The emergence of women as independent economic actors is not depriving children of vital support; it is giving them more powerful defenders. Depriving mothers of an income and influence of their own is harmful to children and a recipe for economic backwardness" (qtd. in Smith 130). To return to the story of Demeter: "It is only because Demeter has autonomy and independent resources," as Smith explains, "that she can protect Persephone" (241). Conversely, "when a culture devalues and enslaves the mother, she can [not] be like Demeter and protect her daughter" (244). Therefore, and as Smith concludes, "If we are really interested in improving the lot of children, our best method would be laws and policy that support mothers and mothering" (187). It is indeed remarkable, as Smith notes, that "[n]o society has ever voluntarily turned its laws and riches toward liberating mothers" (168).

The free mother valued by Smith and recognized as essential for the wellbeing of children, however, will be not found in the patriarchal institution of motherhood. Feminist, or to use Smith's term "free," mothering only becomes possible in and through the destruction of patriarchal motherhood. Such mothers can better protect and defend their children as Smith observes. As well, and as noted above, feminist mothers can make real and lasting changes in society through social and political activism and in the way that they raise their children. More specifically, feminist mothers challenge and change, in the home and in the world at large, the gender roles that straightjacket children and the harm of sexism, racism, classism, and heterosexism more generally. I believe that patriarchy resists feminist mothering precisely because it understands its real power to bring about a true and enduring cultural revolution.

CHALLENGES: THE PARADOX OF FEMINIST MOTHERING AND THE PROMISE OF A FEMINIST MATERNAL PRACTICE

As the above section examines the benefits of feminist mothering for children, this section considers its risks. More specifically, it considers whether feminist mothering fosters or undermines the aims of maternal practice. My writing on feminist mothering frequently draws on my experience of raising my three children—a son and two daughters—in a feminist household. Of interest to me in my reflections is how my children have come to be feminists in a patriarchal culture. All three of my children—my son Jesse, who is thirty-two years old, and my two daughters, Erin and Casey, who are thirty and twenty-seven, respectively—identify as feminists. Over the last several years as my children became teenagers, young adults, and then adults, and the assaults on them as feminist men and women grew more frequent and hateful, I began to reflect on how my feminist mothering seemed to be in conflict with my maternal practice. More specifically, I struggled with how I could reconcile the demands my motherwork—keeping my children safe and ensuring that they have a sense of belonging in their culture—with the desires of my feminism, as in raising my children to challenge that very same culture, which put them at risk in doing so. Preoccupied with and perplexed by this inherent and perhaps irresolvable paradox of feminist mothering I returned to the writing of Sara Ruddick to consider whether feminist mothering could be understood as a form of maternal practice

In *Maternal Thinking: Toward a Politics of Peace,* Sara Ruddick argues that motherwork is characterized by three demands: preservation, growth, and social acceptance. "To be a mother," Ruddick argues, "is to be committed to meeting these demands by works of preservative love, nurturance, and training" (17). The first duty of mothers is to protect and preserve their children: "to keep safe whatever is vulnerable and valuable in a child" (80). "Preserving the lives of children," Ruddick writes, "is the central constitutive, invariant aim of maternal practice: the commitment to achieving that aim is the constitutive maternal act" (19). "The demand to preserve a child's life is quickly supplemented," Ruddick continues, "by the second demand, to nurture its emotional and intellectual growth" (19). The third demand of maternal practice is training and social acceptability of children. About this third demand, Ruddick writes:

> [The demand] is made not by children's needs but by the social groups of which a mother is a member. Social groups require that mothers shape their children's growth in "acceptable" ways. What counts as acceptable varies enormously within and among groups and cultures. The demand for acceptability, however, does not vary, nor does there seem to be much dissent from the belief that

> children cannot "naturally" develop in socially correct ways but must be "trained." I use the neutral, though somewhat harsh, term "training" to underline a mother's active aims to make her children "acceptable." Her training strategies may be persuasive, manipulative, educative, abusive, seductive, or respectful and are typically a mix of most of these. (21)

"In any mother's day," Ruddick concludes, "the demands of preservation, growth and acceptability are intertwined [and] a reflective mother can separately identify each demand, partly because they are often in conflict" (23).

A feminist mother, as a mother, is committed to the safety, wellbeing, and social acceptability of her children, yet as a feminist, that same mother knowingly and deliberately raises her child to be critical of the dominant culture and to cause, as a result possible physical and psychological harm to her children. Rich has argued that as feminist mothers, we worry that we may turn our sons "into misfits and outsiders" (205). I argue that as feminist mothers, we *do* make our children—both sons and daughters—misfits and outsiders and that this is in direct conflict with our responsibility as mothers to ensure safety and social acceptability for our children

Writing on this paradox of feminist mothering, I am reminded of the work of black mothers of sons who speak of a similar paradox. Marita Golden in her book *Saving our Sons: Raising Black Children in a Turbulent World* says this of her son: "The unscathed openness of Michael's demeanour was proof that he had been a protected, loved child. But this same quality was also suddenly a liability, one that he had to mask" (95). Nurturing black sons to be confident and proud, mothers recognize that these same traits—because other black youth, police, or whites may misconstrue them as insolence, obstinacy, or arrogance—put their sons at risk. Golden realizes that this paradox of mothering black sons necessitates a new mode of mothering, which is, perhaps, best expressed by Audre Lorde when she writes, "Black children must be raised as warriors. For survival they must also be raised to recognize the enemy's many faces" (77). She goes on to say:

> The strongest lesson I can teach my son is the same lesson I teach my daughter: how to be who he wishes to be for himself. And the best way I can do this is to be who I am and hope that he will learn from this not how to be me, which is not possible, but how to be himself. And this means to move to that voice from within himself, rather than to those raucous, persuasive, or threatening voices from outside, pressuring him to be what the world wants him to be. (77)

A feminist mother must, likewise, develop new modes of mothering and to teach her children to be true to themselves by modelling such in her own life. This, as Rich has noted, "means that the mother herself is trying to expand the limits of her life. To *refuse to be a victim*: and then to go on from there" (246).

When my daughters were teenagers, I interviewed them on their experience of being raised by a feminist mother for an article I was writing. From their commentary, it became evident that my daughters perceived and experienced their upbringing as antisexist childrearing and that my daughters understood their childhood in this way. They both mentioned several times that my partner and I did not "girl" them in their upbringing. (Casey spoke of how fishing, playing with frogs, and getting dirty in the mud was a normal part of her childhood.) As well, they commented on how they did not experience the "normal" sexist feminization of daughters. (They did not play with Barbies, wear makeup, or listen to the Spice Girls.) As well, both of them emphasized the importance of being offered alternative, or empowered, examples and images of womanhood (feminist books and music, Goddess figures, and so forth). But equally, my daughters spoke about how they learned feminism directly from the way that I lived my life. This came up far more than I had anticipated. What they remember about me is "working, standing up to traditional gender roles and always talking about issues." They saw me living a life outside of motherhood. As Erin remarked: "You had a long relationship with dad, work, friends, partying. You did everything: you never had a shitty nonlife." My daughters, in watching me live my life, learned that feminism was possible, do-able, and normal. And, as importantly, they learned that motherhood does not, and should not, shut down other dimensions of a woman's life: work, sexuality, friendship, activism, leisure, and so forth. Listening over and over again to my daughters' voices as I transcribed the interview, I finally understood Rich's insight at a deeply personal level. To paraphrase Rich: the quality of my life—however, embattled and unprotected it may have been—was my primary bequest to my daughters because in believing in myself, in fighting, and in struggling to create livable space around me, I demonstrated to Erin and Casey that these possibilities exist. Feminist mothering is ultimately not about choosing blue over pink or trucks over dolls but about the mother living her own life, to use the title of Marilyn Waring's work, as if women counted.

WHERE DO WE GO FROM HERE? FEMINIST MOTHERING FOR THE FUTURE

Having spent over thirty years committed to both maternal practice and feminist mothering, I have yet to resolve the paradox of feminist mothering. However, what I have come to understand from interviewing my daughters, rereading Ruddick's theory of maternal practice, and remembering Lorde's and Rich's words on staying true to ourselves is that feminist mothering must be seen an expression of maternal practice. Although feminist mothering does, in the first instance, run counter to the safety and social acceptability requirements of maternal practice, in allowing our children to grow outside and beyond the gender straightjackets of patriarchal culture, it does foster the nurturance of children, the second demand of maternal practice, which enables our children to become happy and healthy adults. Moreover, what I have learned as a feminist mother is that we must teach our children not only how to resist patriarchy but, as importantly, how to keep safe and sane in doing so. We need to model to our children our own lived resistance and to share with them our stories of success and sorrow. And most importantly, we must create a feminist community and work towards a feminist world so that our children will have that sense of belonging, which is essential for wellbeing and makes possible resistance.

In "Developing a Feminist Motherline: Reflections on a Decade of Feminist Parenting," Fiona Joy Green, reflecting on the experiences shared by the feminist mothers that she interviewed, observes, "I am struck by the need to continue sharing and recording feminist motherline stories to ensure that the difficult, yet rewarding work of feminist mothering remains a communal and political endeavour" (18). She goes on to say:

> A feminist motherline provides the space and a place for feminist mothers to record and pass on their own life-cycle perspectives of feminist mothering and to connect with those of other feminist mothers. Additionally, a motherline ensures that feminist mothers have a connection with a worldview that is centered and draws upon feminism's crucial gender based analysis of the world –including parenting. It also promises a legacy of feminist mothering and motherwork for others. (18)

With Green, I believe that "motherline stories contain invaluable lessons and memories of feminist mothering, as well as support for mothers" (18). Looking back at over three decades of feminist mothering, I realize that it has been precisely these stories—shared across telephone lines, kitchen tables and more recently keyboards—that have sustained me as a feminist mother. Building on my work of cultural bearing in African American culture, Green argues that mothers, in sharing their stories of feminist mothering, are similarly cultural bearers of feminism. To borrow from Green, "Through developing a feminist motherline, with feminist mothers being the cultural bearers of feminism in their daily lives, empowerment for mothers and children is surely to follow" (18). For me, this is both the hope and promise of feminist mothering in and for the future.

CONCLUSION: "WORTH IT IN THE END"

As a mother of grown children, I can speak about feminist mothering with a good measure of composure and confidence. My kids have turned out just fine and are, more or less, content with their lives and doing the same things that "normal" people do. They have not sprouted two heads or morphed into antisocial loners as a result of being raised by a feminist mother. This is not to say that feminist mothering has been easy; on the contrary, there were many days, and even more nights, that I wondered and worried whether I was doing right by my children by raising them to be such strong feminists. And, of course, my children also suffered as a result of being raised in a feminist household, particularly as they grew up in a rural and conservative community. But, ultimately, I believe that feminist mothering has made me a better mother and my children, better people. Speaking of her experience of coming to feminism, Erin said: "Feminism did make it harder for me growing up because it made me different, but it was so worth it in the end. I came out the other side of all that. I am my own person." Casey commented: "I feel the same way. Worth it in the end, though going through it was hard.... As you grow older you come to appreciate it more. I live in this world without being swallowed up." Like my daughters, I too believe that feminist mothering is ultimately more about rewards than risks and that it is indeed "worth it in the end."

WORKS CITED

Bort, Julie, et al. *Mommy Guilt: Learn to Worry Less, Focus on What Matters Most and Raise Happier Kids.* American Management Association, 2005.

Bueskens, Petra. "The Impossibility of 'Natural Parenting' for Modern Mothers: On Social Structure and the Formation of Habit." *Journal of the Association for Research on Mothering*, vol. 3, no. 1, 2001, pp. 75-86.

Butterfield, Elizabeth. "Maternal Authenticity." *Encyclopedia of Mothering*, edited by Andrea O'Reilly, Sage Publications, 2010, pp. 700-701.

Collins, Patricia Hill. *Black Feminist Thought.* 2nd ed., Routledge Press, 2000.

Copper, Baba. "The Radical Potential in Lesbian Mothering of Daughters." *Politics of the Heart: A Lesbian Parenting Anthology*, edited by Sandra Pollack and Jeanne Vaughn, Firebrand Books, 1987, pp. 186-193.

Crittenden, Ann. *The Price of Motherhood: Why the Most Important Job in the World is Still the Least Valued*. Henry Holt, 2001.

Douglas, Susan J., and Meredith Micheals. *The Mommy Myth: The Idealization of Motherhood and How It Has Undermined Women*. Free Press, 2004.

Gordon, Tuula. *Feminist Mothers*. New York University Press, 1990.

Glickman, Rose. *Daughters of Feminists: Young Women with Feminist Mothers Talk about Their Lives*. St. Martin's Press, 1993.

Golden, Marita. *Saving Our Sons: Raising Black Children in a Turbulent World*. Anchor Books/Doubleday, 1995.

Gore, Ariel, and Bee Lavender. *Breeder: Real Life Stories from the New Generation of Mothers*. Seal Press, 2001.

Green, Fiona. "Feminist Mothers: Successfully Negotiating the Tensions Between Motherhood and Mothering." *Mother Outlaws: Theories and Practices of Empowered* Mothering, edited by Andrea O'Reilly, Women's Press, 2004, pp. 31-42

Green, Fiona. "Developing a Feminist Motherline: Reflections on a Decade of Feminist Parenting" *Journal of the Association for Research on Mothering*, vol. 8, no. 1-2, 2006, pp. 7-20.

Green, Fiona. *Practicing Feminist Mothering*. Arbeiter Publishing, 2011.

Horwitz, Erika. "Mothers' Resistance to the Western Dominant Discourse on Mothering." Dissertation, Simon Fraser University, 2003

Horwitz, Erika. "Resistance as a Site of Empowerment: The Journey away from Maternal Sacrifice." *Mother Outlaws: Theories and Practices of Empowered Mothering*, edited by Andrea O'Reilly, Women's Press, 2004, pp. 43-58.

hooks, bell. *Talking Feminist, Talking Black*. South Ends Press, 1989.

Kinser, Amber. *Motherhood and Feminism*. Seal Press, 2010.

Lorde, Audre. "Man Child: A Black Lesbian Feminist's Response." *Sister Outsider*, 1993.

MacDonald Strong, Shari. *The Maternal is Political: Women Writers at the Intersection of Motherhood and Social Change*. Seal Press, 2008.

O'Reilly, Andrea. *Mother Outlaws: Theories and Practices of Empowered Mothering*. Women's Press, 2004.

O'Reilly, Andrea. *From Motherhood to Mothering: The Legacy of Adrienne Rich's* Of Woman Born. SUNY Press, 2004.
O'Reilly, Andrea. *Rocking the Cradle: Thoughts on Motherhood, Feminism, and the Possibility of Empowered Mothering.* Demeter Press, 2006.
O'Reilly, Andrea. *Feminist Mothering.* SUNY Press, 2008.
O'Reilly, Andrea. *Maternal Theory: Essential Readings.* Demeter Press, 2007
O'Reilly, Andrea. *The Twenty-First-Century Motherhood Movement: Mothers Speak Out on Why We Need to Change the World and How to Do It.* Demeter Press, 2011.
O'Brien-Hallstein, Lynn. "Maternal Agency." *Encyclopedia of Mothering*, edited by Andrea O'Reilly, Sage Publications, 2010, pp. 697-699.
Reddy, Maureen, et al., editors. *Mother Journeys: Feminists Write about Mothering.* Spinsters Ink, 1994.
Rhine, Davina. *Rebel Moms: The Off-Road Map for the Off-Road Mom.* iUniverse Inc., 2011.
Rich, Adrienne. *Of Woman Born: Motherhood as Experience and Institution.* W.W. Norton, 1986.
Ruddick, Sara. *Maternal Thinking: Toward a Politics of Peace.* 1989. Beacon Press, 2002.
Shields, Juile. *How to Avoid the Mommy Trap: A Roadmap for Shared Parenting and Making it Work.* Capital Books, 2002.
Simpson, Bria. *The Balanced Mom: Raising Your Kids without Losing your Self.* New Harbinger Publications, Inc., 2006.
Smith, Janna Malamud. *A Potent Spell: Mother Love and the Power of Fear.* Houghton Mifflin Company, 2003.
Tiemann, Amy. *Mojo Mom: Nurturing Your Self while Raising a Family.* Spark Press, 2006.

4.
The Potential for Feminist Parenting

LYNN COMERFORD

THE CONSTRUCTION OF "MOTHERING" and "fathering" as separate roles that are coded feminine and masculine respectively is a principle undergirding the current gender order. In this chapter, I explore the binary mother-father in child-custody law in order to see if these subject positions have shifted in a feminist direction over time or if they have remained entrenched in opposition in the prison house of language. Any analysis of difference, such as the difference between mothering and fathering, is made through implicit or explicit contrasts, negations, and oppositions that are more or less enforced in particular contexts (such as the family) (Saussure). Binary oppositions (such as mother-father) are interdependent as Jacques Derrida explains in *Of Grammatology*; however, the interdependence involves hierarchy in that one term in the binary is always dominant or prior ("father") and the opposite term is subordinate or secondary ("mother"). In this chapter, I examine if the father-mother binary holds up over time in the context of changing child custody law in the United States. Are these binary terms always in fixed opposition? Can contrasting terms, such as "mother" and "father," become more fluid in their definitions over time? Has this affected feminist parenting? And if so, how has it?

A fluid notion of gender insists on examining the power relationship between binary terms and deconstructing fixed differences. For example, the leading terms in the following binaries are dominant: male-female, parent-child, heterosexual-homosexual, and identity-difference. These oppositions, according to Derrida, provide insight into how meaning is constructed. In order to uncover meanings, one must reverse and displace binary oppositions. An examination of changing child custody law and feminist parenting requires deconstructing fixed notions of gender and examining mothers as fathers and fathers as mothers. A fluid notion of gender identity—in which mothers are fathers and fathers are mothers—provides a feminist perspective on changes in child custody law in the United States.

In this chapter, I examine the meanings of the terms "mother" and "father" from a fixed theoretical position and then from a fluid theoretical position. After this analysis, I examine the terms in the context of the discourse of child custody law between the years 1800 and 2000. I then reflect on the "fixed" versus "fluid" theoretical descriptions of these terms to try to understand which theoretical position best explains the empirical evidence. Are mothers and fathers trapped in hierarchical binary opposition over centuries? Or have the meanings of these terms shifted over time in a more feminist and less hierarchical and oppositional direction?

GENDER IS FIXED

Nancy Chodorow argues in *The Reproduction of Mothering* that there is an "oedipal causality," which posits a maternal body prior to discourse. Chodorow draws from sociology and post-Freudian psychology, grounded in biological foundationalism, in order to examine and explain women's maternal role and how this role is in opposition to the paternal role. She argues that because the primary caretaker for both sexes in the first three years of life is typically female, the interpersonal dynamics of gender identity formation are different for boys and girls. Chodorow's claim is that the psychoanalytic account of male and female development provides a theory of the reproduction of women's mothering that differs from men's fathering. Women's mothering, she argues, reproduces itself through differing object-relational experiences with differing psychic outcomes in women and men. In her scenario, mothers are the primary caregivers of children and fathers are emotionally distant.

In Chodorow's view, because women were mothered by a woman, women are compelled in a deeply psychological way to also mother. And, because men were mothered by a woman, men are compelled in a deeply psychological way *not* to mother. Women's mothering produces asymmetries in the relational experiences of girls and boys as they grow up that according to Chodorow accounts for differences in feminine and masculine personality. Girls experience themselves as less separate than boys (girls have a close and loving mother, or mother figure, to emulate) and come to define themselves more in relation to others. Boys, on the other hand, experience themselves as more separate than girls because boys have a close and loving mother (or mother figure) that they *do not* emulate. Mothers experience their sons as a "male opposite" and push them out of the pre-Oedipal relationship, and because of this boys lose a sense of connectedness and gain a sense of independence and isolation from others.

Chodorow discusses fathers mostly in terms of their lack of relationship to other family members: "They are not present as much, are not primary caretakers, and their own training for masculinity may have led them to deny emotionality" (193). "Masculine personality" is defined more in terms of denial of relation and connection, and "feminine personality" is defined in terms of self in relationship. The lesson that the boy, and not the girl, learns from primary female mothering is that he must not identify with his mother and must repudiate intimacy in order to become a man. On this view, women "mother" and men "father"; the terms are in stark opposition to one another; and they signify polar opposite parenting behaviour.

GENDER IS FLUID

Michel Foucault, unlike Chodorow, questions psychoanalytic discourse as the explanation for "mother" and "father" difference. In the *The History of Sexuality: An Introduction*, Foucault argues that psychoanalytic explanation creates its own *causal* force in the gendered structure of "maternal" or "paternal" reproductive desires and behaviour. Foucault critiques the repressive hypothesis, which asserts that the structuralist "law" can be thought of as a form of power located in history and points out that the law can be seen as producing or creating the desire it is said to repress. According to Foucault, desire is created and forbidden as a symbolic gesture so that the judicial model can exercise its power. The discursive production of the maternal body by Chodorow conceals the power relations behind the concept of "maternal" and "paternal." Foucault does not see the maternal body as the deep signifier and explanation for all gender difference. In his view, the discourse of sexuality found in the story of psychoanalysis is understood to be an *effect* of power relations and an explanation of the prediscursive maternal body.

In their essay "The Subject and Power," Hubert Dreyfus and Paul Rabinow point out that Foucault examines the power relations and subjectivity at work in scientific discourse. Psychoanalysis is a type of scientific discourse, and one of the things it does is offer an explanation of gendered parenting behaviour. Foucault examines how "[t]he exercise of power consists in guiding the possibility of conduct and putting in order the possible outcome" (221) and studies "the way a human being turns him- or herself into a subject" (208). He is interested in techniques or forms of power that make individuals subjects, and argues that "[t]here are two meanings of the word *subject:* subject to someone else by control and dependence, and tied to his own identity by a conscience or self-knowledge" (212). Sexuality, according to Foucault, produces "sex" as an artificial concept that disguises the power-knowledge mechanisms at work behind the concept and invites a critique of the feminist preoccupation with psychoanalytic maternal identification. In this view, gendered parents (and children) can be understood to be *effects* of the discourses parents find themselves trapped in, such as scientific, psychological, religious, or legal discourses.

Foucault argues that there is nothing stable in the categories "male" and "female." He does not deny the materiality of the body, but he does not give it a fixed biological or prediscursive essence. In *Power/Knowledge*, Foucault writes:

> Each society has its regime of truth, its "general politics" of truth: that is, the types of discourses which it accepts and makes function as true; the mechanisms and instances

> which enable one to distinguish true and false statements, the means by which each is sanctioned; the techniques and procedures accorded value in the acquisition of truth; the status of those who are charged with saying what counts as true. (131)

In this view, discursive formations are not differentiated from the object about which they speak; rather they produce them. In short, what is "true" about mothering and what is "true" about fathering is embattled in discourse. The discourse of child custody law in the United States between 1800 and 2000, therefore, provides an interesting site to examine the "truth" about mothering and fathering over time in order to see if the meanings of these terms have changed in a feminist direction (i.e., have become fluid) or have remained locked in a hierarchical binary (i.e., have stayed fixed).

"FATHERING" AND "MOTHERING" IN CHILD CUSTODY DISCOURSE IN THE UNITED STATES BETWEEN 1800 AND 2000

Pre-1850

Child custody law goes back to common law, derived from Roman law, which gave fathers the unqualified right to child custody in the event of a divorce or separation. In the United States, men were given custody of children throughout the colonial period and the greater part of the nineteenth century. The courts justified this absolute right by arguing that it was divinely ordained, that it was based on natural law, and that it was necessary because fathers had a duty to economically support their children.

William Blackstone in *Commentaries on the Law of England* states simply the English common law on child custody: the father had a natural right to his children and the mother "was entitled to no power, but only to reverence and respect" (453). Before the middle of the nineteenth century, fathers were granted exclusive custody of children because it was argued they were the parents best fit to nurture and care for their children. For example, Lawrence Stone points out in *The Family, Sex and Marriage in England 1500-1800* that in a custody decision in Rhode Island in 1824, a judge determined that the father had an absolute right to custody "not on account of any absolute right of the father, but for the benefit of the infant, the law presuming it be under the *nurture and care* of his natural protector, both for maintenance and education" (38-39, emphasis added). In her book *Towards a Structure of Indifference: The Social Origins of Maternal Custody*, Deborah Friedman, documents that in 1842 a custody decision in the state of New Jersey held the following: "We are informed by the first elementary books we read, that the authority of the father is superior to that of the mother. It is the doctrine of all civilized nations. It is according to the revealed law, the law of nature, and it prevails even with the wandering savage, who has received none to the lights of civilization" (18). Drawing from these arguments, judges ensured that fathers controlled the custody of their children until the late nineteenth century.

John Demos, the historian of early American families, describes fathers in the eighteenth century in his book *Past, Present, and Personal: The Family and the Life Course in American History* as teachers, benefactors, psychologists, moral overseers, example makers, progenitors, companions, and caregivers. He points out that fathers, not mothers, corresponded with their children, and notes that parenting books of the time were primarily written for fathers, which suggests that fathers were interested not only in the labour of their children but in their general wellbeing as well. The literature on childrearing at this time focused on father parenting more than mother parenting. In writings about childhood education after the baby had been nursed, there was an assumption that fathers took care of parenting, or parenting was defined without reference to gender.

In general, prior to the late eighteenth century, motherhood was devalued relative to fatherhood. Mary Ann Mason in *From Father's Property to Children's Rights: A History of Child Custody in the United States* finds that "the ideal images of women appearing in the literature did not focus on women's role as a parent but rather on women as Christians and wives" (38). Women were not depicted in literature as mothers, and little was written about the emotional bonds women had with their children. At this time, when compared to men, women were seen as being less rational and more emotional as well as having less self-disciplined and inferior theological understanding. Mothers typically were busy engaged in work besides childrearing—for example, helping husbands with their trades. In *Governing the Hearth: Law and Family in 19th Century America*, Michael Grossberg argues that father's interest in their children during this time was economic. Most fathers, Grossberg argues, wanted custody of their children because the labour of a child over ten years of age was one of the most valuable assets a male could have in colonial America. Fathers at this time had absolute rights over their children, including the right to sell them and to coerce them into forced labour.

Prior to and during the nineteenth century, Roman, German, and Anglo-Saxon law placed children firmly in the arms of their fathers, both during marriage and after. The presumption of paternal custody reflected the greater access fathers had to legal support than mothers: women were often legal dependents themselves and could not be awarded custody of their children even after the death of the father because a dependent could not get custody of a dependent. Women in colonial America could not fight for custody of their children in the courts because they had no legal individual rights. In the colonial period, a mother's lack of power over her children was an aspect of the general legal impotence of married women. Under English common law, a married woman could not own property, either real or personal—all that she brought to her marriage became her husband's. Nor could married women make a legally binding contract, execute a deed of gift, or write a will, unless the husband consented.

Slave Families

The arbitrariness, contingency, tension, conflict, and struggle underlying the terms "mother" and "father" are particularly explicit in the case of slave families. U.S. family law, until about 1850, did not encompass slave families, who were governed by slave codes and property laws. The institution of slavery *reversed* the standard of fathers having an absolute right to custody. If one was born to a slave mother and had a white father, he did not seek custody, and the state did not grant him custody. Reflecting the economic desires of the white, male, slave owning class, the state created custody laws that stated that the slave child's status should be determined through the child's *mother*, not the father. The discourse of child custody law in colonial America defined "fathering" as the person best fit to nurture, care for, protect, maintain, and educate children, unless the child was a slave. The discourse of child custody in colonial America defined "mothering" as a person due "reverence and respect" from children but not best fit to "nurture and care" for them, unless she was a slave. Slave mothers, on the other hand, nurtured and cared for their children until the owner took possession of, or sold, them.

1850 to1950

As the century wore on, the social facts of fathers leaving the home for work and the declining economic value of children affected the role of the father. During the mid-to-late nineteenth century, the family became conjugal, nuclear, highly differentiated, specialized, private, and child centred. The household changed from a unit of production to a unit of consumption. Men went further from the home for employment. Thus, the management of the family increasingly fell to the mother. In *Mothers and Such: Views of American Women and Why They Changed*, Maxine Margolis notes the striking disappearance of references to fathers in the childrearing advice of the mid-nineteenth century. The elevation of motherhood has been explained as a result, in part, of the waning of home industry and the declining birthrate.

There are a number of factors that explain this shift. First, the absolute right to custody that fathers enjoyed ended in the middle of the nineteenth century when judges were granted the right to make custody decisions. It was then, according to Michael Grossberg, that the state garnered parental power as its own: "custody law transferred that guardianship from husbands to judges" (282). Grossberg argues that "the judge became the buffer and referee between the family and the state" and "family law became their patriarchal domain" (290). And child custody judgements, according to Grossberg, were rooted in middle-class ideology and interests.

The father's obligations to his children were deeply embedded in the institution of the family and the laws that governed it. As long as the social organization of families did not change, the father's status with his children remained unchanged. Yet as the social organization of families changed with increasing divorce, so too did men's status with their children. Also, although the argument that children need their mothers seems self-evident from a modern perspective, this was not always seen to be the case. Modern motherhood was socially and culturally defined, and it was this new conception of motherhood that explained the shift in preference from fathers to mothers in custody at this time. The shift in child custody laws in the 1840s allowed the state to enforce moral standards on mothers wanting custody of their children because, as Maxine Margolis points out, mothering was now defined in terms of women's moral superiority.

During the mid-nineteenth century, the rise of capitalism contributed to the general lengthening of the period of childhood. There were also new scientific studies of childhood that became important in the development of the invention of modern motherhood. Carol Smart in *Feminism and the Power of Law* argues that the sense that there might be an optimal design for raising children meant that socialization could not be left to the idiosyncratic preferences of individual parents. This idea—combined with Christopher Lasch's notion that the task of a parent was to civilize a child rather than break its will and to nurture the child as a distinct person ("Family as a Haven")—meant that a more refined approach to parenting would be required. Fathers were busy working outside the home, so the task was left to mothers. These new ways of thinking about children and childhood isolated mothers in the home. The lengthening of the phase of childhood and the notion that there was a correct way to parent suggested that mothering would have to change. Motherhood, as Barbara Ehrenreich and Deirdre English explain in *For Her Own Good: 150 Years of the Experts' Advice to Women*, would evolve from being a part-time occupation to a noble calling.

In the colonial period, there was little sense that children were a unique group: childhood was short, and children worked at a young age. But between 1785 and 1820, ideologies regarding children began to change. By 1800, Calvinist beliefs in infant damnation had given way to the Lockean doctrine of tabula rasa. In the middle classes, children began to be seen as individuals who needed nurturing rather than as small adults whose natural inclinations towards evil had to be tamed. This new way of thinking about children emphasized the role parents (especially mothers) played in caring for their children, since badly behaved children could no longer be blamed on inborn corruption. Imagining a child as a tabula rasa led to the idea that children were born pure and innocent and only "ruined" by bad parenting.

Within the span of forty years, roughly from 1880 to 1925, the presumption that divorced fathers should be granted custody of their children was changed everywhere. From about the 1850s to 1940s, society's increasing focus on child welfare and the effects of the Industrial Revolution (which encouraged fathers to work beyond the farm or village) increasingly left the care of children to mothers. In her book *Towards a Structure of Indifference: The Social Origins of Maternal Custody*, Debra Friedman points out "new laws were passed upholding the equal claims of mothers and fathers" (17-18). These laws, she argues, provided the basis for maternal custody: "[t]he language of judicial decisions that had once called upon God, Nature, and Reason to undergird paternal custody awards now called upon God, Nature, and Reason to support maternal custody awards" (18). In 1916, in the state of Washington, equally strong language appears to uphold an award of custody to a mother:

> Mother love is a dominant trait even in the weakest of women, and as a general thing surpasses the paternal affection for the common offspring, and, moreover, a child needs a mother's care even more than a father's. For these reasons courts are loathe to deprive the mother of the custody of her children, and will not do so unless it be shown clearly that she is so far an unfit and improper person to be entrusted with custody as to endanger the welfare of the children. (qtd. in Mary Ann Mason 172)

In her essay "American Feminine Ideals in Transition: The Rise of the Moral Mother," Ruth Bloch draws from literature about mothers between the late seventeenth and early nineteenth centuries and traces the development of motherhood. She suggests that the change in the definition of motherhood arose as a result of three factors: the disappearance of servants and other nonkin from the home, the removal of men's work and production from the home, and the increasing depiction of women as morally superior to men. In a reversal of seventeenth-century beliefs, mothers came to be seen as more nurturing and moral than fathers. Suddenly, mothers were granted exclusive custody of children of "tender years" because it was argued that they were the parents best fit to nurture and care for their children. The "tender-years" doctrine (intended to apply to children under six years of age) became the standard for deciding custody in favour of the mother until the children were old enough to be returned to the father.

The patriarchs had high expectations of mothers. Mary Ann Mason in her essay "Motherhood v. Equal Treatment" illustrates the class-based character of child custody law at the time: "English courts in the 1890's would be expected to prefer fathers, particularly elite ones. Sometimes mothers were able to mount effective counter-cases, although the questionable morality of the mother would have weighed against her more than did the questionable morality of the father" (2-3).

The high moral standards attributed to mothers in the nineteenth century allowed judges to view them more positively in custody disputes—but it also meant that they turned harshly against them when they strayed from conventional moral standards. According to Mason, "the two transgressions that most frequently caused women to lose custody of their children were adultery and leaving their husbands without, in the opinion of the judge, just cause" (63). Mason points out that, conversely, in the nineteenth century fathers routinely were not held to the same moral standard as mothers; for example, male adulterers received custody if they wanted it.

Bloch also describes the shift in motherhood in the nineteenth century: fathers sought work outside the home and had less contact with their children, and women became increasingly responsible for childrearing. Because men left the home for work, and women did not, women were less able to assist in economic responsibilities. This new emphasis on the mother-child dyad would have been inconceivable a hundred years earlier because the conditions whereby women could devote themselves exclusively to their children did not exist (Margolis). Carol Smart argues that during this same period, however, feminists made advances in two areas: the increasing demands for married women's rights, and for suffrage. Thus, two conflicting historical movements transformed the status of mothers: the cult of motherhood and the campaign for women's rights.

The turn of the twentieth century was characterized by the increasing demands for married women's rights and for suffrage—both of which had to do with changes in child custody laws. Michael Grossberg draws on family court cases during this time and argues that fathers lost their presumption to custody in the courts in mid-nineteenth century. Grossberg attributes the shift in child custody to forces beyond familial relations. He argues that custody shifts occurred because of expanding legal rights of women, particularly those having to do with women's increasing control over property within marriage. Maternal custody, he argues, became a possibility as women gained more control over property generally. When states gave women the right to control property, the state took that right away from their husbands and extended it to the discretion of the judiciary. When judges were given the right to make custody determinations, it was the state, Grossberg argues, that garnered parental power as its own. There was no consensus on the question of custody of children following divorce, but women's new legal position within marriage, and outside of it, ensured that there would be a battle over property (including children).

If the expansion of the rights of women was behind the shift in child custody rights, why did motherhood become a noble calling during this time? According to Maxine Margolis, the emphasis on maternity helped to solve the so-called woman question. Once women's upper-middle-class, white, heterosexual productive skills were no longer needed, she argues, motherhood was the only role left for women. Margolis notes that outside employment was not considered an option during this time and that "advice givers" argued that paid employment was incompatible with mothering and homemaking. By 1860, there were clearly separated spheres between the public world of work (male) and the private world of work (female). Mary Ryan in *Cradle of the Middle Class: The Family in Oneida County New York, 1790-1865* shows that middle-class women were to devote themselves to producing "high quality" children who would take their husband's place in business and industry. Another factor, Margolis reveals, is that business elites could profit from cornering women into the domestic sphere. Lower wages for working women could be justified by the idea that they were only temporary workers until they became mothers. This also encouraged men and fathers to work harder and longer in order to avoid the stigma of having a working wife.

Another reason for the change in child custody is that children were increasingly seen as national resources. Elisabeth Badinter in *The Myth of Motherhood: An Historical View of the Maternal Instinct* and Anna Davin in her essay "Imperialism and Motherhood" both argue that the self-sacrificing, nurturing, loving mother arose in response to the state's desire to increase the population. High infant mortality rates were blamed on maternal practices (wet nursing, in particular), and it was argued that women's behaviours needed to change. If women behaved with their children more "appropriately maternal," Badinter notes, they were promised prestige, the love of their husbands and children, and the belief that they were making an impact on society. Middle-class women were the first to respond because they had the fewest options. Badinter adds that because the cult of domesticity was a predominantly middle-class phenomenon neither upper-class women nor working-class women were much taken by it. Badinter explains that middle-class women were the last women to give their children up to paid caregivers and the first to take them back from them. In contrast, aristocratic women were the first to give up their children to paid caregivers and the last to take them back. And working-class mothers simply could not afford such an expensive ideology. Christine Bose, in her essay "Dual Spheres" perceptively highlights how the domestic code served to sharpen class distinctions among women.

By 1925, eight states in the United States had custody statutes and seven had no statutory provisions favouring the mother or the father. There was a presumption of custody in favour of the father, but this was based on common law and not statutory provisions. Louisiana was the only state that had a statutory custody provision and that allowed mothers to be custodial parents to children under two years of age and fathers to be custodial parents to children over two years of age. The tender-years doctrine—which determined mothers to be the more suitable caregiver for young children under six years of age but not for older children—modified but did not reverse the traditional notion of the father's rights to custody. The tender-years doctrine refers to the assumption that children up until a particular age should be with their mother.

Determining sole custody for children when the tender-years doctrine was being enforced was based on two simple criteria: the age of the child and who had been the primary caretaker (usually the mother). This meant that if the father wanted custody, he had to prove that the mother was somehow unfit. By about 1925, the courts had nearly reversed the traditional preference for the father as the custodial parent and shifted the award of custody to the mother, unless there were disqualifying factors (e.g., alcoholism or a history of criminal behaviour). The shift to granting mothers, almost exclusively, custody coincided with laws prohibiting child labour. Somebody had to keep an eye on children because the workplace was no longer serving this role.

Husbandless mothers created an even larger problem for the state during this time period. The support of husbandless women was already a public issue by the 1880s. Mother custody created a problem for the state because women started receiving custody but did not have any means of economic support. Father custody demanded that fathers provide protection, material support, and education. Mother custody emphasized only nurturing—not protection, material support, or education (except perhaps moral). Divorce left not only children but also women with no basis of financial support, and providing for divorced women was more serious than the problem of providing for children of divorce because it was more long term. Children could be expected to be self-supporting (either in the labour market or in marriage) by twenty-one years of age at the latest, but this was not the case for their mothers, whose life expectancy was increasing (especially among privileged white women). Mary Anne Mason argues that there were four sources of disadvantage to divorced mothers in the labour market: "First, they were women, second, they had been formerly married, third, they were divorced, and forth, they had children. Each served as a separate impediment to self-support;

together they rendered women nearly economically powerless to provide for themselves and their children" (113).

Theda Skocpol points out in her tome *Protecting Soldiers and Mothers: The Political Origins of Social Policy in the United States* that the state was willing to provide "mother pensions" to women who were widows or had lost their husbands to desertion. However, she notes the state did not help support divorced mothers: fathers were obligated to pay them support. Noncustodial fathers were obligated to financially support both their children and the mothers of their children after divorce. Custodial fathers, however, provided only for their children. Mason highlights that from a social welfare point of view mother custody was a superior arrangement because it provided for not one set of dependents but two. She points out that mother custody (with fathers supporting both their children and their ex-wife) saved the state the economic burden of supporting divorced women for life. According to her, the state wanted this for three reasons: first, it privatized the obligation; second, it solved the problem of support of divorced mothers; and third, it avoided a public debate on the issue of discrimination against women in the labour force. The only responsibility to families left for the state, she explains, was the obligation to educate children.

By the 1920s, maternal preference for custody in American law, regardless of the child's age, became as firmly fixed as the earlier paternal preference and was encoded in statute in all forty-eight states. (Alaska and Hawaii did not become states until the 1950s.) Jacques Donzelot argues in *The Policing of Families* that the assumption that mothers were better suited to raise and nurture children received an intellectual underpinning in the 1930s from the discourse of Freudian psychoanalytic theory (188-209), which focuses exclusively on the mother-child relationship and largely ignores the role of the father in the child's development. At the time, the discourse of Freudian psychoanalytic theories suggested that young children needed their mothers as their primary caregiver in order to become, among other things, heterosexual. By the middle-third of the twentieth century, as divorce became more common, judges began to shift their reasons for giving custody to mothers from their "natural" abilities to what was in "the best interest of the child," which expanded the judges' discretion in child custody decisions. The shift from father custody to mother custody benefited the state in at least three ways: first, it allowed its male citizens to work outside the home unfettered with the responsibilities of caring for children; second, it provided the state, in the form of "patriarchal judges," control over the family (particularly the moral behaviour of mothers); and third, it saved the state from having to provide "divorcee" pensions to mothers.

1950 to 1990

In 1950, the federal government stepped into the arena of child custody. At this time in the United States, only a small minority of children were in mother-only families. Congress amended the Aid to Families with Dependent Children (AFDC) law by requiring state welfare agencies to notify law enforcement officials when benefits were given to a child who had been abandoned by one or both of his or her parents so that local officials could find the nonresident parents and make them pay child support. From 1950 to 1975, the federal government helped welfare families collect child support from the absent parent but did not help nonwelfare families collect child support. By the early 1970s, however, Congress recognized that the composition of the AFDC caseload had changed. In the 1950s, the majority of children needed financial help because their fathers had died. By the 1970s, the majority needed aid because their parents were separated, divorced, or never married.

The Child Support Enforcement and Paternity Establishment Program (CSE), enacted in 1975, was a response by Congress to reduce money spent on welfare by obtaining child support from noncustodial parents, which helped non-AFDC families get support so they could stay off public assistance and established paternity for children born outside of marriage so that child support could be obtained for them. For the first time, the state became involved in financially supporting divorced family members. During this time period, the tender-years doctrine was found to be discriminatory and was rejected by California courts in the 1950s and by the New York and Illinois courts in the 1970s. By 1982, two-thirds of the states had rejected the tender-years doctrine as not in the child's best interest.

The tender-years doctrine gave way to the "best interest" doctrine; the best interest doctrine gave judges the power to decide who would be the primary or sole custodial parent based on a vague notion of what was in the best interest of the child. Deborah Friedman points out that "the 'best interest' doctrine permitted judges to use their own discretion in their decisions" (34). She highlights the lack of directives in child custody policy with regards to exactly what obligations come with parenting as well as the flaws inherent in basing decisions on children's welfare rather than on parents' obligations.

With the advent of "no fault" divorce, the presumption that the interests of a child of tender years is best served in the custody of the mother was legally abolished or demoted to a "factor to be considered" in nearly all states between 1960 and 1990. Friedman raises some concerns regarding what is meant by "best interest." For example, she wonders if the judge's estimation of a child's happiness with one parent as against another should be the guiding criterion, or if the judge should be concerned with the material advantages associated with one parent. What about the child's future needs? Nurturing? Emotional wellbeing? The "different" and stereotypical contributions from mothers and fathers to their children's welfare in intact families are optimized; however, in divorced families, how does a judge, Friedman wonders, decide which type of contribution is best? The best interest argument is so symbolically and rhetorically compelling that the argument continues to be raised in custody decisions today.

In his book *Haven in a Heartless World: The Family Besieged*, Christopher Lasch addresses the fears working-class parents had when they were held to middle-class parenting standards during custody cases. Judges, social workers, juvenile courts and family visits "sought to counteract the widespread lack of wisdom and understanding on the part of parents, teachers, and others, while reassuring the mother who feared, with good reason, that the social worker meant to take her place in the home" (14). The "best interest" shift in custody law also began the history of state resources being used by the family. The state took an active role as super parent by providing more economic support while dictating stricter standards of behaviour to mostly poor families.

By the 1970s, as mothers increasingly worked outside of the home and the feminist movement challenged the presumption that only women could care for children and do housework, the "best interests of the child" argument had replaced the "tender years" presumption in most states. For the first time in history, child custody decision making was rooted in a consideration of the child's needs and interests rather than on the gender of the parent. Although the principle of "equal treatment" of the sexes in child custody cases had been incorporated into statutory law in a number of states in the 1920s and had received legislative support earlier, it was not until the 1960s and 1970s that equality became a principle doctrine. In 1979, California was one of the first states to adopt a joint custody law that made a distinction between physical and legal joint custody. By 1988, thirty-four states had adopted some form of joint custody. Beginning with a California law passed in 1969, the advent of "no fault" divorce throughout the United States shifted child custody results. Before "no fault" divorce, a parent was found to be "at fault" and stigmatized as the "bad" parent and usually automatically lost a custody battle. California was the first state to enact a child custody law that explicitly stated that the gender of a parent had no barring on the child custody decisions (see California Civil Code Section 3040 listed below).

In 1980, California went one step further in its effort to increase the participation of the noncustodial parent in cases in which there was no joint custody, and enacted a law that granted noncustodial parents access to medical, school, and legal records. This law also favoured granting custody to the parent most likely to encourage contact with the noncustodial parent. In the 1980s, as Scott Coltrane and Neal Hickman suggest in their article "The Rhetoric of Rights and Needs: Moral Discourse in the Reform of Child Custody and Child Support Laws," judges suddenly began to focus on the "need" for children to maintain a close relationship with both parents. Joint legal and physical custody was made an explicit preference in law at this point, but only about 20 percent of California divorce decrees provided for joint physical custody.

In the 1970s and 1980s, there was also reform in child support. As divorce became the norm, the refusal on the part of fathers to pay child support created a national scandal. In 1974, the U.S. Congress initiated a "parent locator" service for fathers who were delinquent in their child-support payments and whose children were relying on AFDC, according to Judith Cassetty in her book *Child Support and Public Policy.* By 1984, Congress mandated withholding money from all delinquent parents' paychecks and income tax refunds to force payment of child support. In 1988, as Lynda Walters and Carla Abshire describe in their article "Single Parenthood and the Law," Congress passed legislation regulating how the courts award and collect child custody support payments and required that by 1994 all new or modified child-support orders could be collected by automatic wage withholding if necessary. Custody law reforms occurred at the state level, but child support enforcement reform occurred at the federal level. States had to comply with child-support enforcement laws, or they would not receive federal subsidies for Aid to Families with Dependent Children (AFDC).

The legal changes in child custody and child support and new developments in genetic testing led to laws enforcing the establishment of paternity due to the Child Support Enforcement Program of the Ways and Means Committee. According to the Committee on Ways and Means of the U.S. House of Representatives, *2004 Green Book*, Public Law 98-378 was enacted that contained provisions aimed at increasing the number of paternity suits established, as was the Child Support Enforcement Amendments of 1984 that required states to implement laws that permitted paternity to be established until a child's eighteenth birthday. Under the *Family Support Act* of 1988 (Public Law 100-485), states have to establish paternity for all children under eighteen years of age. The 1988 law, according to the Department of Health and Human Services, encourages those in contested paternity cases to take a genetic test upon the request of any party and also requires the federal government to pay for 90 percent of the lab costs of the tests. Fathers, like mothers, were identified as parents.

1990 to the Present

By 1991, according to Greer Fox and Priscilla Blanton's article "Noncustodial fathers following divorce," more than thirty-five states had shared parenting statutes in which joint legal and physical custody was either an option or preference. Joint legal custody means that both parents share in making important decisions for their children, such as in the areas of health, education, and travel. This arrangement became important because of the enormous demographic changes in the U.S. family composition. Mary Ann Mason, in her book *From Father's Property to Children's Rights*, suggests that joint legal custody in the state of California, for example, quickly became as "natural" as "father only" custody had been in the early nineteenth century or "mother only" custody in the 1950s. Legal custody of children is usually jointly held between parents and allows parents to equally contribute to nonemergency life decisions affecting the child, including religious training, education and medical treatment. Physical custody of a child is also called "time sharing." Primary custody must be assigned when a county has to determine who is rewarded public assistance.

Joint legal and physical custody was a welcome change for many judges who had grown wary of making sole custody decisions. The feminist revolution, the father movement, working mothers, increases in divorce and single parenthood, and the shift from an adversarial to a mediation approach in family court, brought about a shift in child custody decisions from primary custody to shared custody. With the abolition of fault-based divorce and the maternal presumption (which made custody decisions fairly routine), judgs increasingly became dependent on the social sciences. Martha Fineman points out in her book *The Neutered Mother*, that by 1990, one-third of all child custody cases on appeal had been tried with the aid of some sort of expert testimony. Fineman argues that state legislatures and courts weakened mothers' legal claims to primary custody of their children following divorce actions, this systematically wiped out the maternal preference with new gender-neutral preferences, such as joint physical custody. The new goal, according to Fineman, was to provide consistency in decision-making in which there was no longer an easy choice based on gender; arguments that there were differences between mothering and fathering fell on deaf ears in family courts across the country.

"MOTHERS AND FATHERS" OR "FEMINIST GENDER-NEUTRAL PARENTS"?

Does the shift in legal discourse from automatic father custody to automatic mother custody to "gender-neutral" custody reflect the fluid nature of the meaning of "mother" and "father"? Or do mothers continue to remain subordinate or secondary to fathers in the mother-father binary in U.S. child custody legal decisions? Has systematically wiping out the maternal preference for a gender-neutral preference signified a feminist shift in parenting?

The material concept of "sex"—which Monique Wittig in her essay "The Straight Mind" calls a thoroughly political category and which Michel Foucault in *The History of Sexuality* calls a regulatory and "fictitious unity"—does not describe a prior materiality, according to these theorists, but produces and regulates the intelligibility of the materiality of bodies. The above review of the history of custody law in the U.S. illustrates that the categories of "mothering" and "fathering" impose a gendered duality and a uniformity on bodies that is violent in its restrictions. Parents lost primary custody of their children because of a parent's gender. Custody law describes fathers as the nurturers in the family in the nineteenth century, mothers as the nurturers in the family in the twentieth century and, with a stroke of the pen, nurturing becomes gender-neutral in the U.S. in the twenty-first century.

In my effort to expose as nonfoundational the categories of "mother" and "father" and examine the lives of parents in child custody discourse, I find that both a fixed and fluid understanding of gender is helpful. An examination of the history of mothers and fathers in custody exposes the political aspects of the origins and causes of identity categories, which Michel Foucault charges are in fact contingent and the effects of institutions, practices, and discourses. And, at the same time, one observes that mothers and fathers, as distinct groups over time, tend to be victims of patriarchal norms codified through child custody law. The processes, procedures, and mechanisms—whereby truth, knowledge, and beliefs are produced in child custody discourse—reveal that gendered norms are imposed on individuals as members of a particular sex. This reveals both the fluid *and* fixed nature of gender. The history of child custody law decentres child custody as a practice involving coherent gender norms that change over time and emphasizes how parenting (i.e., mothering and fathering) is both an *effect* of institutions and practices and, at the same time, accomplished by active agents and social movements making choices that challenge the binary.

Co-custody policy, as a disciplinary cultural practice, constitutes subjects who become gender-neutral co-parents; however, it also constitutes subjects who resist. What is interesting from a feminist perspective is that some of the disciplinary practices of custody law have the potential to emancipate gendered parenting and make family life more equal (50-50 physical and legal custody can open up parents' schedules, for example.) However, if fathers, for example, take the opportunity to physically and legally co-parent their children equally (and thus save a lot on child support) but pass the actual carework on to new wives, girlfriends, grandmothers, or paid female caregivers, the "neutral" in gender-neutral co-parenting is troubled.

As a result of gendered custody policy historically and gender-neutral custody policy today in California, parents can creatively navigate their way in and through legal discursive formations that define their parenting. In this view, the language of parenting is neither a closed system nor a unitary force because it constitutes subjects differently. The force of the legal discourse of custody on particular parents varies in degree and effect, and exerts more control over some subjects than others. The question of whether parents become objects of co-custody policies or subjects who resist them illuminates the idea that in any social context, multiple forces are at work, and the cause-effect relationship is never unitary.

The point here is that the force of custody policies on subjectivity is multiple, uneven, at times contradictory, and does not uniformly determine subjectivity. There is no question that subjects change when they come into contact with gender-neutral custody law, but the way that they change may or not be in a feminist direction. Mothers and fathers are not neatly turned into gender-neutral, equal feminist co-parents because a judge provides them with equal physical and legal custody of their children. In fact, the changes in child custody law in the United States have historically led to women's material disadvantage. Co-custody policy—which is gender-neutral legally and has the potential to emancipate women and men from disciplining maternal and paternal discourses—only works if equal physical and legal child custody does not have the effect of impoverishing women and children or increasing women in the role of parent because men neglect and/or delegate their custodial parenting responsibilities. In child custody law today, mothers and fathers are not automatically gender-neutral feminist co-parents, but the potential is there.

WORKS CITED

Badinter, Elisabeth. *The Myth of Motherhood: An Historical View of the Maternal Instinct.* Souvenir Press, 1981.

Blackstone, William. *Commentaries on the Law of England.* 1765. University of Chicago Press, 1979.

Bloch, Ruth. "American Feminine Ideals in Transition: The Rise of the Moral Mother, 1785-1815." *Feminist Studies*, vol. 2, no 2, 1978, pp. 101-126.

Bose, Christine. "Dual Spheres." *Analyzing Gender: A Handbook of Social Science Research*, edited by Beth Hess and Uyra M. Ferree, Sage, 1987, pp. 267-285.

Brown, June Gibbs. *Paternity Establishment: State Use of Genetic Testing.* Office of Inspector General, Department of Health and Human Services. OEI – 06-98-00054, September, 1999.

Cassetty, Judith. *Child Support and Public Policy.* Lexington Books, 1978.

Chodorow, Nancy. *The Reproduction of Mothering: Psychoanalysis and the Sociology of Gender.* University of California Press, 1978.

Coltrane, Scott, and Neal Hickman. "The Rhetoric of Rights and Needs: Moral Discourse in the Reform of Child Custody and Child Support Laws." Social Problems, vol. 4, no 39, 1992, pp. 400-419.

Committee on Ways and Means. *2004 Green Book.* U.S. Government Printing Office. March, 2004.

Demos, John. *Past, Present, and Personal: The Family and the Life Course in American History.* Oxford University Press, 1986.

Derrida, Jacques. *Of Grammatology.* John Hopkins University Press, 1976.

Donzelot, Jacques. *The Policing of Families.* Johns Hopkins University Press, 1979.

Dreyfus, Hubert, and Paul Rabinow. *Michel Foucault: Beyond Structuralism and Hermeneutics.* University of Chicago Press, 1983.

Ehrenreich, Barbara, and Deirdre English. *For Her Own Good: 150 Years of the Experts' Advice to Women.* Anchor Press, 1978.

Fineman, Martha. *The Neutered Mother, The Sexual Family and other Twentieth Century Tragedies.* Routledge. 1995.

Foucault, Michel. *The History of Sexuality.* New York: Vintage Press, 1978.

Foucault, Michel. *Power/Knowledge.* Edited by C. Gordon. Pantheon, 1980.

Fox, Greer and Priscilla Blanton. "Noncustodial Fathers Following Divorce." *Marriage and Family Review*, vol. 20, pp. 257-282.

Friedman, Deborah. *Towards a Structure of Indifference: The Social Origins of Maternal Custody.* Aldine De Gruyter Press, 1995.

Furukawa, Stacy. "The Diverse Living Arrangements of Children." U.S. Bureau of the Census, Current Population Reports, pp. 70-78. Government Printing Office, 1994.

Grossberg, Michael. *Governing the Hearth: Law and Family in 19th Century America.* The University of North Carolina Press, 1985.

Lasch, Christopher. "The Family as a Haven in a Heartless World." *Family in Transition: Rethinking Marriage, Sexuality, Child Rearing, and Family Organization.* 4th eds., edited by Arlene S. Skolnick and Jerome H. Skolnick, Little, Brown, 1983, pp. 102-113.

Lasch, Christopher. *Haven in a Heartless World: The Family Besieged.* Basic Books, 1977.

Margolis, Maxine. *Mothers and Such: Views of American Women and Why They Changed.* University of California Press, 1984.

Mason, Mary Ann. *From Father's Property to Children's Rights: A History of Child Custody in the United States.* Columbia University Press, 1994.

Mason, Mary Ann. "Motherhood v. Equal Treatment." *Journal of Family Law*, vol. 29, no. 1, 1991, pp. 1-50.

Morris, Linda. U.S. Bureau of the Census. "Current Population Reports." U.S. Government Printing Office, Washington, DC, pp. 23-192, 1996.

Rawlings, Steve and Arlene Saluter. "Household and Family Characteristics: March 1994." U.S. Bureau of the Census, Current Population Reports. U.S. Government Printing Office, Washington, DC, pp. 20-483, 1995.

Ryan, Mary. *Cradle of the Middle Class: The Family in Onedia County, New York, 1790-1865*. Cambridge University Press, 1981.

Saussure, Ferdinand. *Course in General Linguistics*. La Salle, Illinois, 1986.

Skocpol, Theda. *Protecting Soldiers and Mothers: The Political Origins of Social Policy in the United States*. Harvard University Press, 1992.

Smart, Carol. *Feminism and the Power of Law*. Routledge, 1989.

Stone, Lawrence. *The Family, Sex and Marriage in England 1500-1800*. Knopf, 1977.

Walters, Lynda Henley and Carla Rae Abshire. "Single Parenthood and the Law." *Marriage and Family Review*, vol. 20, no. 1-2. 1995, pp. 161-188.

Wittig, Monique. "The Straight Mind." *Feminist Issues*, vol. 1, no. 1, 1980, pp. 106- 107.

LEGAL CODES CITED

California Family Code 3040:

(A) Custody should be granted in the following order of preference according to the best interest of the child as provided in Sections 3011 and 3020:

> To both parents jointly pursuant to Chapter 4 (commencing with Section 3080) or to either parent. In making an order granting custody to either parent, the court shall consider, among other factors, which parent is more likely to allow the child frequent and continuing contact with the non-custodial parent, consistent with Section 3011 and 3020, and shall not prefer a parent as custodian because of that

parent's sex. The court, in its discretion, may require the parents to submit to the court a plan for the implementation of the custody order.

If to neither parent, to the person or persons in whose home the child has been living in a wholesome and stable environment.

To any other person or persons deemed by the court to be suitable and able to provide adequate and proper care and guidance for the child.

(B) This section establishes neither a preference nor a presumption for or against joint legal custody, joint physical custody, or sole custody, but allows the court and the family the widest discretion to choose a parenting plan that is in the best interest of the child.

5.
Before You

I never noticed parks
or other pregnant women.
I was a passenger in a red convertible,
circling fast around the Arc de Triomphe.
My sunny skies a different hue,
free and cloudless.
Chasing ideas, adventure, love
Little reflection; often alone.

Parks are everywhere now.
And, global warming, warming, warming.
And, Iraq, Afghanistan, Gaza, Libya and Syria.
The red slide you're on distracts for a moment,
Your face hurling toward me.
Your lovely face.

My love and fear in a swirl.
The weight of the responsibility,
a constant cloud,
weighs on me more.
I've always been
the first line of defense.

Our long days and short years;
the grinding exhaustion of motherwork.
Air strikes, rapprochement,

The park's dry grass,
The drone in the blue sky,
We must share responsibility.

—Lynn Comerford

II.
RESISTANCE

6.
powerful autonomy

becoming a teen mom
and giving birth to a baby
shortly after high school graduation
made me a better mother

to experience something as powerful
as deciding to become a mother
in a world that told me I shouldn't
was a strong and defiant choice

all the world wanted to do
was to prevent a birth like my daughter's
my existence was not good enough
teen moms are never given a chance

but teen motherhood is a feminist act
using that powerful autonomy
and choosing to raise a child
in a world that tells us we shouldn't

it is a defiant, radical, and feminist act.

—Heather Jackson

7.
Mothering on Their Own Terms

How Single, Queer, and Feminist Mothering Deconstruct Patriarchy, Gender, and the Nuclear Family

HEATHER JACKSON

MULTIPLE CONNOTATIONS attach themselves to the term "motherhood." Motherhood, defined by society, contains an ever-changing set of "instructions" to judge mothers. These instructions are created and shared by society in many different venues, such as pop culture, academe, the work place, and media. Social constructions of "who is a good or bad mother" are fabricated as ideals. Not only have mothers internalized these ideals, but society uses them to define mothers. Adrienne Rich notes that motherhood is "a patriarchal institution that is oppressive to women" (13). Andrea O'Reilly expands on this notion and argues that "while motherhood as an institution, is a male-defined site of oppression, women's own experiences of mothering could nonetheless be a source of power if they were experienced outside of motherhood" ("This Is What Feminism Is" 192).

Motherhood, as an institution, is patriarchal and oppressive to women. Patriarchy defines how mothers should behave in the mother role. Motherhood is a social construction. As O'Reilly argues:

> Most agree that motherhood is primarily not a natural or biological function; rather, it is specifically and fundamentally a cultural practice that is continuously redesigned in response to changing economic and societal factors. As a cultural construction, its meaning varies with time and place; there is no essential or universal experience of motherhood. (*Mother Outlaws* 5)

Social constructions ascribe appropriate behaviours to mothers, such as being married to a cisgender[1] man and having children after marriage. Frequently excluded are mothers who do not fit within these socially constructed norms. As Love and Shanklin explain: "Patriarchy and patriarchal motherhood are embedded in institutions and in families. [This] implies the expropriation of the child and the exploitation of women as mothers. Patriarchy, then, refers not only to male domination, but to a specific set of institutions that ensures the alienation of the child from the mother" (276).

Thus, the daughter will be socialized to marry a man and to be "given away" by her father to another man through the marriage ceremony, just as her mother was expected to do. Mothers raise their children in a patriarchal society, even if the mothers are single or have gained custody of the children. They must navigate within a patriarchal society. Queer and lesbian women also choose to become mothers. However, these mothers may not have a man or traditional father figure involved in their own or their children's lives. As Love and Shanklin explain further: "For the lesbian relationship implies commitment to denial of male authority over the mother's own and her child's life. Therefore, the lesbian mother constitutes a threat to the continuation of patriarchal society" (277). The lesbian mother threatens patriarchy. Lesbian mothering does not involve a father figure and can involve one or two mothers, which demonstrates that children can be raised without fathers. Not only is this true with lesbian mothers but with single mothers as well. As Monica Nolan argues, "A single mom and her kids are by definition a family without a father, and the female-headed household is destruction of the patriarchy at its most basic level" (245). Nolan claims that since these mothers are not partnered or married specifically to men, single mothering breaks down patriarchy. Because lesbian, queer, and single mothers may not have a father in their households, this means these women and their children are not subject to the direct control of men.

In this chapter, I focus on how single, queer, and feminist mothering deconstructs patriarchy, gender, and the nuclear family by breaking down the "appropriate-ness" that has been ascribed to mothers by patriarchal society. I begin the chapter with my theoretical approach and define the terms that I use and follow with a literature review of journal articles, books, and other sources that have explored the subject. Following this, I explain my methods of qualitative research—my interviewing of ten mothers. Finally, I describe my findings on how these mothers have deconstructed these normalized roles of mothering. I draw from queer theory and my interviews with mothers to deconstruct social norms of mothering.

THEORETICAL APPROACH: QUEER AND FEMINIST THEORY

Queer theory deconstructs traditional and heteronormative views of the family, individuals, sexuality, and gender. Queer theory is "demonstrating the impossibility of any 'natural' sexuality and it calls into question even such apparently unproblematic terms as 'man' and 'woman'" (Jagose 3). Queer theory questions language and identity within a world of social and cultural norms. Therefore, disassembling the norms is exactly what queer theory aims to do.

Chris Ingraham explains that "Heteronormativity is an ideology that promotes gender conventionality, heterosexuality, and the family traditionalism as the correct way for people to be" (169). Moreover, it is the "implicit moral system or value framework that surrounds the practice of heterosexuality" (Oswald et al. 144). This system marks heterosexuality as the norm and "more natural" of sexualities; every other sexual identity, therefore, becomes the "other" or is seen as deviant.

This theoretical approach also discusses the importance of people who build families on their own terms and are "queering" the world around them. Queering the world involves resisting heteronormativity through sexuality, gender identities, and family structures. For example, the mothers I interviewed have queered their lives and families with their own identities by being feminists, single mothers, queer, and by questioning the gender binary. Even with small revolutionary acts—such as being a mother-headed household with no father involved, identifying as a feminist queer mother, or creating a family as a transman mother[2]—these mothers queer the world around them. Thus, they are mothering on their own terms and deconstruct the gender binary, the family, and sexuality. As Nancy Naples states, "Queering family and parenting, and destabilizing the powerful hegemony of heteronormativity, involves daily negotiations, strategic choices, and a commitment to challenging heterosexual privilege in everyday life" (638).

Finally, as a feminist, I do not want to forget the importance of feminist theory in regards to patriarchy, power, privilege, and oppression. Some feminist theorists have had concerns with queer theory and that it "risks paying insufficient attention to gender in its analyses of sexuality and that, as a consequence, will/may lead to the construction of a universal male subject at the heart of its theorizing" (Richard et al. 7). My intent is to use queer theory as an approach to this topic as well as to develop a way to deconstruct the social norms that I question.

LITERATURE REVIEW

Although there is a lot of research on mothering, empirical research on feminist, queer, and single mothering continues to grow. Valerie Mannis and Maureen Sullivan explore the question of how mothers make the choice to be single or be a lesbian and chose to become mothers, and explore what types of support that they receive from other family members, their jobs, churches, and physicians. Gillian Dunne, Amy Hequembourg and Michael Ferrell, Angela Wilson, Susan Bell, and Sudan Dalton and Denise Bielby all use qualitative research in their work to explore the social constructions of "lesbian" and "mother." The authors agree that these social constructs deconstruct the patriarchal and heterosexist views of mainstream parenting. Lesbian and queer mothering also deconstruct patriarchal kinship and family lines.

Fiona Green and Andrea O'Reilly ("This Is What Feminism Is") analyze feminism and the effect it has had on mothers and children. Green interviews self-identified feminist mothers and focuses her qualitative research on how the mothers see that identifying as a feminist is important to how they rear their children and break down patriarchy because it can ultimately lead to empowerment for women and children. In "This Is What Feminism Is," O'Reilly concludes that motherhood is a patriarchal institution for women. She discusses how she raised her children using feminist principles and the implications it has had—such as how her daughters are assertive and have self-esteem. She explains how other mothers can do the same by practicing feminist mothering.

Mothers hail from all walks of life. Being queer, lesbian, single, transgender, feminist, *and* a mother can be alienating, especially since those constructions do not fit into the normative discourse of motherhood. Such experiences need to be heard because these mothers do not fit into a specific mold, and their experiences deconstruct the patriarchal and heteronormative notions of motherhood. It is important to hear the voices of mothers and to read their words to see how they construct mothering on their own terms.

Many of the journals, books, and essays I have come across in regards to single, feminist, or queer parenting are personal reflections and qualitative research. I read a few theoretical papers on how these types of constructions radicalize or deconstruct patriarchy, heteronormativity, gender, and the nuclear family. These voices of mothers (and parents) are being heard through additional research and essays, and this paper will continue this trend and further explore the subject.

METHOD

The data for this paper come from the interviews of ten mothers whom I personally know. The interviewed mothers live in the United States and Canada and were chosen because I knew that they identified as feminist, queer, and/or single (or did so at one point). After obtaining institutional review board approval, I emailed each mother individually about the project and sent other information about the study. I also do not use their real names and have chosen a pseudonym for mothers.

The interviews took place over the phone or in person and lasted one to two hours. I began by asking their basic background information, such as their age, the number of children they had, whether they were a student or worker, their race, their relationship status, and their gender and sexuality identities. After this, I asked them a series of open-ended questions, including the following ones: "Because of your age, race, sexuality, or gender identity, have you ever felt you were perceived differently from others toward your parenting?"; "How does feminism inform your parenting?"; and

"How do you approach gender and sexuality with your child?"

As a whole, the mothers were cooperative in answering the questions and sharing their experiences. This willingness may have come from the personal connections and understandings that we shared. Sometimes, we exchanged stories that involved children and the frustrations of mothering. I felt this was important because the mothers felt comfortable with me and had confidence that they would be understood.

These mothers resided in several different locations in the United States and Canada: four in Minnesota, one in North Dakota, one in California, two in Massachusetts, one in Ontario, and one in Saskatchewan. Four of the mothers were pursuing college degrees while working; one was in school full time; one was a physician in residency; and the other four were working full time. Each mother was on, or previously had been on, some sort public assistance.

The respondents varied in age from twenty to thirty-five. The ages of their children ranged from one year to ten years. The number of children each mother had was either one or two. When I asked about their race or ethnicity, four identified as white, two identified as white and Jewish, two identified as Native American, and two identified as mixed (one as white and Latina and the other as white, Middle Eastern, Jewish, and black). When I asked about their relationship status, the mothers replied with varied answers, such as single, dating, married, engaged, polyamorous, and in open relationships. However, most had experienced being a single mother at some point in their lives. When I asked about gender identity, eight identified as female or women, one as "gender queer-ish-like butchy girl," and one as female-to-male transgender. Five mothers identified as straight, and five identified as queer or bisexual.

The sample of these mothers is skewed in the direction of a group of mothers who are not heard from often. Most of the qualitative research that I found focused on women who were white and middle to upper class, were partnered in heterosexual or lesbian relationships, were educated with at least a bachelor's degree, and were homeowners. The mothers in this study, however, are young, queer, and from lower socioeconomic backgrounds. Some are mothers of colour; most of them had their children as teenagers; and some of them have constructed their lives and families without the help of a father or a partner at some point in their lives.

Although this sample is small compared to the actual number of single, queer, and/or feminist mothers, these mothers' experiences are still relevant. Their experiences are completely different from the experiences of the women represented in the other qualitative research that I read. Their voices are important and could potentially be generalized to other mothers who share their unique and underrepresented situations.

FINDINGS

Four major themes emerged from the interviews: (1) externalized and internalized pressures about being single and/or young mothers; (2) gender neutral parenting; (3) the value and encouragement of autonomy, honesty, and respect in their children; and (4) assumed heterosexuality towards the queer mothers. Almost every mother embraced feminism as a way of mothering, even if the mothers did not identify as feminist. Some of these findings parallel the interviews that Green and O'Reilly did. The mothers in their studies embraced feminist mothering because it led to self-esteem and assertiveness. In my study, the mothers of daughters embraced feminist mothering because of patriarchy and sexism. In the following four sections, I discuss the findings of each of the themes that emerged from my interviews.

Being a Single Mother: The Ups and Downs of Creating a Family Without a Partner

Many of the mothers had been single parents of their children at one point or another. Becoming a single mother was not necessarily a choice but resulted when the relationship with the father ended, either during pregnancy or after the birth. Many mothers were teenagers or in their early twenties when they got pregnant. The external reactions were positive for a few of the mothers. For instance, one mother stated: "I don't get the stereotypical, 'that's bad.' I get things like, 'that's really awesome you can do that by yourself', more positive than negative." However, many participants negatively internalized the experience of being a single mother. As Ranae explained: "I felt that I wasn't as good as a partnered parent, that I didn't spend enough time/money on my kid (or) that I did something wrong by having a kid and not staying with his father. I was unstable. I was looking for a father for my kid."

Matthias (a female to male trans parent[3]) elaborated on the externalized pressures and judgement experienced from others on a daily basis:

> Since she [daughter] was born, I have dealt with discrimination because of my single parent status. People always ask about her other parent. And when they hear that he is not around they treat me differently. As if I am somehow less capable as a parent because it is just me. People are not friendly at school events and the ones who are friendly are the exception.

Kaia, a mother in a committed relationship, explained the assumptions regarding her sex life because of her age and being a single mother. She stated, "Well, I guess as a single parent who is kind of young, the kind with a kid out of wedlock—you must sleep around."

Casey talked about the constraints that she faced as a single mother. She moved to another state, transferred to another college, and did not have the support that she had in her old city:

> I think a lot of people don't think about the constraints, so it's hard to schedule anything in evenings, especially last year, and I had no family here from moving, didn't know anyone, didn't go to lectures much. Now I can because my partner is here.... Judgement perceptions—only gotten that from a few people, on the fringe of things like, conservative Christians "you're not married?"

Casey explained that having her partner made it easier for her to go to evening school activities. The external pressures towards single mothers, especially young mothers, make everyday life more difficult than for partnered individuals.

The experiences of the women I interviewed contradict the findings from Mannis, whose qualitative research shows that a lot of the single mothers had a strong support system and did not experience much judgement. However, the single mothers she interviewed were financially well off, well educated, and in their thirties and forties. In contrast, most of the mothers from my interviews were younger, on welfare, and/or in college, which may account for the different findings.

A single mom and her kids are by definition a family without a father, and the female-headed household is destruction of the patriarchy at its most basic level (Nolan 245). Although these mothers have been subject to judgement and external and internalized pressures, and do not have help from the other parent, their families are female (or transgender) headed. Their identities and families break down patriarchy because their families do not rely on a cisgender male or father to construct their lives. They are running their households without a male and as Nolan states, this is the "destruction of patriarchy" (245).

Reflecting on Ginny Vida's comment that "matriarchy is a form of power that mothers can use to form their lives and families for themselves, not influenced by males" (qtd. in Love and Shanklin 277), I understood that the mothers I interviewed were doing that act; men did not influence them. Not only do the mothers' identities and families deconstruct patriarchy, but they also queer their families. Being single, these mothers have created a family without a second parent. They have built their families based on their own views of what a family is—thus queering their families.

Not Old Enough to Be a Mom

A surprising theme emerged from my study. Many of the mothers explained that their abilities were questioned more often than other mothers, and they felt as if they needed to prove themselves more because of their age. They felt more pressure and judgement because their youthful age than being a single mother. Kaia elaborated, "When bringing my daughter to school, other parents are way older, the way they look at you, don't really talk to you."

When I asked Casey—who had her son at sixteen but is now in college—about judgement that she had received about her age, she explained:

> All the time, that might be why the single thing didn't come up—too many people are focused on age. An article got published about me ... and the comments said, I must have a trust fund and my parents raised my kid. I haven't lived with parents since I was sixteen. Any time my son has a temper tantrum, people don't see a normal toddler, they see a fault in parenting ... especially when I am younger, I felt like I had to prove myself as a good parent and if he was well-behaved that was reflected on me as a good parent and vice versa.

People focused more on her age rather than her singleness. She said people were confused by the fact that she actually chose to get pregnant as a teenager. They also assumed that her young age would negatively affect her parenting abilities.

Some mothers I interviewed described the daily judgements they face because of their age and lifestyle. They found these judgements to be frustrating and alienating at times. One mother elaborated on this by explaining her experience of dropping off her child at daycare: "Now she's in preschool and the other moms that are there ... in military, married and have one or two kids, I am the only single parent and the youngest. When I walk in, they usually are singing their last songs, moms are talking, I am not introduced, not talked to, I know I am newer there, but it's been a month. I don't fit in." Ranae, a thirty-year-old mother of a ten-year-old child and a resident physician, spoke about the judgement that she felt working as a physician and having a preteen child. She explained, "I look younger [than she actually is] and in my career I was young for having a kid. I get lots of disbelief, like, 'you mean you have a ten-month-old, right?'" Many people have a hard time believing she has a ten-year-old child, not a ten-month-old one.

Another youthful mother, Elise, described how people reacted to her being pregnant and not getting married:

> I remember when I was pregnant with number one, and I was not married. Everyone was like, "you have to get married" ... they just assumed I had gotten pregnant by accident, or that I didn't really want to be a mom, not

> going to be successful, because of my age, children would be harmed, was going to be lazy because I wanted to stay home with my baby … with my profession, most people are older in midwifery in mainstream society. They think I am too young and incapable, how can you be old enough to have two kids? People do not trust me; they want a forty-five-year-old woman. They ask how can you be old enough to have this experience? I was told this at the hospital and my baby was given formula without my consent. She did not want to latch. I was twenty years old, and I should not breastfeed, according to the nurses.

Matthias elaborated on this theme and stated: "I have always looked too young. I think that my opinions are dismissed by many people because they think that I am several years younger than I am."

Age also queers the traditional notion of motherhood. Not only are some of these mothers single but they are also young. Their ages defy traditional notions of motherhood. That is, they are not the typically appropriate age for being a mother.

Feminist Mothering: "My Daughter Can Do It; She Can Do Anything"

Although not every mother in my study identified as a feminist, most of them still embraced feminist values. These findings were parallel to the findings of Green and O'Reilly ("This Is What Feminism Is"), whose qualitative research explores the feminist values of mothers raising children. Most of the mothers realized that feminism can empower their children (especially their daughters) and can break down the implications that patriarchy may have on them.

Mathias did not identify as a feminist because the feminist movement had not treated him, as a trans male, very well," but he nevertheless remarked: "I am more aware of disadvantages that will face my daughter as she grows up. Although transitioning has made a lot of those things even more clear. I've also been really aware of the fights that are most important to me. Such as reproductive rights that I want to be sure that she will have."

Most mothers I interviewed also explained that they do not subscribe to the gender binary. Their children can play with whatever toys they want to and wear whatever they want to; they would not treat their children any differently if their child were another gender. Eva explained: "I don't really push him into a boy-girl role at all; I just treat any child the same, in a disciplinary or nondisciplinary role. Whether they are a boy or a girl." Each mother I talked with was supportive of their children no matter what their gender identities were, and they taught their children to express their gender how they wanted to. They explained that it was more important that their children be happy and respectful. So long as their kids were developing their own autonomy, their gender identity did not matter to them as parents.

Chloe, who did not identify as a feminist because she felt that feminism only catered to white, privileged women, elaborated: "Even though I do not identify as feminist, feminism still affects me because I still do believe in equality for women. I teach my children that things are not gender focused, that gender is fluid, and to not make assumptions or preconceived notions based on gender." Casey explained the ways that she approached gender with her son: "Not a big deal. I use gendered pronouns with him. It's because I know I am raising him in a way ... we talk about trans and genderqueers—how that's a choice then. He knows that about choices and gender. Gendered preferences—we don't really subscribe to that or influence that." Ranae also discussed how she approached gender with her son and some of the implications that feminism and gender-neutral parenting have had on him:

> I try to create a space where my kid can express his own gender identity in the way he wants. So he can dress the way he wants. He used to choose to wear a lot of pink and Hello Kitty. Today with his long hair a lot of people think he's a girl. He tells me 'its ok that people think I'm a girl, but I'm not a girl, but there isn't anything wrong with being a girl. I just feel so bad for people when they realize I'm a boy and then they get all flustered. So usually I just don't bother correcting them, if I don't have to see them again like it's at a store or something.

Other mothers did identify as feminist and explained that feminism had a huge role in their parenting. As Kaia explained, "I feel like the same reason that my daughter identifies as a girl, teach her to be strong, she can do what she wants to do, basically girls can do anything. I really try to challenge her on her gender roles that she assigns to people." Elise, a married mother who identified as a feminist and who is in school for midwifery, explained how feminism has affected her parenting: "Everything that I do is an attempt to empower to my daughters as future women or whatever. Everything. I hear ... 'too bad she was girl ... you must want a boy to take on the family farm.' But my daughter can do it, she goes out with her dad, follows him around on the farm. She can do anything that a boy can do. She can probably do it fucking better."

Although I did not find as many qualitative studies on feminist mothering as I did with single and queer mothering, these mothers' experiences are very similar to the mothers in the previous studies. Feminist mothering has influenced their parenting, as they parent with gender-neutral approaches, which has produced autonomy, honesty, and respect in their children. It has also encouraged their sons to be respectful towards girls and has encouraged their girls to be strong and courageous.

In my sample, the mother's ways of approaching parenting deconstruct gender and the nuclear family. They are queering gender by letting their children express their gender in whatever way they choose, and they queer the nuclear family by encouraging values, such as autonomy, respect, and gender fluidity, which break down traditional notions of mothering.

"What? You Can't Be Queer and a Mom."

As with other studies that focus on lesbian, bisexual, or queer mothers, these mothers do feel judgement and pressure, as well. Hequembourg and Ferrell argue that "lesbian motherhood is often depicted as an oxymoron" (541). I found that this was often the way some of the mothers felt in my sample—the assumption being that they cannot be lesbian, bisexual, or queer because they are mothers. As Mathias elaborated: "I have been treated differently because I was perceived as a lesbian. And somehow that made my parenting more suspect." Kaia, who is bisexual and in a relationship with a trans man, elaborated on pressures and judgement from her family: "when people find out that my partner is trans, there is a weird vibe ... my daughter's paternal grandmother was very rude and horrible about it, to a point where I had to stop talking to her."

Whereas the other studies focus on lesbian, bisexual, or queer mothers making the decision to become mothers, my study has focused on the judgements that they might have felt for being queer. The assumption of heterosexuality among my participants emerged as a theme. Ranae, for example, explained the assumptions that have resulted from others even within the dating scene. She mentioned that she had to be more assertive when trying to date women: "I felt that because I was a mom, I was perceived as a hetero and thus lots of heterosexual discussions about boys ensued. I like girls too and sometimes I have to be very proactive in dating women because it is assumed I only date boys."

Because some of the mothers I interviewed were in relationships with cisgender men, they explained it was hard for them to perceive any judgement from anyone for that reason. Since five of the mothers identified as queer, I did not get as much data as I did with the other questions. However, a theme of assumed heterosexuality still emerged, and I felt it was important to address because it was similar to the experiences of other lesbian, bisexual, or queer mothers in other studies. Their queer identities break down the traditional notion of motherhood; they are queering the heterosexual assumption of motherhood as well as the institution of heteronormativity.

CONCLUSIONS

This study of young, single, queer, and/or feminist mothers has demonstrated the ways that these mothers' identities deconstruct patriarchy, gender, and the nuclear family. I focused on these mothers because, as the literature review reveals, not a lot of research in this area exists. A mother's identity, childrearing choices, and how she queers the world around her by breaking down the traditional notions of motherhood have not been explored by researchers as much as they could be. With this study, I hope to add to the discussion of mothers' identities and how their experiences deconstruct traditional notions of motherhood.

I also chose to focus mostly on young and poor mothers because the mothers in the other qualitative studies were not, and the experiences of the mothers in my study were different. Surprisingly, the experience of ageism emerged as a theme with every mother I interviewed, more so than bias based on single parenting.

Although all these mothers faced internalized and externalized pressures because they did not fit into the traditional notion of who a mother should be, they still took their childrearing choices seriously. They have made important points about the daily pressures and joys of their lives as mothers and as individuals.

Even though the sample size may be small, the fact that the mothers come from several different locations is important. Their experiences are not specific to a geographical location. These mothers experienced similar things while being in different locations; they also experienced things that could be studied further for the same reason. For instance, studies could further examine the differences between similar experiences of mothers from the United States and mothers from Canada.

This study may have helped to close the gap on lingering questions regarding the experiences of young, single, queer, and/or feminist mothers. However, this study also opens space to continue these types of studies and exposes something else to explore within feminist, maternal, and queer theory. Future research questions could include the following: what is the experience of a transitioning transgender parent? What are the experiences of their children? What are the externalized and internalized pressures for teen mothers and low-income mothers? What are the externalized and internalized pressures of mothers to appear or look like a mother to others?

Finally, the findings demonstrate that heteronormativity, patriarchy, gender, and the nuclear family still reign in society. Mothers who do not fit into these roles are judged and perceived as being unacceptable. I further believe that these mothers' identities and childrearing choices are fundamental in deconstructing societal views of young, single, queer, and/or feminist mothers. I also believe their identities and childrearing choices break down patriarchy, gender, and the nuclear family. Their identities challenge traditional notions of motherhood and force society to acknowledge their presence as individuals and mothers.

NOTES

[1]Cisgender relates to a person whose gender identity corresponds with their biological sex.
[2]A trans man mother is someone who has transitioned from female to male, but still identifies as a mother.
[3]Matthias was born female and identified as a woman until he transitioned to being male. He identifies as "parent" as opposed to "mother" or "father" and uses male pronouns.

WORKS CITED

Bell, Susan E. "Intensive Performance of Mothering: A Sociological Perspective." *Qualitative Research*, vol. 4, no. 1, 2004, pp. 45-75.

"Cisgender." *Oxford Dictionaries*. Oxford University Press, 2016, en.oxforddictionaries.com/definition/cisgender. Accessed 5 July 2016.

Dalton, Susan E., and Denise D. Dielby. "'That's Our Kind of Constellation' Lesbian Mothers Negotiate Institutionalized Understandings of Gender within the Family." *Gender and Society*, vol. 14, no. 1, 2000, pp. 36-61.

Dunne, Gillian. A. "Opting Into Motherhood Lesbians Blurring the Boundaries and Transforming the Meaning of Parenthood and Kinship." *Gender and Society*, vol. 14, no. 1, 2000, pp. 11-35.

Green, Fiona Joy. "Feminist Motherline." *Feminist Mothering*, edited by Andrea O'Reilly, State University of New York Press, 2008, pp. 161-175.

Green, Fiona J. "Developing a Feminist Motherline: Reflections on a decade of feminist parenting," *Journal for the Association for Research on Mothering*. vol. 8 (1/2), 2006, pp. 7-20.

Hequembourgh, Amy, and Michael Farrell. "Lesbian Motherhood Negotiating Marginal-Mainstream Identities." *Gender and Society*, vol. 13, no. 4, 1999, pp. 540-547.

Ingraham, Chyrs. "The Heterosexual Imaginary: Feminist Sociology and Theories of Gender." *Queer Theory/Sociology*, edited by

Steven Seidman, Blackwell Publishers Inc., 1997, pp. 168-193.
Jagose, Annamrie. *Queer Theory*. New York University Press, 1996.
Love, Barbara, and Elizabeth Shanklin. "The Answer is Matriarchy." *Mothering: Essays in Feminist Theory*, edited by Joyce Trebilcot, Rowman & Allanheld, 1982, pp. 275-283,
Mannis, Valerie. "Single Mothers by Choice." *Family Relations*, vol. 48, no. 2, 1999, pp. 121-128.
Naples, Nancy. "Queer Parenting in the New Millennium." *Gender and Society*, vol. 18, no.6, 2004, pp. 679-684.
Nolan, Monica. "Mother Inferior: How Hollywood Keeps Single Moms In Their Place." *BITCHfest: Ten Years of Cultural Criticism from the Pages of Bitch Magazine*, edited by Lisa Jervis and Andi Ziesler, Farrar, Straus, and Giroux, 2006, pp. 240-246.
O'Reilly, Andrea. "'This Is What Feminism Is—The Acting and Living and Not Just The Told': Modeling and Mentoring Feminism." *Feminist Mothering*, edited by Andrea O'Reilly, State University of New York Press, 2008, pp. 191-202.
O'Reilly, Andrea. *Mother Outlaws: Theories and Practices of Empowered Mothering*. Women's Press, 2004.
Oswald, Ramonda Faith, et al. "Decentering Heteronormativity: A Model for Family Studies." *Sourcebook of Family Theory and Research*, edited by Alan Acock et al., Sage Publications, Inc., 2004, pp. 143-165.
Rich, Adrienne. *Of Woman Born: Motherhood As Experience and Institution*. W.W. Norton & Company, Inc. 1976.
Sullivan, Maureen. "Rozzie and Harriet? Gender and Family Patterns of Lesbian Coparents." *Gender and Society vol.* 10, no. 6, 1996, pp. 747-767.
Wilson, Angela. "With Friends Like These: The Liberalization of Queer Family Policy." *Critical Social Policy*, vol. 27, no. 1 2007, pp. 50-76.

8.
Wild, Child

Reflections at the Intersections of Nature, Gender, Race, and Parenthood

KATE PARSONS

AT TWILIGHT, on a springtime stroll in our city neighbourhood, I spot a bunny and silently halt Kira, my three-year-old, to point it out. She sees it, her eyes widen, and she whisper-shouts, "Mommy, can I pet it?"

"No, sorry, honey. We can't pet it; it's a wild bunny."

She turns to me, vexed, and protests: "Mommy! It's not scary; it's nice!" Its nose is twitching and it's indisputably cute. I see her point and offer, "Well, wild doesn't have to mean scary; it just means that it doesn't live with humans."

Her brow furrows at my apparent lack of common sense; the bunny is half a block from our house, hopping in our neighbour's carefully cultivated flowers. If it's not living with these humans, it's at least a frequent visitor.

I try again: "Wild also means it might not want to be touched ... it's not like the bunnies at the zoo." This satisfies her somewhat: "Like Jester," she says, matter-of-factly. (She's referring to our family dog.) "Sometimes he doesn't like to be touched," she informs me with grave authority. (Er ... well, he doesn't like to be ridden like a horse, but sure.)

The bunny hops away, and Kira finds something else that captures her interest. I follow her up the hill, bemused. In my day job, as a philosophy professor who teaches environmental ethics, I think I do a fairly good job of helping students clarify and reconstruct our thinking about the so-called natural world; alas, in my job as a parent, I seem only to muddy the waters. In my feminist theory classes, I aim to break down and elucidate the public-private split, and this would have been a perfect opportunity to explore a related binary—the split between the ferocious "wild" and the cuddly confines of the "domesticated." But I had lost her at my knee-jerk "no." My parental blunders multiplying, I hear faint echoes of Debbie Downer's theme song.

Of course, she's three, and I'm being slightly dramatic; I have lots to learn about how to talk to preschoolers, and this isn't my one and only chance to help her become the next Rachel Carson. And I remind myself that often I'm tickled and inspired by the sagacity of Kira's three-year-old protests; she recently responded to my plea to stop running with, "Mommy, just because it's a sidewalk doesn't mean you have to walk!" Still, her indignation about the bunny in this case engenders more maternal consternation than admiration. Her question—what is "wild"? —has, on some level, stumped me, and has raised a question that I feel I should be better able to handle.

As a philosopher, I've trained myself to digest deep questions (and also feelings of inadequacy) through obsessive analysis. Parenting a three-year-old, I've learned, provides plenty of fodder, so I launch into the process as we proceed up the hill. First step: analysis. Why does wild seem incompatible with bunny? I start with the known, making a mental list of the "wild" animals in preschool books and cartoons that have sharp, dripping teeth, and are coldly indifferent: lions, tigers, coyotes, hyenas. Bunnies—innocent, cute, cuddly—are typically portrayed as their opposites: prey to, not perpetrators of, wildness. "Wild bunny," I realize, would clearly yield preschool cognitive dissonance.

Step two: alternatives. How else might I have defined it? I ponder some synonyms for wild—harsh, savage, fierce, rough, severe, absurd, bizarre. Hmm, not quite. The more fitting terms all start with "un": untamed, undomesticated, uncontrolled, unpredictable, unrestrained, undisciplined, uncultivated, uninhabited, unsettled, undeveloped, uncivilized, unkempt, unruly, unchecked. It seems "wild" is, in many cases, nothing more than the un-doing or undone state of what is praiseworthy, known, controlled, and good.

Step three: relevance. So what? Who cares? This is all mildly interesting but may amount to no more than self-soothing for a professor mom who lives and works mostly in her head. Although

I love philosophizing and think it is a deeply underappreciated and underutilized skill, I am mindful of its risks. As philosopher Kate Rawles notes, "Philosophy has a way of retreating away from the question it is trying to answer" (542) as one conceptual question leads to another, and another. Does it really matter that in my aim to raise an intelligent, strong, thoughtful, inquisitive girl, I have failed to enlighten on this one question?

My sense, inarticulate yet pressing, is that such weirdness about wildness is more than trivial; larger issues of environmental justice, as well as gender justice, seem to be lurking in the background. Many environmental ethicists—deep ecologists and ecofeminists especially[1]—maintain that we must stop thinking of ourselves as "separate" from nature if we have any hope of reversing the rapid rate at which we are effecting climate change, decreasing the diversity of the earth's flora and fauna, depleting the fertility of our soil, releasing toxicants into the air, and diminishing the availability of fresh water. When we align ourselves with the culture side of the culture-nature binary and with the domestic of the domestic-wild split, and when we see ourselves as fundamentally superior to other living beings on earth, we fail to see our connection with the species and entities with which we are inextricably linked and on which we ultimately depend. We praise good behaviour selectively and shamelessly as "humane" and characterize depraved behavior as "animalistic."[2] In doing so, we conveniently ignore the complex social and communicative systems of bonobos, chimpanzees, elephants, dolphins, and other sophisticated beings, or, at best, consider their behaviour anomalous to the rest of the animal kingdom.

Sometimes, in its best iterations, nature—even "the wild" —is what people "get back to" or "get away to." It can relax, rejuvenate, connect, and ground us. But it is a type of relaxation made possible through its temporariness, by only relatively short hiatuses from indoor plumbing, electrical outlets, and HVAC systems. The escape into nature is a growing and unique (though not exclusive) narrative of people in the Global North and in Western cultures, particularly the subset living above the poverty line and not working with the land on a daily basis. Those who extol the relaxing effects of getting back to, or away to, nature and of going into the "wild" are typically those who have the luxury of owning cars (it's harder to access and carry gear to campgrounds and nature reserves by bus); of having leisure time (vacation time, one job instead of two—or a job at all); of being able bodied or freed from primary caregiving (for babies or ill parents); and of having a host of other privileges typically shaped by class, race, ethnicity, gender, and physical ability.

This demographic—mostly male, white, and relatively wealthy, and sustained by writers, politicians, and policymakers who are similarly situated—reinforces the culture-nature and the domestic-wild binaries by often romanticizing the second half in each pair. Ramachandra Guha and Joan Martínez-Alier note that environmentalism in the Global North typically centres on wistfulness over spaces distinct from, and untouched by, humans; environmentalism in the Global South typically stems from immediate shortages in resources and/or their distribution. The latter conception of the environment is not exclusive to the Global South. It is also found in the concerns of the environmental justice movement in the U.S—led primarily by people of colour and include a significantly high number of women[3]—to keep toxins dumped by chemical companies out of water sources, out of homes, and out of children's playgrounds. Yet these are not typically considered environmental concerns in mainstream (Western and white) media. Since these concerns are considered human rights issues (if at all) rather than environmental ones, the dominant ideology remains intact; nature is primarily conceived as something apart from most of "us," distinct from where most of "us" live, and outside of our daily comfort zones. Those of us defining the terms typically fail to see how the invisibility of white, suburban, wealth privileges shape a particular view of what constitutes the environment or the wilderness in the first place.[4]

What does this have to do with the bunny, if anything? The dissonance that "wild bunny" produces seems largely tied to these binaries and Western conceptions of them; my sense is that perhaps some creative thinking about wildness, in particular, could help break them down. Just as small farmers have worked hard in the past several decades on mending the sharp disconnect many of us have from our food sources—small, local, and organic farmer's markets are increasingly popular, and more people are planting vegetable gardens—kindergarten through grade-twelve educators have been working to de-emphasize the "domesticated" nature of our children's educational system. Books, such Richard Louv's *Last Child in the Woods* and more recently Scott Sampson's *How to Raise a Wild Child,* extol the benefits of encouraging our children to dig in the dirt, to learn the names of native and local flora and fauna, and experience more unstructured time to explore the outdoors. For our children's physical and mental development, we are encouraged to let our children roam free. We are encouraged to let, as one of my daughter's favorite books by Starhawk suggests, "just a bit of wildness get inside them" (28).

Letting conventionally understood "wildness" into their lives may be particularly challenging for those of us whose children are girls and for those of us who engage in feminist parenting. These days, as I watch Kira run with complete abandon, oblivious to her flailing arms and disproportionately long legs, I often cringe at the clock ticking on her gender-neutral youth. Eventually, despite my best efforts to stock her closet with more shorts than skirts, to cultivate a love of pet rocks over pining princesses, she'll learn to see herself from outside herself. She'll absorb her culture's norms for what *girls* do, and she'll learn to see them as incompatible with her own wildness. Wild is what boys may be when they're being boys. Wildness, she'll be told, is not compatible with being, or behaving, as a girl. As a teenager and a woman, she'll learn that attempts to forge compatibility between "wildness" and "girl" can be a liability; "wild girls" can end up victims of a range of harms, from social ostracism to rape.

Gender norms will constrain her ability to embrace any wildness she may still seek, and race-ethnicity will further complicate it. Famously, Patricia Hill Collins has pointed to the ways in which whiteness in our culture has served as a distinguishing marker between "civilized" (white) women and "wild" (black) women; whiteness produces distance (culture) from those that are supposedly closer to nature. As a person of Latina heritage, my daughter may similarly have some wildness assigned to her, and rarely in complimentary terms. Her skin colour is light, due to her mother's Anglo heritage, yet to the extent that she chooses to self-identify with and/or is labeled as "mixed"—as also "brown"—she will find herself at the intersection of gendered and raced conceptions. Wild is not what (white) girls are, but it is what brown and black (especially Latina/o, African American, and indigenous) people are. So some of her wildness may be "excused" with a shrug, though not the esteemed version that comes with the (white) boys-will-be-(white)-boys rhetoric.

When I think about how these raced, gendered, and ecological binaries will shape my daughter's future in ways that I will ultimately be unable to control, I feel desperate, helpless, and angry. My impulse is to encourage her, despite the risks and the denigrating associations, to be wild as long as she can—to resist the "civilizing" forces that will tamp down her confidence, her curiosity, and that will circumscribe her sense of adventure and comfort in the world. When I pair "wild" with "child" in conventional terms, I envision a kid who runs with abandon and joy, who flaunts authority, who shouts first and reflects later, who jumps often and revels in getting dirty. When I add "girl" to that child, I envision (a complicatedly white) Pippi Longstocking; she does what she pleases, is unconstrained by gendered or domestic expectations, and is a creative, insightful, inventive leader. I loved Pippi as a kid, and hope that my daughter will love her, too. In a sense, I want my daughter to be Pippi (even if I prefer she not live on her own until she's eighteen!). Yet as much as I love Pippi and aspire for Kira to have all of the confidence and comfort that it takes to be like her, it occurs to me that Pippi—even as a wild child—is modelled on a conventional interpretation of wildness. In encouraging my child to be like Pippi, I realize that I reinforce the culture-nature and domestic-wild binaries (even though I disrupt the white, masculine associations with them). Akin to my lack of clarity about the wildness of the neighbourhood bunny, I don't have a satisfying model for understanding (let alone cultivating) a wildness for my daughter that challenges the binary.

Can there be a useful sense of wildness that is captured by the neighbourhood bunny? Is there any sense in which my daughter may cultivate its skills in a manner I would endorse? It occurs to me that in the model of Pippi as wild child, it is hard to locate my daughter's admirable tendency to watch quietly. Where is the side of her that pays tentative and keen attention to what the other children are doing before she joins in? Where is the side of my daughter that would sit for hours, if I let her, digging for rocks and sorting them into piles? Where is the side of her that is unafraid of worms or beetles and will pick them up without hesitation? In her watchfulness, patience, astute tentativeness, and curiosity, does she not also display some traits of wild, (nonhuman) animals, of her neighbourhood bunny?

I don't mean to suggest that wildness is hardly different from domestication or that it can or should be reinterpreted to capture everything my daughter already does. I also don't want to rest too quickly on the notion that because we're animals (albeit human ones), the binary has no meaning. Although I believe that the binaries between nature-culture and domestic life-wild life are largely constructed, they still have profound cultural meaning and shape us in important ways that deserve analysis and reinterpretation. Yet I do think that she could be wild in some nonconventional ways and that alternative conceptions of wildness might be worth exploring. Karen Warren's rock-climbing example—through which she illustrates an ecofeminist shift from climbing with arrogant perception to climbing with loving perception (inspired by Marilyn Frye's arrogant vs. loving eye)—would seem to contain a fertile seed for thinking through alternative conceptions of wildness. Warren's example offers a shift from day one—wherein the narrator says, "I climbed with intense determination," and was moved by the driving goal of making it to the top—to day two—wherein the narrator perceives herself and her surroundings differently: "I looked all around me—really looked—and listened" (558). On the first approach, on day one, she aims to conquer the rock, and with a version of Frye's "arrogant eye" reduces the rock "to the size of the seer's desire" (Frye 76). On the second approach, in climbing with Frye's "loving eye," she is compelled to "look and listen and check and question" (Frye 75). The climber, according to Warren, sees herself in a caring relationship with the rock, not as its conqueror. Most of the paradigmatic examples of wild beings that come to mind (even to the mind of a three-year-old)—the dangerous, threatening ones that are not under our control—would seem to be shaped by the dominant conception of an arrogant eye, an eye that feels threatened by difference rather than appreciative of it. Yet to view the bunny as wild requires a shift not unlike the one Warren's climber undergoes; it means not just seeing difference but seeing *differently*. In particular, it rests on the inspiration of thinking carefully about what a nondominant group and pairing is like—in this case considering nonparadigmatic conceptions of the bunny as wild—and, in particular, what the wild bunny does well.

Rather than conceive of wildness as a lack—of predictability, control, sensitivity, deference, or sociality—part of the bunny's wildness may be located in its rapt attention and watchfulness. Not only do such skills help many wild animals survive, but they are also skills that in children may form the basis for deeper ecological learning and awareness. To identify a bird's song requires a keen, trained ear; to recognize different species of grasses and flowers requires attentive eyes; to sit and watch a worm travel across the sidewalk requires patience and an alternate view of progress. People who develop these skills, who are good at watching, listening, focusing on the world around them, may not seem wild by dominant standards. (And it is worth keeping in mind that such skills are often developed by women and people of colour under oppressive conditions and are honed and employed for the sake of survival.) Yet these are also skills that may lead us to some of the values extolled by those hoping to bring wildness back into our lives; by cultivating understanding of, respect for, and connection to the natural world, we slowly break down the culture/nature and domestic/wild binaries.

The deeper aim of promoting wildness lies in cultivating respect for our differences from, and also interdependence with, other species. These are some of the patterns and insights that some of our most important scientists and environmentalists advocate for coming generations; they suggest we embrace the wild, and our own wildness, by slowing down and sinking into our environment.[5] This suggestion is at the heart of Scott Sampson's recent recommendations and instructions for how to raise "a wild child." Early in the book, he sets up a brief contrast between a paradigmatic wild child—one peripheral to civilization, abused, isolated, and damaged after having lived alone in the woods—and instead claims that his "use of the term *wild child* refers to something entirely different—a child sharing deep connections with nature *and* people" (15). This strikes me as an incredibly hopeful shift in a book that will undoubtedly have an influence on Western popular culture; Sampson's wild child bucks beautifully the associations that all of the "un" words that I drummed up earlier bring to mind.

Sampson's vision seems like a crucial step towards breaking down the domestic-wild binary; it offers a calmer, quieter, more reflective, and introspective version of wildness that is respectful of the world around us. Yet aside from merely mentioning that the paradigmatic wild child to whom he draws his contrast is a boy, Sampson offers no analysis of the paradigm's gendered associations. Presumably anyone can be wild, and he notes that his deepest inspirations for the book come from his interactions with his daughter, but I would suggest that it is important to note that in advocating this new type of wildness, we are not only bucking the standard of the dripping-jawed, menacing predator, we are also bucking the dominant standards of someone who is portrayed as reckless and carefree—and who has a race and gender. If we want girls to see themselves in Sampson's vision (and I do), we need to be talking more about their gender and race, about the importance of watching insects, but also of watching (cute) bunnies. I want a conception of wild that makes room for the bunny, in all of its dimensions, including its gendered ones, and I want a model for my daughter that allows her to be wild—perhaps dissonantly at first but uniquely—like the bunny.

NOTES

[1]Although the interests of deep ecologists (sometimes social ecologists) and ecofeminists converge, I do not mean to suggest that all of their claims or assumptions are identical or even always compatible. Ynestra King notes, for instance: "Social ecology challenges the dualistic belief that nature and culture are separate and opposed. Ecofeminism finds misogyny at the root of that opposition" (408).

[2]Franz de Waal notes, "We would much rather blame nature for what we don't like in ourselves than credit it for what we do like" (1).

[3]The Citizens Clearinghouse for Hazardous Wastes has estimated that 80 percent of leaders of grass-roots environmental justice

protests have been women (Krauss).

[4]Robert Verchick claims the following:

> Traditional environmentalists often promoted an image of 'environment' as something removed from everyday experience. The word conjured images of undeveloped, exotic, and sometimes faraway places—Yellowstone, the Oregon Coast, or the Florida Everglades. Similarly, environmental "harm" suggested harm to these places or to the wildlife that inhabited them. This telescopic view of environmentalism significantly influenced the direction of environmental policy in the United States. Environmental justice activists expand this view of the environment. For them environment also means the places where they live and work—an Indian reservation, an African American neighborhood in Dallas, or the barrios of South Central Los Angeles. Harm to that environment includes not only the contamination of natural resources (toxic soil, poisoned water, dirty air), but anything in the environment that threatens human health and safety. (66)

Also, Robin Morris Collin and Robert Collin note:

> Racist views and practices, both individually and institutionally, produce at least two outcomes in the environmental movement. First, whites ignore or discount the distinctively different orientations of people of color to nature and the environment as less important than those presented by whites. For example, when asked to define environment and nature, people of color across many ranges of ethnicity include a broad range of phenomena: the creations of nature, living and dead, contemporary and future, flora and fauna, where we live, work, learn, and play. The conservation-based environmental movement focuses instead on so-called wilderness, wild places, and wild things. (212)

[5]Jeannine Atkins introduces her inspiring book for children, *Girls Who Looked Under Rocks*: "The six women portrayed in this book all grew up to become award-winning scientists and writers, as comfortable with a pen as with a magnifying glass. They all started out as girls who didn't run from spiders or snakes, but crouched down to take a closer look" (4). Atkins profiles Maria

Sibylla Merian, Anna Comstock, Frances Hamerstrom, Miriam Rothschild, Rachel Carson, and Jane Goodall.

WORKS CITED

Atkins, Jeannine. *Girls Who Looked Under Rocks: The Lives of Six Pioneering Naturalists*. DAWN Publications, 2000.

Collin, Robin Morris and Robert Collin. "Environmental Reparations." *The Quest for Environmental Justice: Human Rights and the Politics of Pollution*, edited by Robert D. Bullard, Sierra Club Books, 2005, pp. 209-221.

Collins, Patricia Hill. "The Sexual Politics of Black Womanhood." *Black Feminist Thought*. 2000. Routledge, 2009, pp. 133-160.

Frye, Marilyn. *The Politics of Reality: Essays in Feminist Theory*, The Crossing Press, 1983.

Guha, Ramachandra, and Juan Martinez Alier. "The Environmentalism of the Poor." *Earthcare: An Anthology in Environmental Ethics*, edited by David Clowney and Patricia Mosto, Rowman & Littlefield, 2009, pp. 297-314.

King, Ynestra. "The Ecology of Feminism and the Feminism of Ecology." *Feminist Theory: A Reader*. 3rd ed., edited by Wendy K. Kolmar and Frances Bartkowski, McGraw-Hill, 2010, pp. 407-412.

Krauss, Celene. "Blue-Collar Women and Toxic-Waste Protests: The Process of Politicizatoin." *Toxic Struggles: The Theory and Practice of Environmental Justice*, edited by Richard Hofrichter, The University of Utah Press, 2002, pp. 107-117.

Louv, Richard. *Last Child in the Woods: Saving Our Children from Nature-Deficit Disorder*. Algonquin Books, 2008.

Rawles, Kate. "The Missing Shade of Green" *Environmental Ethics: What Really Matters, What Really Works*, edited by David Schmidtz and Elizabeth Willott, Oxford University Press, 2002, pp. 535-546.

Sampson, Scott D. *How to Raise a Wild Child: The Art and Science of Falling in Love with Nature*. Houghton Mifflin Harcourt, 2015.

Starhawk. *The Last Wild Witch*. Mother Tongue Ink, 2009.

Verchick, Robert R. M. "Feminist Theory and Environmental Justice." *New Perspectives on Environmental Justice: Gender,*

Sexuality, and Activism, edited by Rachel Stein, Rutgers University Press, 2004, pp. 63-77.

Waal, Franz. *Our Inner Ape: A Leading Primatologist Explains Why We Are Who We Are.* Riverhead Books, 2005.

Warren, Karen J. "The Power and Promise of Ecological Feminism." *Ethics: The Big Questions, Second Edition*, edited by James P. Sterba, Wiley-Blackwell, 2009, pp. 552-562.

9.
Childhood Phobia

SHANNON DRURY

ALL SEEMED CALM the frosty February morning I tossed my two-year-old daughter's pajamas and reached for her shirt and pants combo of the day, until she surprised me with a determined "No." Her jaw set firmly in her chubby cheeks, Miriam announced: "Wear dress."

"No," I echoed. "Today you're wearing these."

"*No*," Miriam growled. "Wear *dress*. WEAR DRESS!"

As a lifelong feminist, a child of the second wave and a college student of the third, I had only one interpretation of this standoff: panic. I wasn't afraid of frozen knees; I was afraid of engaging my feminist parenthood politics before my second pot of coffee. She said *wear dress* but I heard *I hope you're ready for this, Mama*.

I wasn't ready when I gave birth to my first child—a boy, whom I hoped to dress in tasteful shades of yellow and green. I didn't realize that twenty-first-century America demands rigid adherence to gender performance, which made reproducing the gender neutral wardrobe of my "*Free to Be ... You and Me*" youth an exercise in futility. After the living hell of wandering the pink and blue stores of Mall of America while postpartum depressed, I gave up and ceded control of his wardrobe to my mother-in-law. Elliott spent his infancy and toddlerhood in clothes of azure, sapphire, and indigo from the boys' department at Kohl's.

With Miriam, I thought I'd do better, although there were more than a few Grandma Anne-purchased pink dresses in her closet. "No," I repeated, "it's too cold today. We're wearing pants." To avoid a meltdown (my own), I left her bedroom for the coffee I so desperately needed. She marched out a few minutes later in the outfit I selected—rebellion forgotten.

Not long after the dress standoff, I watched as Miriam played with her doll-sized airplane, perhaps giving Ken and Sporty Spice a flight to Rio, where no one of any gender required pants. She placed the tail wing between her legs and began to chant: "I have a penis, I have a penis."

"No, you don't," I said while my husband cracked up. "You have an airplane."

"I HAVE A PENIS. I HAVE A PENIS," she sang happily.

I support trans folks as much as anyone with a personally signed copy of Kate Bornstein's *A Queer and Pleasant Danger*, but even dear Aunt Kate would be alarmed at a substitute penis that was large enough to fit several Barbie dolls. I told myself that sometimes a cigar is just a cigar is a toy airplane until she waddled off and started throwing Legos at her big brother's head.

These incidents troubled me, more so than I could have imagined. I searched in my heart for homophobia and/or transphobia, finding instead a different terrifying phenomenon: *childhood phobia*.

I know I'll be happy with the adult that Miriam grows to be—whether girl, boy, grrrl, boy, gay, straight, or any colour in the rainbow. I'm her mom, and I accept her. What I can't yet accept is the torture she will endure until she gets there. Much is written about a mother's heart beating on the outside of her body— in my case there seems to be not only heart but soul and gut and every other physical metaphor for emotional vulnerability.

When Miriam demands a dress, I envision her blossoming into a Girly Girl, the type who plays into gender expectations a little too well. This girl's rigidity makes her particularly vulnerable to the ugly aftermath of female stereotypes, including fatal eating disorders and the unquestioning support of machismo. When Miriam waggles around a fake penis, I see my baby become a Baby Butch, the tuff grrrl marching at Pride in combat boots. This type's personal experience makes her less likely to accept things at face value but far more likely to be beaten to a bloody pulp in a vicious hate crime.

The movement for LGBT civil rights reminds us that gender and sexuality are a spectrum as lovely and fluid as a rainbow, but anxious parents, even feminist ones, have a hard time with nuance. When we're trying to protect our kids, we see through two lenses: Bad and Very Bad. For between the rainbow's extremes are millions of soul-killing experiences that are endured as just (*just*!) a part of modern American maturation: "gay" still in use as a synonym for "wrong," Miley Cyrus pole-dancing at an awards show for young children, *Teen Vogue*, the unstoppable Disney Princess machine, the phrase "boys will be boys," a mother regularly suggesting that one may be less lonely on Saturday nights if one acted more feminine and wore a thicker coating of makeup. Oh, I'm sorry: were we talking about me? We weren't? Back to Miriam, then.

I want my daughter to be Who! She! Is! *without* the heartbreak needed to get there. In short, I want her to be a post-therapy, fully realized forty-year-old.

Childhood should be a time for exploration, but even kindergarteners know that true freedom is not allowed. Every mother who shrieks that Legos can be enjoyed by boys *and* girls is undone the minute she rolls her cart into Target, where even those simple bricks have now been gender coded. When even usually sensible Danes fold to North American consumer pressures, you know our kids are in trouble.

Stereotyping hurts everyone—from girls who die emulating fashion models, to boys like Lawrence King, who was shot dead in his classroom in 2008 by another boy who feared his romantic advances. Someday when my twelve-year-old daughter cries herself to sleep in her bedroom, it won't make the news. What is a concerted effort to stop gender programming entirely, starting in the layette aisle? I should have picketed the Mall of America back in the day, my wailing infant on my hip, chanting: "PINK AND BLUE, WON'T DO! DON'T BE MEAN, BUY YELLOW AND GREEN!" I bet that slogan would look great on a T-shirt ... *or* a dress.

In the mood for nostalgia, not regret, Miriam and I recently flipped through a book of family photographs. She pointed to an old bathtub shot of her big brother. "Look," she said, as matter-of-fact as ever. "I have a penis."

"That's not you, sweetheart," I corrected. "That's Elliott when he was little."

"*My* penis," she repeated. I decided not to argue with her; maybe this stubbornness was the very thing needed to inoculate her against what lies ahead.

"Sure, honey," I said. "You're right. It *is* your penis. You can do whatever you want with it." This made her happy, and she hugged me.

Postscript, several weeks later: Miriam tripped over the too-large Hanna Andersson clogs handed down from an older friend and landed squarely on her diaper-cushioned baby butt. "I fell on my penis," she snickered.

I checked that she wasn't hurt, and then asked: "Did you really?"

"Yep."

I thought I might as well follow up. "Do you even *have* a penis, Miriam?"

"No," she laughed. "I don't have a penis. I'm a *girl*, you silly." She picked herself up and announced, "I fell on my nutsack." Then she clogged away.

10.
My Grandmothers

The Real Powerholders in the Family

QUINCIE MELVILLE

I COULD FEEL pressure in the cabin as the plane tilted back to begin its ascent into the sky. The early morning sunlight filtered into the cabin, highlighting the dust floating in the air. Butterflies fluttered through my insides as a wave of emotions flooded my body and my brain. Suddenly, that pit of sickness took hold deep inside my stomach—self-doubt. What had made me think that I could become a single parent to this child? He would depend on me to be his EVERYTHING! Panic settled in. Blinking back tears, I replayed the life changing events of the past week.

It all began with a phone call. She was in her thirty-sixth week. She had made the decision to place her child into adoption. She wanted to choose the family that would raise her baby. She needed to be certain that this child would be raised with similar values to her own. Right away, my letter stood out to her. She was a single mother with the support of her family. I, too, would raise her child as a single mother with the support of my family. She liked that I lived in a nice neighbourhood with a good school district because education was important to her. She appreciated my personal letter, and she felt in our hearts that we shared common morals and values. She believed that if she could not raise this child, I could do an equivalent job. When we spoke, we realized there were many coincidences and similarities between our families.

When she shared her decision with our adoption agency, it scoffed at her choice. She was living in the Deep South, and although it has been racially integrated "in law" for some time, the culture, in fact, is not always integrated. The agency felt that she should choose a family of the same race, made up of two parents, to raise her child. Her social worker sent her letters composed by adoptive parents that she felt would better fit her child's profile—of African American couples. My son's birthmother obliged her by reading the new packets. However, she continued to feel a strong pull to that single mother in California (me), whom she had spoken to once for five minutes. The fact that our races were different was not of concern to her. Our conversations had made her feel confident that even though I was Caucasian, I would raise her child to know his identity. She knew I would value her baby's heritage, and that as a family, we would celebrate culture. I had been raised amid transracial families, and there would be many examples of integration and acceptance in her child's life. She called me again, and we spoke for only a few minutes more, but that conversation changed all of our lives forever. She told me what happened with the agency, but said that if I wasn't working with any other birthmothers, she would like to move forward with me. She shared that she was going to be induced in a week's time and asked that I come to Georgia for the birth because she did not want her child to go into any sort of foster care for any length of time. I agreed, and she called the agency. Against the advice of her social worker, we moved forward. The next day, she called to tell me that she had a final ultrasound and that the baby was a boy, so I should come prepared to be the mother of a *son*.

We both spent the remainder of that week preparing for what lay ahead: the creation of a new family. The birthmother spent her last week carrying her baby boy, and I spent the week preparing to hold my son for the first time. As mothers, we shared the common goal of giving this child the best that life has to offer.

All-consuming nausea began to set in as the plane levelled out and reached cruising altitude. I looked at my mom, who was sitting next to me, and she said, "Are you ready?" *Ready?* I thought. *What had I done? How would I care for a baby on my own?* I responded with a smile, but inside I was shriveling. It was in that moment that my mom looked at me and said, "Mother would have been so excited." Indeed, my maternal grandmother would have been beside herself with delight at the thought of me becoming a mother, and she would have had every confidence in me.

In the sixties, at a time when most white, middle-class women stayed home to raise a family, my maternal grandmother (Mamaw) and my Aunt Jean were working mothers. Both had given birth to a single child. Both were married to adventurous husbands. Both women continued to work full time when their marriages ended. My Mamaw raised my mother, and my Aunt Jean raised my cousin in single-parent households with absentee fathers.

These two women were pillars of strength. Nothing scared them. They played many roles to those who had the pleasure of encountering them. Always dressed impeccably, these women held their own while living in a man's world. As single income parents, they provided their children with nice homes, vacations, cars, and college educations.

In her youth, Mamaw had done everything that her perfect southern family had asked, until she didn't. She was the oldest of three spirited children, she graduated early from high school, dated the boys her parents expected, and had done exactly as they wanted. One day, she met a boy from the other side of town. He was handsome and had dimples that would weaken any woman's knees. Their courtship was fast, and it ended in marriage. Soon after, she left home and began to follow her new husband all over the United States as he left and returned from war. It was during his leaves of duty that the less attractive side of his personality came out. These were the moments that made Mamaw consider leaving the marriage. However, her family was not supportive of this idea. For the most part, they thought that she had created her situation and therefore she should make the best of it. For several miserable years, she carried on. She found places for her and her husband to live, she maintained jobs, and miscarried a son, nearly losing her own life in the process. Mamaw's final move brought her and my grandfather to California, where she would stay, mostly without him, for the rest of her years.

Throughout her life, Mamaw, made wise investments, and she purchased her own home, cars, designer clothes, and wonderful family vacations. After the Northridge earthquake in 1994, her home was condemned. Some of my friends from college came to help me evacuate her, since she had only one hour to take whatever she could. As one of my kind friends opened her closet, his eyes bulged in disbelief. He turned to me and said, "There can't really be shoes in all those boxes?" He counted as he unloaded her trove and later reported that there were 472 pairs of Italian designer shoes in that closet. All of this from a woman who worked for an hourly wage; she had previously been supporting her husband, and continued keeping her daughter and granddaughter in the best that money could buy. Nothing was too good for her family. In return, she expected good posture, good manners, and a southern, lady-like etiquette in all situations.

While we were packing up her things from her condemned home, Mamaw stood there, after an hour, watching her belongings rifled through; some were loaded onto a truck, whereas others were left lying in the rubble. She handed out one hundred dollar bills to anyone who came to help us. She always kept them stashed in her cedar chest for emergencies. She said that this was an emergency and that those people had helped us in one of our darkest hours. It was all that she could do to thank them. My grandmother's grace was astounding that day. She came dressed nicely, with her hair done, and made sure that everyone was taken care of with a thank you and a smile. She might have been in a dark time, but she never let it show for one moment. Her shoulders were back, and her head was high. She was always the epitome of a lady, both when life was at its best and at its worst.

Although Mamaw might have been intimidating to some, I frequently witnessed her many softer sides. As a child, I knew that every Wednesday, I would come home to a new treasure on my bed because Wednesdays were her shopping days with her best girlfriend. As I matured, my Mamaw taught me that I could have a man in my life for companionship, but that I didn't have to depend on him to take care of me. At that time, she had a lovely gentleman friend, but she never did remarry. She had decided that it was far better to be self-sufficient. She had earned her stripes as a woman who could stand on her own, and she, in turn, ingrained in me that the most important gift that I could give myself was an education. With this, I, too, could sustain my independence.

My grandmother was an icon to the modern feminist. She was way ahead of her time. Mamaw's saddest day was the day she was diagnosed with dementia, for she knew that her sharp wit and propensity for numbers and decision making would come to an end. This dignified lady reeled in what would come. She did not go out without a fight, however. She kept her wit, her southern charm, and her strength until the end.

I can remember the last time that I saw her. Her memory was gone, except for fleeting glimpses. She did not know us, and looked at things that we could not see in the room. She was in pain, and we had asked for a dose of medication to ease it. My mother and I usually held vigil by her bedside. However, that night, we decided to go home and try to get a little bit of sleep. As I left her room, I turned over my shoulder and looked at her one last time and said, "I love you, Mamaw." To my surprise, she looked me straight in the eyes and said, "I love you, too, darlin'." It was her only moment of clarity that day, or that week for that matter. A few short hours after I slid into my bed that night, the phone rang. I knew before I picked it up. She was gone.

My mother has always told me that my Mamaw could take on the world with one hand tied behind her back. Flying somewhere over the middle of the United States early that morning, I knew that Mamaw was nudging me to recall the lessons that she had taught me. I knew that I had the makings to be a strong woman in a man's world and to be a loving mother to my child at the same time.

I was brought back to the present when I overheard my mom telling the woman next to her that we were flying to Georgia for me to adopt a baby. The woman congratulated me and asked if I knew whether it was a girl or a boy. I told her that tomorrow I would have a son. She responded that she hoped that I had plenty of energy because boys took a lot of work. I smiled back, it being one of those parenting comments that we all receive, whether we want them or not.

As I settled back into my seat, self-doubt kept me wondering if I truly had what it took to raise a son as a single mother. I had taken classes through my adoption agency. I knew that I would provide a host of male role models as father figures for this child and had conversations with these men to assure their support, but I wondered if that would be enough for him. It was then that I remembered my other lessons of strength; these were taught from a mother of two sons.

My paternal grandmother, my Mimi, was another beacon for her time. Although she chose more traditional roles as a wife and stay-at-home mother, her strength was revealed to me in different ways. She was the first American-born child of Irish immigrant parents, and she grew up learning to appreciate America's gifts. Mimi was one of ten children, and her parents raised her to think independently and to speak her mind. She always had an Irish twinkle in her eye. It was that sparkle in my grandmother's personality that drew her loved ones in like moths to a flame.

At a time when girls were taught to be proper and demure, she was enrolling in sports leagues, climbing trees, and constantly coming home with skinned knees. She was late to marry; late for her time, that is. Her first son was born when her husband was at war. She and her child had two years alone together. When my grandfather returned from overseas, another son, my father, graced the family.

It is my belief that it was during these years that she developed with her sons what became known in our family as "Mimi's backdoor." My grandfather was the kind of man who liked to feel that he was in charge, so she found a way around that. It didn't matter what you needed; it was to Mimi that you would place your request. She always found just the right manner to present it my grandfather. She could always garner a yes out of him. He idolized her. He had her on a pedestal, and there she stayed even after she passed away. She held all of the power in the family in her quiet, unassuming way.

All of the business of the family was conducted in the kitchen. She was an avid cook and a remarkable baker. She spent hours immersed in culinary pursuits. It was there that she would slip money into my pocket and whisper, "Don't tell Grandpa." If there was ever anything anyone needed, the kitchen was the place to ask it. He stayed away until it was time to do the dishes, so it was the safety zone for business.

After she died, my grandfather handed me an envelope one day. He said, "It's money from Mimi and me." He knew. In fact, he had known about our secret tactics all along. He admired her uncompromising spirit and her ability to fight for what she wanted. It had been one of the reasons that he loved her so much. Thus adored, she raised two boys and managed a household dominated by men. She taught them to respect strong women and to treat them well. She taught me how to raise a son that is drawn to powerful women and to teach him how to treat women with respect. She taught us all that battles of consequence are few, but are worthy of time and cunning. From Mimi's silent power came my quiet strength.

The flight attendants came around with another round of beverages by the time the sun was straight overhead. A movie was playing on the projector in the plane, but I was unable to focus on it. Laughter came and went, and I could hear the jostling of the cart and clinking of ice in cups. The scent of forced air was getting stronger as we travelled further away from my home and closer to something that I had never known. This was not, of course, the first time in my life that I had experienced a significant and life-altering change. I had come of age years earlier with the support of my amazing grandmothers. My life did change, but their devotion to me did not.

Divorce. It's a word that plagues every family. Sometimes, it can be more of a blessing than a detriment. As time has marched on, society has become more accepting of the process: seeing it within each family and accepting families from every walk of life with branches strewn out across the wind.

When my father first uttered the word "divorce," it felt like a crack in the universe. As if everything I had known had somehow ended and the world I knew would never be the same. In some ways, that was true. It was the women in my family who picked up those pieces and put my world back together after my father walked out of my home.

The day after his announcement, my Mamaw took me shopping in Beverly Hills and to lunch at the Bullocks Wilshire Tearoom. This was usually our Christmas tradition. However, since he had chosen to give me this news just before my twelfth birthday, we broke tradition. I spent the day looking at jewelry and china, and trying on clothes. She bought me an outfit that made me feel pretty. We had ice cream sundaes for lunch that day. When I asked her if we needed to eat lunch first, she asked, "Why?" That was the kind of woman Mamaw had become.

She broke the rules. She made her own money so that she could spend it however she wanted. She spoiled me to no end. I was a very lucky little girl. She taught me how to treat the ones you love and how to be strong in any situation.

Mamaw assisted my broken mother in a similar fashion. While eating dinner at my Aunt Jean's house, my mother could barely speak through all her tears. The time had come to remind my mother precisely what she was made of. The lesson was given in story form through a conversation between Mamaw and my Aunt Jean. In hindsight, at the age of twelve, I might not have been quite old enough to hear it. The women did not send me away, so I sat and listened intently. The telling of that story marked a pinnacle moment in my education on being an independent woman.

The story began with my Aunt Jean following her (then) husband as he parked outside of an apartment building. She knew about the woman who lived in this building, and she knew why her husband was there. He disappeared into the apartment for what must have been hours, given the events that followed. My aunt drove to pick up my Mamaw and together they went to my aunt's house. Here, they collected every single item of her cheating husband's belongings and then loaded them into her car. They drove back to that apartment and stuffed his car with all of his worldly possessions. Then, they sat, waited, and watched. Eventually, he emerged, with tousled hair and an untucked shirt. When he saw his car, he was furious and proceeded to go into a full rage in the middle of the street right in front of the home of his mistress, while they sat giggling a block away. Mamaw said there were tears running down their cheeks from the laughter. He had been caught, and the message was clear. He was no longer welcome in the house that my Aunt Jean had supported. The time had come for him to move on. The ride was over.

My father's mother, Mimi, took the news of my parents' divorce differently. She and my grandfather had moved away recently. For my entire life, they lived within a mile of my childhood home. Around the time when my parents divorced, they moved a few hours south to a beach community. While it was difficult to adjust to them being so far away, I could see how relaxed and happy they were. They joked. They golfed. They did things together. It was the happiest they had ever been.

Mimi made sure that I spent parts of my summers with them and that I saw them frequently. She forced my father to step up and to keep them involved in my life. They remained a constant for holidays, special events, and everyday life. In fact, it was during those years that her backdoor policy was in its fullest effect. Mimi taught me that it didn't matter the convenience of things; that if something is important, you have to stick with it. People are important, and you cannot give up on them, even if it's easier to do so.

Together, my grandmothers saw to it that I had everything that I wanted and needed. Phone calls, discussions, and letters passed between these two women. They provided magical moments in my teen years and beyond because they felt that I should not pay for the choices of others. They never asked for credit, and they simply did what they felt was right. Unconditional love abounded from the souls of these women. They each held their heads high in their own right, and they shared a common bond.

As the plane began its final descent that morning, a flurry of emotions flooded over me. This time I would be embarking on my life-changing journey without them, and it terrified me. Then, it occurred to me. When it came time for me to become a mother, I chose to adopt without thinking twice. At the time, I did not even question whether I could raise a child on my own because I had these strong women who had guided me on my journey. They had taught me that I could do anything in life, as long as I decided to do it. I had the support of my own mother, who was sitting right next to me on the plane that day. She had raised me alone from the time that I was twelve; plus, I had some very special angels looking down on me to guide me in all that they had taught me. When the wheels touched down in Georgia, my mom took my hand and squeezed it and asked me if I was ready. I answered as honestly as any new parent could: "I don't know. Let's go."

The next few days were a whirr of news, activity, and emotion. Eventually, I received a phone call from my son's birthmother announcing his arrival. She reported that the delivery had gone well. He was a good eater and had strong lungs. I could hear his noises in the background. I will admit that even though I was very happy, I did not feel very much like his mother. In that conversation, he was still her son. My moment would not come until the next day.

The sterility of the hospital was overwhelming. The pungent odor of disinfectant hung in the air, and the white glow of iridescent lights cast a glaring hue on everything in my line of sight. I approached the window of the nursery, searching intently for his name on the bassinettes. I could not see it anywhere. Within a few moments, a woman with a kind smile came towards me, asked my name, and then invited me into the maternity ward. As I followed her, I felt as if my heart was about to explode from my chest. A nurse appeared down the hall rolling a baby in a clear, plastic bassinette. She smiled and said, "Here is your son." Examining him closely, I noticed the name on the card did not match his birthmother's, so I told her that this was the wrong baby. She explained that children who are to be placed for adoption in that hospital are assigned the last name of *Givens*. This was indeed baby Givens, and, yes, he was mine. We moved into a nearby hospital room. His birthmother wanted us to have privacy. I was told we could stay together there as long as I liked. With that, the nurse left the room, congratulating me with a smile.

Having gone through some near misses, I still didn't quite believe that this could be happening, that this little boy could be my son. That feeling of doubt only lasted for a few seconds, though. I picked him up from the bassinette, my hand cupping the back of his head. He was wrapped so tightly in the white blanket with the blue and pink stripes. I placed him carefully on the bed and unwrapped him. For the first time, I could see his fingers, his toes, his skinny little arms, and wrinkly legs. He stretched his toes out just the way he still does today. As I was staring at him, he grasped my finger and held fast to it, pulling it towards his mouth. Then, he searched my face with his little eyes. In a heartbeat, I became his mother. He was mine, and I was his. Nothing was ever going to change that.

From the very beginning of his life, my son has been governed by strong women. First, his birthmother chose to place him with me. Adoption had not been an easy choice for her. Her decision was wrought with personal agony and scrutiny from her friends and family. She was even judged by the social workers, whose job it had been to assist her. Yet she stood firm because she knew that for her child, I was the right choice.

She was his first mother and will always be an important part of his life. I am blessed that she chose me to be his mommy. I do my best each day to guide him through his decisions and to teach him to be a good man and citizen. I hope to pass down to him the important lessons that were given to me. These lessons on courage, grace, dignity, kindness, strength, and unconditional love have molded me into the person that I am today. His grandmother, my mom, teaches him the things that I cannot. Together, we work to weave our best intentions into him. I know that one day, he will emerge in his best, most perfect form, ready to create his own family and to continue to pass on our traditions.

Raising him with my family's values has defined me as his mother. It has affected our relationship, and it is my hope that it has affected how he will interact with the world. I especially want him to see women as strong, each in their own way, and beautiful for having this strength. I also want him to appreciate the sacrifices that were made by previous generations in our family in order to instill these feminist values within him. Although my son is young, he will learn to respect the people around him and emulate kindness and great compassion. As a man, it will be his task to continue to pay these gifts forward into society and to raise his own family. I hope that he will follow the path that Mamaw, Aunt Jean, Mimi, my mother, and I have paved for him, and our legacy of feminist parenting will continue with future generations.

11.
The Whole of My Child

JANA BÜHLMANN

MY LITTLE GIRL can be powerful. My little girl can be angry. Before she was born, I felt strongly about not owning my daughter. I thought it my job to own parenthood more particularly. I was a mother; I did not HAVE a daughter. Now, after almost seven years, I have come to embrace that she is mine. She is mine right now, until she is ready to be more fully her own. My job—deep breath—is to guide and interpret each active movement, each dialogue, each heartfelt expression that she shares with me. Sometimes, I don't fare so well. Such moments are most forgiving when I take them on as mothering myself.

My daughter is an explosive child. Or at least she is as such if I choose to apply a label to those moments when she is brave enough to swirl in her own chaos. Her huge chaos. Sometimes, I wonder if she has a choice, and then I think about those moments in which I, too, feel myself launch into an abyss, a place I know I have no choice but to go—noncontextualized feeling.

Is my daughter a mirror of who I am or of humanity? I watch her and think about my own intense personality, my own self-expression. She parents me just in her living, if I so choose. I have said out loud on more than one occasion that she arrived whole, and the world is chipping away at her. Is it my job to shield her from this process, or to simply show her that it is ok to be nicked and to actively engage with discomfort just as equally as joy?

Her last explosive moment felt the most intense to date, yet I did not feel as afraid or overwhelmed as in the past, when she would crawl across the floor in her rage and lash out at me. Now, I feel as if I go there with her. I dance with her anger so that we can play out my words to her: *tell yourself that you are angry, tell an adult that you trust, then find somewhere safe to let your anger out so that it does not hurt your body nor someone else.*

Most recently, I trusted us both to let her release the worst of her fears on her own, to step up only when it felt right to offer comfort. The next day, the related dialogue began—the momma narration and the observance of the words in my child's eyes. I told her: "Your anger is just your own sweetheart. As big as it gets, your anger is just simply yours. And so it becomes your job to find a way to take care of your anger, and everything else you feel. And Momma is here to help you right now so that in the moments when I am not there, you will trust yourself."

I am reading about collaborative decision-making, and thinking about the strength and intellect of my child. It plays out one way on the websites I am finding and another in my internal monologue. It furthers my thoughts about the impossibility of controlling my child and the humility of motherhood—parenthood—being just simply a process of active learning. Together.

My daughter is mine, yet she will never be. I am always and forever her mother and my own.

12.
The Skin of Your Hand

The skin of your hand is paper
where dark words were written
by us, mother and daughter, together.
What we had, your dad and I, is over.
I look out the window at coming
green grass, and my anger
is gone. I am full with what
his eyes gave me when he gave me
to you. I cannot pretend anymore.
My mouth of soft mothering words
is empty now, and you are dark
in the silence. Spring comes fast,
my daughter. But for now, it is winter
and we are no longer together.
The snow is white like a ceiling.
Take the skin of your hand and
write the words upon it. Continue
what I began. Begin with the feelings.

—Cassie Premo Steele

III.
STORIES OF POWER AND INEQUALITY

13.
Tomatoes: *A Sonnet*

I set the toddler on the kitchen floor
so I can turn the handle, crank the teeth.
When I can see them, bobbing large and round
I realize I've bought the wrong tomatoes.
At the store, the toddler had been screaming,
crying, plucking at my pregnant gut.
I was tempted to throw up, or sleep
on cool and grimy-smooth linoleum
right there next to the full grocery cart
and I grabbed whole instead of diced. Dammit.
Fleshy red gobbets, globes like fresh placentas
I grab the kitchen shears and plunge them, savage
scissoring red fruit to tiny, bloody bits.
Next time, I think, *I'll buy the right tomatoes.*

—Sara Hardin Keeth

14.
Embodying Feminist Mothering

Narratives of Resistance through Patriarchal Terrorism from Both a Mother's and Child's Perspective

MARILYN METTA WITH MAE[1]

THIS CHAPTER is a collaborative co-scripting of narratives of resistance from both a mother's and child's perspective as survivors of domestic violence and patriarchal terrorism. This chapter weaves the autoethnographical narratives of resistance from contemporary feminist perspectives to unpack the systematic male control and violent characteristics of patriarchal terrorism. In this chapter, the term "patriarchal terrorism" is used in preference to the more commonly used term "domestic violence" because patriarchal terrorism better reflects and encompasses our experiences. The term "domestic violence" appears throughout the chapter as the common term referred to in existing literature. Johnson first introduced the term "patriarchal terrorism" in 1995 to describe the "patriarchal traditions of men's rights to control 'their' women" ("Patriarchal Terrorism" 284). It is "a form of terroristic control" of women by their male partners, which involves "the systematic use of not only violence, but economic subordination, threats, isolation, and other control tactics" (284).

This chapter is written as a direct response to the gaps in existing literature and scholarship on domestic violence, and address these three themes: first, the voices of children and young people who have experienced patriarchal terrorism speaking in their own terms; second, the complex and crucial role of mothers and mother-figures in the survival as well as recovery process of children and young people; and third, the nature of the more invisible and insidious forms of abuse and control through the eyes of survivors of patriarchal terrorism.

This chapter draws on contemporary research in autoethnography and narratives of resistance in women's lives, and is framed within contemporary feminist and reflexive philosophies. The chapter puts the voices of children and young people at the centre of their own knowledge making, which creates the space and forum for them to speak on their own behalf and in their own terms. This framing is fundamental to our feminist approaches and to our positionings in challenging patriarchal terrorism.

Marilyn: I position myself as a feminist academic and researcher, as an advocate and activist for women and children's rights, and as a survivor of patriarchal terrorism. I explore some of my personal, embodied, and therapeutic journeys as a woman, mother, and stepmother, who has experienced patriarchal and intimate terrorism; and as a narrative therapist who works with mothers and children who have experienced and/or witnessed patriarchal terrorism. I draw from the works of contemporary feminist scholars and the practice of mindful, agential, and embodied parenting to explore different ways of thinking about parenting and motherhood. My narratives of resistance offered here in both prose and poetic forms frame the discussion and exploration of feminist parenting through and beyond patriarchal terrorism. I am Mae's stepmom.

Mae: I position myself as a young adult survivor of patriarchal terrorism and as a young scholar and activist calling for action against patriarchal terrorism. I aim to use my voice and my lived experiences as a platform to speak on my own behalf as a young adult survivor of patriarchal terrorism.

We explore alternative voices, narratives, and perspectives from a feminist mother and stepmother and from a feminist young adult survivor of patriarchal terrorism, who both seek to challenge dominant masculinist narratives and histories. This feminist stor*ymaking* speaks from an intergenerational and Asian Australian perspective. We argue that these embodied and relational ways of feminist parenting have much to inform the philosophical, conceptual, and scholarly understandings of parenting.

Furthermore, feminist relational story*making* creates spaces for the rewriting of personal, gendered, cultural, racial, and hybridized histories that act as narratives of resistance to discourses of racism, sexism, and violence. By placing the personal and embodied narratives of resistance of women at the centre of story*making*, we are challenging the dominant masculinist and patriarchal discourses of knowledge making within scholarly paradigms.

As such, the autoethnographical story*making* takes centre stage in this chapter. As a narrative therapist, researcher and storymaker, narrative ways of working with stories have been an integral and important part of Marilyn's personal, professional and research epistemologies and practice (Metta, "Writing against" 263). The autoethnographical narratives from Mae have emerged from personal journal excerpts and from two narrative-based interviews conducted with Mae by Marilyn. The interviews are framed within a narrative framework and form part of an ongoing narratively informed and dialogical conversation between Marilyn and Mae. The narrative methodological frameworks adopted are discussed later in the chapter.

By examining the relational ethics and practice within the parent-child relational narratives, the chapter foregrounds the importance of relational knowing and engaged practice and pedagogy in the production and transmission of knowledge across difference. In the context of domestic violence—where isolation and separation of self and other dominate both the experience and narratives—this relational story*making* is a deliberate methodological strategy and framework to counter and mitigate the abusive patterns of control and systematic isolation characteristic of patriarchal terrorism.

This chapter argues that embodied feminist lifewriting occupies an important and pivotal place within contemporary feminist scholarship and contemporary scholarly knowledge making. To place women at the centre of scholarly texts, critical analysis, and knowledge making is a political act, which challenges histories that have long erased marginalized women and subjugated their experiences. This challenges the taken-for-granted location of ethnic minority women's lifewriting at the margins of culture, which can further subjugate and marginalize ethnic minority women's lives and experiences (Metta, "Writing against" 29-30).

RELATIONAL ETHICS

It is important for both of us to carefully consider the relational ethics of collaborating on this chapter. The personal relationship and histories that we both share as stepmother and stepdaughter are an integral part of this collaboration and co-scripting. This whole process of working together and co-writing this chapter has emerged out of a long journey that spans over two decades and would not be possible without the level of trust, respect, integrity, and mindful relational ethics that are at the core of our relationship. Our reconnection since 2012 has provided a powerful and rigorous space for both of us to engage and explore the different layers of storytelling and story*making* together and separately. As the parent, I (Marilyn) am fully aware of the power relations that are embedded in our relationship and collaboration. I would not have attempted this collaboration without having the level and depth of experience, which comes from working with people's life stories as both a lifewriting researcher and scholar, or without being a narrative therapist who has worked in the field of domestic and family violence for the past fifteen years. I have researched and written extensively about relational ethics, and I am deeply committed to the duty of care and the practice of relational ethics, especially when working with people and stories within the domestic violence and patriarchal terrorism paradigms. My work and practice have always been deeply grounded in and guided by Trinh Minh-ha's philosophy encapsulated by what she describes as the "maternal touch," which "is neither possessed nor possessive, neither binding nor detached nor neutral. For a life to maintain another life, the touch has to be infinitely delicate: precise, attentive, and swift, so as not to pull, track, rush, crush, or smother" (38).

CHILDREN LIVING WITH PATRIARCHAL TERRORISM

Emerging research from the past two decades has focused on the impact of domestic violence on children and young people living with it (McGee; Pearson et al.; Hayes and Jeffries; Mullender; Gillinder and Goddard; Holt et al.; Øverlien; Fantuzzo et al.). The recognition of children as victims of domestic violence emerged following the United Nations 1989 Convention on the Rights of the Child, which brought international attention to the rights of children and prompted the emergence of "a discourse of childhood and children in research" across a range of disciplines in the 1980s (Morris et al. 126). The rise of the discourse of childhood and children in research created opportunities for "collaborative approaches" in research with children that is centred on "children's own experiences of domestic violence and children's agency in keeping themselves and others safe" (Morris et al. 126). Holt et al. have found in existing literature that children and adolescents living with domestic violence are "at increased risk of experiencing emotional, physical and sexual abuse, of developing emotional and behavioral problems and of increased exposure to the presence of other adversities in their lives" (797). The authors also stress that one of the most important protective factors that can mitigate against these impacts is "a strong relationship with and attachment to a caring adult, usually the mother" (797).

Øverlien points to the growing body of research in the field of domestic violence showing that the negative impact of being exposed to the abuse of one's primary caregiver has previously been "grossly underestimated" (277). Research has also shown that "children who experience domestic violence are at increased risk of developing psychological and behavioral difficulties such as anxiety, depression and aggression and of becoming victims of physical violence and sexual abuse themselves" (Øverlien 277).

Children living with patriarchal terrorism are witnesses of and are exposed to multiple aspects of violence and abuse within the family. Children are often directly or indirectly involved in the violence and abuse by being forced to witness the control used by men to threaten, manipulate, intimidate, and control their partners. Children are often also used as bait or guilt traps to stop women from leaving abusive relationships or to lure them back to the relationships.

COERCIVE CONTROL

As stated previously, Johnson has coined the term "patriarchal terrorism" as a way to highlight the historical and cultural roots of family and domestic violence: "The term patriarchal terrorism has the advantage of keeping the focus on the perpetrator and of keeping our attention on the systematic, intentional nature of this form of violence. Of course, the term also forces us to attend routinely to the historical and cultural roots of this form of family violence" ("Patriarchal Terrorism" 284). Johnson describes how "the causal dynamic of patriarchal terrorism is rooted in patriarchal traditions, adopted with a vengeance by men who feel that they must control 'their' women by any means necessary" ("Patriarchal Terrorism" 286). He describes this system of controlling tactics as coercive control, which is a form of emotional abuse. Many women living with patriarchal terrorism describe "patterns of abusive control" in every aspect of their lives, including financial control. These patterns of abusive control also extend to "freedom of movement, manner of dressing and self-enhancement, going to, or not going to work, shopping, leisure activities, contact with family, friends and professional systems, contraception and childbearing" (Allen 52).

Drawing from Johnson's work, Øverlien argues that children living with patriarchal terrorism are subjected to coercive control, which characterizes the violence they are exposed to: "The degrading words and actions, the demand to be perfect, the bizarre acts, and oscillation between rage and tenderness are all parts of a terror aimed at controlling the children" (285). For Mae, this coercive control is often unpredictable and permeates her everyday life.

I think his moods ... they were getting more and more frequent ... Mood would consist of him just bringing the whole house down and dragging everyone into it ... but we all would have no idea what happened... and it was out of nowhere and for no reason ... and we all thought, who did something wrong ... so everyone would be punished ... and I mean this would frequently happen, celebration days, birthdays, Christmas, New Year's but frequently throughout, it's kind of every day.

Many children and young people living with patriarchal terrorism experience a deep sense of grief and loss of innocence and a normal childhood.

To be able to just live carelessly, and freely as a child... [she cries]... it was like living ... always having to watch out ... to keep ears and eyes open, you never really know what to expect

... living in fear all the time.

Children living patriarchal terrorism often experience the loss of control and an overwhelming sense of helplessness.

I was so angry, frustrated, and frustration was probably the biggest emotion... I felt, just all the time, just why, why is this happening, Why us, why can't we stop it?

MOTHERING THROUGH PATRIARCHAL TERRORISM

Mothering through patriarchal terrorism is complex and multi-layered. The physical, psychological, and emotional impacts of patriarchal terrorism on mothering are complicated. Some mothers interviewed by a study by Radford and Hester describe the detrimental effects of domestic violence on their mothering, such as "losing their confidence as mothers, being emotionally drained and with little to give their children" ("Mothering through Domestic Violence" 29-30).

For many women, mothering and their relationships with their children can also be an enormous source of strength, resilience, and comfort. For Marilyn, mothering through domestic violence was a delicate act and art of love for self and other.

> Embodied mothering, for me and for many of the women I work with, is multi-layered and is often an extraordinary journey. The mundane, daily embodied rituals of a mother feeding, bathing, clothing, attending to and caring for herself and for her children become central to the recovery process. The act of combing my children's hair every morning before school became a mindful and deliberate process of connection, soothing, and healing. Embodied mothering is about dealing with the confusion, trauma, fears, and sometimes anger embodied by her children. It is also about the delicate tender and intimate exchanges that are vital in keeping the woman and her children alive and in hope. Motherhood and mothering, for many of these women, become a key source of hope, courage, strength, and resilience for survival and recovery. (Metta, "Putting the Body" 504)

Captured in this new poem are Marilyn's reflections on her experiences of mothering through domestic violence.

Mothering with Clipped Wings

My heart breaking
As the little hands held mine
The sad young eyes tugged at my heartstrings
I returned again and again
To the wolf's den

He knows the bait, the innocent younglings
I gathered them close to my heart
I tried to speak but I had no voice
Yet they knew
They knew all along

He clipped my wings so I couldn't fly
He thought he could clip my spirit too
Swallowing me whole
Grinding me down, and down and down
Driving me to the brink of insanity

Mothering with clipped wings
I built a fragile cocoon of love around my little ones
We stole moments of tenderness
Amidst the brutality and violence
It has a name—patriarchal terrorism

Mothering with clipped wings
The day came when I took flight
My only chance of freedom
I had to leave all my younglings behind
My heart bled that day

Found my little cave on the hill
Where I hid and hibernated
Days, months and years passed

My wings slowly healed and I waited
For the day when I soared

We now know what he could never touch
Our cocoon of love and tenderness
Even after years of separation
With my babies safely tucked under my wings
It's now time to heal your young wings.
(by Marilyn)

ETHICS OF DISCLOSURE

The question of the ethics of disclosure for women and children who have experienced patriarchal terrorism is a complex and highly contested issue. This is an issue that I have previously written about and unpacked in my earlier autobiographical writings when I first wrote about my experiences of domestic violence:

> In the writing of my autobiography, I have had to negotiate the ethical dilemmas involved in the breaking of many silences. In breaking my silence about my experiences of domestic violence, I inevitably have to disclose my ex-partner as a person who has perpetrated domestic abuse. This has always been a huge risk that many women who have experienced domestic violence face in any disclosure about their perpetrator. While I have taken the necessary steps to protect my ex-partner's identity in this research, it is impossible to conceal his identity to people who knew of our relationship. (Metta, "Writing Against" 58-59)

For many children and young people, disclosure about the violence involves risks and ramifications. Every disclosure requires enormous courage and is never taken lightly. In the writing of this piece, the risks, possible ramifications and the ethical considerations of her disclosure were discussed with Mae. One of the most challenging considerations for Mae was the possibility of her dad reading the piece.

Well, I guess I've avoided doing that ... because I feel like this is my journey, I'm taking the control over it ... but I do understand that it will have consequences, but I feel like I'm equipped with support networks at the moment to deal with whatever comes my way and I feel confident that I'll be able to deal with it, and I know it's not going to be easy.... But I want to take power, and it's not his choice whether I'm going to share my story or not. It's not his story, it's mine.... So it's up to him how it's going to affect him ... but it's out of my hands. I can't tell him how to feel ... or tell him what's right or wrong ... that's not my responsibility and I'm an adult, and I can make my own choices on what I want to do with my past experiences and how I'm going to let that affect me.... So yeah, I guess it's a risk but its one that I'm willing to take and I'm willing to be able to deal with myself....

TACTICS OF DENIAL

Johnson provides a detailed description of the tactics of coercive control that forms a pattern of power and control and a "web of abuse" used in patriarchal terrorism ("Typology" 9). The perpetrator uses tactics of isolation, surveillance, and a range of emotional abuse to exercise coercive control over his partner. A recurring tactic that is often used by perpetrator to exercise control over the victim is denial.

> Related to this emotional abuse is minimizing or denying his own abuse, and blaming her for what is going on in the relationship. It's her crazy behavior or incompetence or sexual misconduct that requires him to control her the way he does, in her own best interests. How could she see him as abusive? He's never really hurt her. In the contrary, she's the abusive partner. She's so out of touch with reality that maybe she should get some help. (Johnson, *Typology* 9)

Denial

The dark clouds of denial descend
Looming, swallowing up

My truth, my voice
The ultimate attempt of erasure

The patriarchal denial
The charming god of glib tongue
The Zeus who swallowed Metis whole
To erase her existence, *herstory*

Desperate to hide his dark secrets
And clean up the evidence
Consumed by his obsession
To mask the truth with a false script

To convince the world she never existed
"*But, it never happened!*"
"*But she was mad!*"
"*But, but, but …*"

The villain turned himself the victim
The wolf dressed up as Little Red
The story must not be changed
At all costs.

Shocked he was when she not only survived but thrived
Agitating the patriarchal stomach, she created a storm
She roared with a power he never saw coming
Upheavals raged through history.

She refused to be silenced
Herstory refused to be erased
She stands now at the centre of her story
Her voice and legacy powerful and strong

He who tried to swallow, beware
Of the crack threatening to burst open
Spilling the dark secrets out into the world
Denial, your time is up.
(By Marilyn)

THE AFTERMATH

Many women who have escaped abusive relationships and homes often have to be separated from their children, loved ones, and pets for long periods of time. Many women have managed escape with only the clothes on their backs and whatever they were able to grab. The separation from children and loved ones is one of the major reasons why women have found it so hard to leave the abusive relationships. Many have had multiple failed attempts to escape and even when they do succeed in escaping, the guilt and sense of responsibility for children and loved ones often lead to them returning to the abusive relationship.

One of the most devastating and heartbreaking costs when a woman ultimately leaves the abusive relationship is the forced separation from her children and loved ones. In the case of stepmothers, this can mean long separations that span years. In my case, when I left the abusive relationship in 2005, I knew that would mean separation from my three stepchildren whom I had loved and looked after for nearly twelve years, and for whom I was Mama. Mae was the youngest of my stepchildren. The aftermath of leaving the relationship becomes one of the most dangerous periods for the women and children living with patriarchal terrorism.

The Aftermath

9 April 2005 was the day
She found her freedom
She saw the narrow chance to slip
Out of her cage

Purse and keys I grabbed and ran to the car
Had no choice but to leave my babies behind
I will come back for you, I promise!

I drove aimlessly for hours
Paralyzed with fear and trepidation
My mind threatened to explode
Into a million pieces

My life hung perilously on a thin rope
Threatening to snap any moment
As I continue to face daily and hourly torments
I hung on for my children

As he pushed and shoved me
Restrained for hours in my car
Snatched my keys and phone
Pummelling at my door at nights
As I crouched in fear

Pick-up and drop-off times
Became my weekly nightmares
As I struggled to breathe through that choking sensation
I felt the world closing in on me

I never felt more alone in my life
All I could hang onto was my wings
They grew stronger every day I was out of that cage
I kept faith as I faced the aftermath of leaving him

Fear for my life, I wrote my will
And began a long and painful process
Restraining orders Police 000
Family Court Lawyers

But each day, my wings grew stronger
I could fly longer and farther
And dream of the day I would soar through the skies
With my babies tucked under their mother's wings
(Metta, "Writing against" 121)

In the aftermath of leaving the relationship, the power and control perpetrated on the woman often gets transferred onto the next most vulnerable targets—the children who are left behind. For Mae, the aftermath became one of the most traumatic periods of living with patriarchal terrorism.

It was filled with lots of lectures, lots of talking, lots of us sitting there in silence for hours and hours ... listening to his, I guess his grief, you leaving, his feelings about it ... lots of car drives. I don't remember which times, whether it was the final time or ... but we went searching for you... in the car. He went to all the places he thought you'd be... [she cries] and it's all vivid but there were so many memories of you leaving. It was so many different occasions, just you trying to get out the door with the keys, trying to get in the car, trying to get him out of the car ... and then giving up, and saying "you've won" and you would come back inside.

For the children who are living with patriarchal terrorism, the aftermath also means the loss of their primary caregivers, which is often devastating.

I guess you were that mother-figure at dad's house. You did everything he didn't know how to. But I think you weren't able to fully because of the situation. I think we felt that ... you were also the person that would consume him in a way that would give us a break from him... so I feel like I wasn't able to have that full connection with you... then and when you left. It was weird because I grieved the loss of that mother-figure at dad's house ... the person that would cook and clean for me, and I guess all of a sudden, I had to do it for myself, at that young age, and look after the kids and step up. I think we all did.

Children living with patriarchal terrorism often experience the loss of innocence and their childhood, which is especially heightened after a woman leaves the abusive relationship and the children are left behind and alone with the perpetrator. Children often experience the loss of childhood and often have to take over household chores, childminding responsibilities for younger siblings as well as taking care of themselves.

So the relationship stopped, turned into us becoming adults as children ... and then after so many years, we got used to it and we dealt with it the best way we knew how to.... I mean we still had to deal with dad and deal with him still wanting you to come home.

LONG-TERM IMPACTS OF LIVING WITH PATRIARCHAL TERRORISM

Living with and being exposed to patriarchal terrorism has been shown to have serious and devastating effects on the children and young people's physical, emotional, social and mental health and development. As Carolina Øverlien explains:

> the finding that no children can remember and describe feeling happy or at peace when spending time with or being around their fathers/stepfathers tells us that fathers who are patriarchal terrorists do not just add something toxic to their children's lives, they also take away things all children have a right to: feeling safe, loved and protected. (285)

Various studies have found that children who repeatedly witnessed violence within the family perceive each incident as "a traumatic episode" and some children can go on to develop post-traumatic stress disorder (PTSD) (Brandon and Lewis 35). Children who have been exposed to violence are also vulnerable to developing a range of psychological and emotional issues, such as anxiety and low self-esteem.

My confidence ... I think when I'm in big groups, I tend to be quite reserved. I'll just listen, won't really speak up, and I think that stems from being forced to sit there listening, so many times.

These children often carry embodied memories of trauma, which can be retriggered by being back to or near the place or house where the original trauma took place or by being around the perpetrator.

It's hard, like walking through the gate, walking inside but what gets me through is that the kids are there when I go, and it gives me time to be with them and just, I do feel down when I leave... it puts me in a mood, and it's hard to shake off, times like...

Many children and young people living with patriarchal terrorism also experience nightmares, which are often symptomatic of the embodied trauma.

I used to get nightmares I guess, about dad ... different scenarios. They would always come after an argument with him, after coming back from the house, after witnessing how he is again. I think I have certainly distanced myself from him in recent years ... so I haven't had them for a while.

Children and young people living with patriarchal terrorism are often felt "split" and confused with conflicting emotions towards both parents. For these children and young people, their parental experiences that are "tainted with sadness, fear, confusion and disappointment ... and ambivalent attitudes towards both their parents, including fear and empathy towards their father, and compassion coupled with a sense of obligation to protect their mother" (qtd. in Holt et al. 802).

LIVING WITH INVISIBLE SCARS

One of the key aims of this chapter is to shed light on the more invisible and insidious forms of abuse and control through the eyes of children and young adult survivors of patriarchal terrorism. As Øverlien explains: "The violence cannot be described by counting the blows or measuring the physical and psychological harm. In line with women victimized by patriarchal terrorism, the children describe the violence as pervasive, as influencing every aspect of his/her life to the point of eradicating all possible positive and/or pleasant contact with the father" (285).

I was always in fear. But I think it's crazy because part of me wanted something to happen because that would have been the ability for us to get out of that situation.... When I told you about the situation the other day, about how I left and I asked him if he would physically hurt me and he said "No," and I was like oh, then I will leave... and I was thinking, but if you do physically hurt me then, good, then I have the evidence.

For many children and young people living with patriarchal terrorism, their relationships and feelings towards their fathers are often conflicted and fraught. "Children are clearly struggling with trying to understand how someone they loved could behave so horribly. Conflict was also created for children by the abuser trying to turn them against their mother, or takes sides against her" (McGee 86).

I was like, how could you treat your own kids like this? And how can anyone treat anyone like that? And why? We were just kids ... and till now I don't understand. I still don't understand today ... how it's possible ... [I] feel frustrated.

NARRATIVES OF RESISTANCE

> If personal stories offer a powerful tool in the therapeutic context as in narrative therapy, and if lifewriting as a reflexive feminist act of resistance through the re-scripting of dominant themes and identities, offers the possibilities of change, resistance and healing, then we need to examine the many different ways a story can be told and retold. (Metta, "Writing against" 262)

Narrative ways of working with stories, memories, and life narratives form the central epistemological and methodological frameworks of this chapter. The process of using a narrative approach and framework allows dominant narratives we are working with to be rescripted through reflexive feminist consciousness to craft alternative viewpoints, voices, and life scripts that not only challenge the structures and systems of patriarchal terrorism but are deeply grounded in reclaiming agency and power. We have chosen a relational story*making* approach to writing this chapter, which draws from the notion that storytelling can function as "collaborative social performance" (Rober and Van Eesbeek 313).

Marilyn devised the term story*making* to suggest "a kind of doing and an act of making something—it implies an active process and/or even a conscious act" and the notion of story*making* also suggests "how we *make* stories and how stories *make* us" (Metta, "Writing against" 286).

> I see story*making* as a two-fold process: firstly, it is a creative, intuitive and imaginative process of storying; and secondly, it is very much about *representations*—how we represent our stories and how our stories represent us. In other words, how we make sense of our life stories is related to how we *tell* the story and how we *represent* the stories. (Metta, "Writing against" 287)

In narrative therapy terms, the notion of resistance is central to the process of rescripting life narratives in ways that challenge "dominant narratives and discourses by deconstructing the ideological, cultural and social constructions of identity scripts and stories" (Metta, "Writing against" 175). Wade aptly describes resistance as "any attempt to imagine or establish a life based on respect and equality" (qtd. in Allen, 56).

For Mae, many of the stories in this chapter have been told for the first time.

When I started looking into domestic violence, when I was in university ... and really looked at what it meant and what it was, and I realized that that was what we went through. I guess it was always hard growing up knowing that things weren't right but not knowing what it was. So when I started looking at it through uni, and I had the ability to explore its meanings and the constructions of DV [domestic violence] and what it was really like ... [it was] a little surprising and shocking that to realize and to believe that was what we went through. So yeah [it is] only the last few years, four to five, that I really looked into it and understood it.

AGENCY

For Mae, her decision to break her silence and tell her story is a remarkable and courageous act of resistance and agency.

For me to share my story, it does give me a sense of like, it's reality, it happened and I'm acknowledging it and I think that's really important ... to dig up those memories and acknowledge that they happened and to be able to make peace with them and don't let them affect me anymore... because that's what's been affecting me all these years... growing up and going through work and uni life and having it affect my confidence, ability to speak out. So yeah I think I'm come to a point where I've had enough of it affecting me, and I want to acknowledge it and move forward ... and I guess writing this paper, [it will] not only help me but it'll also help others, so that's a good opportunity for me, again turning my negative experience into a positive, into a paper, and I mean this is what I want to do when I'm older, well, in a few years ... [she laughs] ... it's a good starting point I guess [she laughs].

One of the prevailing myths about domestic violence we want to highlight here is the myth that women and children do not resist the violence and stay with the perpetrator. The fact is that women and children resist the violence in a myriad of explicit and implicit ways. Øverlien writes:

> Research has shown that children are far more active in regards to the violence that takes place in their homes than we have known. They try to protect themselves, their siblings and their mothers; they physically and verbally intervene during the violent episodes; and they call out for help, often at the risk of being abused themselves. (277)

I remember when I would react the least during conversations and then when I start getting older, I start talking back and he wasn't expecting it ... and it would stun him, and he would stop... I think the last kind of chain I took down was Chucky [her dog]... Chucky was one of the only reasons besides the kids why I would go back there. I narrowed it down to only during the day when I went back home... and then I thought, no, Chucky is better off with me.... I don't have to go back there anymore.

The following story is a powerful narrative of resistance in Mae's re-scripting of her life and experiences as an adult survivor of domestic violence. It is the story of the day she made the pivotal and life-changing decision to leave her dad's house for good. She was 17 years old at the time.

Something inside me snapped. I couldn't take it any longer. Today would change my life.

The words that I unleashed onto you that day escape my memory. But even so many years later, I can't shake that feeling I get in my chest every time I think about it. The feelings, the emotions, will forever be imprinted on my mind. The muffles of arguing and fighting followed by the sudden slam of the front door and the fierce sound of your car engine screeching off the driveway and down the street. I ran to my room, desperate to disappear. I wanted to dissolve beneath those dark, cold wooden floorboards.

Every time I thought peace had finally come, there would be another fault, another element wrong with life that you just did not agree with. You would never listen; you could hear words that would come from my mouth, but you never really listened. You were right, and the world was wrong and that was that. It frustrated and angered me because none of this was new.

A build up of anger and frustration took over my mind, my body. I felt like exploding. I needed to get away from this house.

Freedom was near; it was always near, just a twenty-minute drive away. This freedom was a breath of fresh air every alternate week. It was time to rest my mind, rest my heart, and prepare myself for what may lie ahead. This freedom was only temporary, but I had decided that day to make it permanent. With this decision, I would not have to suffer in this place any longer. I would not have to sit through hours and hours of your lecturing, about how I am not good enough and how I needed to change. I would not have to feel degraded and listen to you tell me how to live my life. I would be free of your negative, controlling, and hurtful words.

But this decision brought feelings of grief. Huge grief. I soon realized what this freedom would cost me. Did I have the strength to leave behind the two people I loved the most and could not live without? Two troubled and fragile siblings would have to learn how to survive in this place without me. I know I am the youngest, but I still felt responsible for them. Would they crumble without me? I knew I would not be able to live with myself if anything were to happen to them. Tears rushed to my eyes, I just did not know what to do anymore. I felt helpless, angry, scared, and frustrated.

I collapsed to the floor; my head was spinning, I was so angry.

Moments later, I was sitting on my bed, and my head felt like it was going to explode. My sister and brother were talking to me. I could hear words of kindness and understanding escape their mouths; tears welled up in their eyes but didn't seem to be able to break away. I sensed strength within them, and I knew what they were thinking. We spoke together for a long time, sharing our feelings of concern. I was reminded that I would see them every week and if anything, I was just a phone call away. They reassured me and told me everything would be okay. I felt like the youngest sibling again; it was calming, and I knew my decision was final.

With a short note and a packed bag, I left.

(by Mae)

RECOVERY

The process of recovery for women and children who live with patriarchal terrorism is often difficult and complex. Holt et al. have found that a "secure attachment to a non-violent parent or other significant carer has been cited consistently in the literature as an important protective factor in mitigating trauma and distress" (806). Siblings have also been identified as an importance source of comfort, support, and solidarity for many children and young people living with patriarchal terrorism. Mullender et al.'s research has also found that children and young people often cite mothers as "their most important source of help than anyone else in their lives" (210). Children's relationships with their mothers and mother-figures form the most significant source of support in coping with the trauma. Mullender et al. assert that it is important that both policy and practice recognize the significance of the mother-child relationship and "not cut across this one element of continuity and hope" (211). The recovery and restorative process for many parents and children living with patriarchal terrorism can often come after leaving the abusive home.

I don't want it to affect me, to not have control over my emotions, and whenever I have a difficult situation to deal with, I wouldn't be able to control the tears in my eyes, shaking, and I want to be able to have control over that and be able to choose to be strong, to be able to deal with difficult things.

REUNION

After Marilyn left for good in 2005, she was separated from her three stepchildren for seven years before they reunited in 2012. The moments of reunion were overwhelming for all of them. Alisha came to visit her one evening in September 2012. Marilyn remembered that moment very vividly; opening the front door and standing in front of her was this beautiful young woman holding a bunch of flowers. Tears started flowing in her eyes and time stood still. They hugged and talked for a long time that evening. For Mae, the reunion was a deeply emotional experience.

It was hard to describe, overwhelming ... and to see that you were so well. It provided so much hope for me ... that you made it ... and you went through all of that. And as I got to know you again, it gave me inspiration to think about how my life could be, eventually ... and seeing you with the kids just reassured me how they have that in their lives and how we had that in our lives when we were at dad's house and at mum's. It's been amazing getting to know you again.... I mean really getting to know you ... getting to know how you survived it all and how you've grown so much from it... and now you're helping me to do my recovery from it and I don't know how else I would have done it. If we didn't build our relationship up again ... I don't think I would have thought about doing it, just trapped, feeling angry, frustrated, and not knowing what to do with myself.

I think I realized then you were such a big part of us when we were growing up... and we didn't deal with it then, the grief of losing that. And to go through all of that as children... and being able to get through it and see you again ... it was pretty cool.

CONCLUSION

Putting women and children at the centre of their own storymaking is critical in addressing the pressing global issue of domestic and family violence. Listening to children and young people and taking their voices, experiences and responses seriously are vital to how we may respond as a society to their plight and how we might support their recovery.

> We no longer think of children as the silent witnesses of domestic violence but as social actors who have their own perceptions and understandings, their own strength and resilience, and their own coping strategies on which to draw. They are involved in their own situations; they have an effect on the circumstances of their own lives. Above all, from their experience of living with it, they can tell us a great deal about domestic violence. They can enable us to understand what helps and what does not, what they want and what they need from us as professionals. (Humphreys and Stanley 66)

In conclusion, feminist story*making* offers a powerful site and tool to reclaim women's and children's lives from the impacts of patriarchal terrorism. Through relational co-scripting of narratives of resistance from the perspectives of survivors of patriarchal terrorism, we have unpacked and challenged the systematic coercive control and violence characteristic of patriarchal terrorism. Feminist narratives of resistance that position women and children at the centre of their own knowledge making challenge the fundamental hegemonic and masculinist discourses around motherhood, selfhood, and childhood. In doing so, feminist story*making* has many sociocultural and political implications for the ways we read history, construct knowledge, and imagine future generations.

NOTES

[1]"Mae" is a pseudonym used for the co-author to protect her identity.

WORKS CITED

Allen, Mary. *Narrative Therapy for Women Experiencing Domestic Violence: Supporting Women's Transit*. Jessica Kingsley Publishers, 2011.

Fantuzzo, John W. et al. "Domestic Violence and Children's Presence: A Population-Based Study of Law Enforcement Surveillance of Domestic Violence." *Journal of Family Violence*, vol. 22, no. 6, 2007, pp. 331-340.

Gillinder, Bedi, and Chris Goddard. "Intimate Partner Violence: What Are the Impacts on Children?" *Australian Psychologist*, vol. 42, no. 1, 2007, pp. 66-77.

Hayes, Sharon, and Samantha Jeffries. *Romantic Terrorism: An Auto-Ethnography of Domestic Violence, Victimization and Survival*. Palgrave Macmillan, 2015.

Holt, Stephanie, et al. "The Impact of Exposure to Domestic Violence on Children and Young People: A Review of the Literature." *Child Abuse & Neglect*, vol. 32, no. 8, 2008, pp. 797-810.

Humphreys, Catherine, and Nicky Stanley, editors. *Domestic Violence and Child Protection; Directions for Good Practice*.

Jessica Kingsley Publishers, 2006.
Johnson, Michael P. *Typology of Domestic Violence: Intimate Terrorism, Violent Resistance, and Situational Couple Violence.* Northeastern, 2008.
Johnson, Michael P. "Patriarchal Terrorism and Common Couple Violence: Two Forms of Violence against Women." *Journal of Marriage and the Family*, vol. 57, no. 2, 1995, pp. 283-94.
McGee, C. *Childhood Experiences of Domestic Violence*. Jessica Kingsley Publishers, 2000.
Metta, Marilyn. "Putting the Body on the Line: Embodied Writing and Recovery through Domestic Violence." *Handbook of Autoethnography*, edited by Stacy Holman Jones et al., Left Coast Press, 2013, pp. 486-509.
Metta, Marilyn. *Writing against, Alongside and Beyond Memory: Lifewriting as Reflexive, Poststructuralist Feminist Research Practice*. Peter Lang, 2010.
Mullender, Andrey. "'He Said He Was Going to Kill Our Mum.'" *Domestic Violence and Child Protection: Directions for Good Practice*, edited by Catherine Humphreys and Nicky Stanley, Jessica Kingsley Publishers, 2006.
Mullender, Andrey, et al. *Children's Perspectives on Domestic Violence*. Sage Publications, 2003.
Øverlien, Carolina. "The Children of Patriarchal Terrorism." *Journal of Family Violence* vol. 28, no. 3, 2013, pp. 277-87.
Pearson, Chris, et al. *Making an Impact—Children and Domestic Violence: A Reader*. Jessical Kingsley Publishers, 2006.
Radford, Lorraine, and Marianne Hester. *Mothering through Domestic Violence*. Epub, 2006.
Rober, Peter, and Dominiek Van Eesbeek. "Talking About Violence: A Microanalysis of Narrative Processes in a Family Therapy Session." *Journal of Marital and Family Therapy*, vol. 32, no. 3, 2006, pp. 313-28.
Trinh, T. Minh-ha. *Woman, Native, Other: Writing Postcoloniality and Feminism*. Indiana University Press, 1989.

15.
"That's Not What Boys Do"

Mothering a Boy Child, Resisting Masculinity, and Coming to Terms with Manhood

RACHEL O'DONNELL

IT WAS A HOT Saturday in the summer when my father took me to the amusement park. He never took me anywhere by himself, and I don't know where my mother was that day—maybe working at Kmart, maybe cleaning the house, maybe she couldn't get off the couch—I can't remember. It was a small park with a handful of rides—a rickety wooden roller coaster called the Valley Volcano, a haunted house with cars on a track, a small train that went around in a circle. When we got out of the car, he said, "Now you go off on your own." He gave me ten dollars, which was enough for a seven dollar unlimited ride ticket and an ice cream sandwich—a real one with a layer of ice cream between two hot waffles. By the time the ticket attendant snapped the plastic bracelet around my wrist so I could go on all of the rides I wanted to, I could see my father standing against a picnic table with a clear plastic cup of beer in his hand, and I knew that when I went to look for him after dark, I would find him slumped over in a plastic chair, asleep.

These were Irish festivals that my father enjoyed often, where there was loud music and drinking songs and men my father's age talking and laughing and enjoying pitcher after pitcher of beer. Each pitcher was only five dollars, so my father could have enough beer for what he called "a good time."

This is how I remember my father throughout most of my childhood—asleep. He fell asleep one time when he took me to the circus. He always had a few beers after dinner, and I distinctly remember having to wake him up if I needed something.

Later, as an adult going off to graduate school, he confessed to me that he used to take a swig of whiskey in the middle of his workday. Much of what I remember about him was in extremes: asleep or wide awake and yelling. I remember getting dragged around by my ear when I was in "his" chair. A lot of what happened in our house stayed well hidden behind closed doors. There was a lot of yelling, cursing, and threats. "Do you want a divorce?" "Get out of my chair." "Leave me alone!"

This brand of violent masculinity shaped the world of my childhood, in a sense. I was muscled around as a child, pulled by my ear off a chair that I did not want to get out of, or shown a muscle or a shillelagh if I was not behaving the right way. Is it only men who claim their own living room chairs? Is it only men who leave their beer bottles for women to pick up? This is the world I grew up in, where men in my poor neighbourhood, these beings of testosterone, overemphasized masculinity, power, and gender-role extremes, and displayed homophobia, restricted emotion, and, sometimes, violence and aggression.

Now, I am the parent of a son. As a baby and toddler, Finnegan was delightful, and I relished saying or singing his name. When I was pregnant, I often said it was important that we pick a name that sounded like a "nice boy," not something traditionally masculine. Motherhood is glorious in so many ways: I could imagine it, but I could never really picture it for what it is. There is a very real joy in meeting someone's needs and doing the actual comforting and caregiving, and I loved having a baby boy.

Now, he is almost six and wiggles his front tooth to show me how much it moves. He runs alongside me to catch up and hold my hand. It is sometimes hard to realize that I have grown up, that I am the mother of a tall and lanky five-year-old who knows how to get his own clothes on, who can walk closely enough in the parking lot instead of holding hands, who can do not only addition and subtraction but multiplication too, and who can wash his own dishes and brush his own teeth. I watch him as he gracefully uses scissors, cutting computer paper into long white strips. He sits at the table making bubble letters with a pen clutched in his hand. I can watch him and then go back to reading or cooking at the stove: he doesn't need attention more than the occasional "Mom, look at this!" He even helps his little sister up and down the stairs.

When my parents came to visit for his third birthday, I was already pregnant again. Finnegan had a paper airplane that he flew in front of my father's face. His Grampy, who was trying to sleep from having too much beer, shoved Finnegan's hand away unkindly. "Why don't you go down to the basement futon to rest?" my mother said gently, and my father growled, "I don't feel like it!"

My childhood had a lot of grumbling and growling. My mother would say my father talks like a bear, or would call him Oscar the Grouch from my favourite television show. In my family, violence took many forms. It was there in the growling, in the dragging, in the throwing of items, in the threats from my father and in the quiet reservation and depression of my mother.

When I was pregnant, there was an ultrasound in which a penis appeared on the screen. In that moment, I went from being a pregnant woman to the mother of a son. I do not admit this to many people, but gaining that information made me cry. A yellow circle was made on an ultrasound image on a tiny fetus with male genitalia. Later, at dinner with my husband at our favourite Italian restaurant, he told the owner that we were there to celebrate our son. He had gone from a bump and a kicking baby in my belly to a son that afternoon, through the yellow circle and the "Oh boy!" note the doctor placed next to the ultrasound picture in a sealed envelope four months before he was born. Friends would say, "Wow, you are growing a penis!"—as if to say, well, what is more amusing than a feminist having a son? Did I have a vested interest in constructing and promoting a specific form of masculinity? What specific form was it? I cannot recall.

When Finnegan was born, there was nothing particularly boyish about our beautiful baby, although I could commiserate with other mothers about getting urinated on during diaper changes, circumcision decisions, and good boy names. He was a beautiful squishy baby with fluffy hair that stood straight up, strong nursing reflexes, and tiny hands and feet. He had a baby cry, and I thought *this is how many men begin, in the arms of their mother*. It must be later that they somehow become what I despise: drunks, domestic abusers, emotionally stunted beings, which were the only forms of masculinity that I knew as a child.

When he was four, Finnegan wore one of his sister's barrettes to school, and two boys, his friends, told him that he looked like a girl and a boy, and that he had to "pick a team." His teacher was wonderful and said to him, "Well, you know something that they don't know. You know that you can be both if you want to be." When Finnegan was two, I decided he would never play contact sports, mostly because I once overheard the football coach insult the players, boys of seven or eight, with "Okay, ladies!" I could not bear the thought of my son being put down in such a stereotypically sexist fashion. Instead, Finnegan takes ballet lessons and plays the violin. He is loving and gentle and longs to wear an "outside dress," his dress-up princess clothes, to school. He keeps his hair long and is proud of it. When he met the new pediatrician, he said first, "I want to keep my hair long," as if understanding that doctors have historically been supportive of gender binaries.

Of course, men I have known well have never been particularly masculine, especially men I have dated. Finnegan's father is gentle and kind and that is what attracted me to him, I am certain. At Finnegan's Montessori school, fathers can be seen dropping their children in the morning, and I have seen many of them skipping in parking lots, climbing snow banks, racing to the playground, and giving hugs and kisses goodbye.

Socially defined or biologically created, masculinity in some forms scares me, especially as I recall it in the violent forms of my childhood. I even reprimanded our babysitter for admitting she goes to fraternity parties.

My father was once arrested for public drunkenness, when he stopped at a sandwich shop after the bar to get a sandwich and fell asleep. He also got drunk at all the family parties and slept through those, too. He fell asleep, perhaps because the Irish tended to be perceived as a violent lot and he found himself in competition with another performance of Irish masculinity: drinking. Perhaps, the social scientist in me finds this kind of emotional and social withdrawal developed from centuries of Irish starvation.

In many ways, the boy child was a surprise and a disappointment. Now, of course, it is pure bliss to have a son. What is lovely is that he still crawls in my lap to snuggle and I still sing him his baby song—"Oh our little Finnegan, he's our little Finnegan, how we love our baby, baby Finnegan." And I think that is what surprised me most: a baby boy is just a baby, a tiny innocent being who has no masculine characteristics at all. I would nurse him and hold him, and duck down behind the side of the car to play peek-a-boo while I pumped gas to keep him laughing until I was done. I love holding his hand, sitting with him in my lap to read stories, and falling asleep cuddled next to him. He has always been my sweet, sweet boy.

When my father is visiting, he falls asleep in the chair sitting up, chin to chest, when the children are playing. Sometimes, he is snoring, sometimes not, which leads me to think he is just looking for a way out, a way to be more internal and avoid the craziness of the children. Still, he does a lot of unnecessary shushing of the children, orders them not to cry, and makes gendered insults of my parenting: "You dress him like a girl." One year, I asked my mother to make Finnegan a baby carrier for his doll, one that looked like one I used to carry him in when he was a baby. My father followed up in an email:

> *Dear Rachel,*
> *Your Mom said she will look at the patterns and see if she can do it. She'll let you know. I don't know if I approve of this. You seem to be trying to turn my grandchild into a queer.*
> *Love, Daddy*

This is a perfect example of our complicated relationship: the "Love, Daddy" sign off after he made hateful and gendered assumptions of what a boy should do.

Finnegan's father and I both make an effort to parent with kindness and without violence, and teach our son self-respect and that violence is never a correct response. Still, there is something frightening about watching a boy grow up and the fear that he will become what you despise: masculinity in all its most militaristic forms. I have already told him about the dangers of gender roles, and I have worked hard to make sure he enjoys being in the kitchen. When he comes home with sewing work, I am especially proud. It is as though he has seen into my soul and done something so traditionally feminine and something I cannot even do myself—something from a previous generation of women that has disappeared.

What is most important to me, perhaps, is that I have a son who does not think of women as lesser beings. My mother always said that my father had little respect for women except for his daughters, but to me, it has always seemed that his daughters have been included in this lack of respect for the feminine. There must have been moments that he attempted to be a good father and the pictures, I guess, show this: a small child being held in his arms, face buried in his beard, or a child sitting on his lap and reading. Moments of tenderness and love must have been there during my childhood, but I cannot remember them.

What I do remember is the awkwardness that came with beginning puberty. I remember getting my period and telling my mother and realizing with horror, at some point later, that she must have shared that with my father. My mother said to me more recently, "Your father was a good father when you were young," as if to forgive the disinterested and distracted person he had become. Emotional neglect was a term I learned much later on, and associated it with memories of my parents laughing when I was crying, taking little time to engage in my life, and, as a teenager, barely speaking to me.

During a visit with my half-sister during college, she told me that she had to tell me something. She fumbled for a minute over her words, and her husband encouraged her. What came out was that our father had beaten up her mother, and this is why she left him. The violence in my house had taken many forms, although I don't recall him ever hitting my mother. I do remember a lot of grumbling and a tremendous amount of yelling, even over simple things; the phrases "Leave it alone!" and "Ok, leave it!" came up a lot. In retrospect, I wonder how much hitting there actually was. I remember his inability to not be frustrated in the kitchen, with the computer, over simple conversations and decision making. This is how drinking and emotional withdrawal rear their ugly head.

It was only as an adult that I learned to ask friendly questions in social situations. I was lucky to be around men, mostly teachers, who demonstrated kindness and respect for women. I had a high school friend who would take weekend trips with her dad; they would drive and talk and spend time together. I was jealous of this and was always embarrassed by my father, not by his tracksuits, as he suspected, but by his unfriendliness. Other dads did not always seem so gruff.

When I left for graduate school, my father drove a van to the university. When I went inside the housing unit, he opened a beer in the car and drank it, desperate for a drink. He just could not wait and could not seem to manage to put my needs before his beer. I came back and cried—it had been such a stressful day travelling on a hot day in August, and he just had to open that beer. It was not enough to stop him that I was moving to begin a new life for myself in a big city far away. That night, he got drunk and told me stories of my sister's mother's first husband, which I had never heard before. Even as an adult, I have never been sure what to make of him.

Still, when he came to visit me in Guatemala when I lived there, I brought two men in I knew to show them that my father was cooking. They were amazed, and said they had never seen a man cook before.

Other men in my family just make me nervous. My uncles did not interact with me much other than to say hello and even if years go by without seeing them, they still do not ask many questions. At family parties, the men are in the kitchen drinking alcohol in its many forms, and the women stay in the living room and talk or play games. The men don't do much of either. And this is often joked about: how the men and women separate. The men mostly ask questions, such as "Can I get you another beer?," and much of the discussion, so I've heard, involves what is wrong with their wives.

In my house, a general disrespect for women took hold early on. Comments that she "drives like a woman" or "looks like a little Lolita" abounded. There were other gendered messages too, mainly that my mother was stupid. Since she read romance novels, worked a service job, and did housework, the messages were clear: man is the judge, and woman is the judged. As a child, I thought that my mother worried and cleaned the house, and my father worked to provide for us. Mothers take care of the house and often, it seems, are embarrassed by it. Fathers have no need for that—they work all day and come home and drink beer. To this day, my father looks up from his paper that he hides behind while my mother is talking and mouths to me: "She never shuts up." There is no need to respect women in his mind; they are lesser beings. Look at her cleaning on her hands and knees, making grocery lists, filling the sink with soapy water as if it is her job. It was as if he said, "A woman with children does not deserve my respect." It was as if he said, "This is how women are treated. Do not expect to be treated any better than this."

There was a moment when I was watching Finnegan swim in the YMCA pool, a tiny little boy in a pair of red shorts with a white stripe around his waist. He was swimming down at the other end in the deep end. On the way out, I was delighted when he held my hand and answered my questions about his swim class.

He once rode his bicycle across the street when I was not watching. I was standing there talking, and suddenly he was there on the other side of the street. No car had hit him, but what if one had? My whole life would have been gone.

My father was always too grouchy to do things for himself. When I was about twenty, I went to a conference in Massachusetts. I took the bus there from a friend's house, and my parents were planning to make the drive to pick me up. When they arrived, I suggested we take the ferry to Martha's Vineyard and walk around before going home. When we arrived, we saw a sign that it was three miles to the next town and began walking. It was a beautiful day. My father had recently had prostate surgery, and as he began to walk, his pants got wet. I was nervous because I knew he would be angry. He walked way ahead of us, like he always did, and I remember my mother coming up to me and whispering, "look at your father," as if it had been my fault. I saw him, and I just felt afraid of his anger. He could not take care of this himself like a reasonable adult. Like many things, he just got angry and yelled, and my mother would fix it. She walked into one of the shops in town—I think it was Banana Republic or J Crew—and asked them if they could please sell her a pair of pants. "My husband has just had surgery," she said.

Part of parenting well, I think, is the waiting. I am often in a hurry to get out the door, but I have a toddler who wants to put on his own shoes. Or he wants to stop to look at a stick while I am walking quickly down the street. I want to finish the grocery shopping, but he is busy fingering the apples. I am driving, but he is asking questions. Parenting with kindness is in the patient discomfort and the endless waiting. My father was always walking way ahead of me; always, I was too slow to keep up.

Recently, my father declared to my son, "That's not what boys do." I do not even remember what it was about—maybe his clothing, his toys, his schoolwork. I cannot remember. And there was an opening to have the same kind of family that I grew up in: loud, depressed, angry, with beer bottles on every open surface, adults sleeping in front of the television, and gendered expectations at a young age. My mother makes excuses for all of this. "Well, when you're old, you get tired," and for my father explicitly, "His drinking got worse when he stopped working."

Now, I dread how my father interacts with my son, and Finnegan has complained to me about him. Once, when he would not get off the bed, my father smacked my precious son on the behind. I wasn't there, and I don't know how hard it was, but it upset Finnegan, and he remembers it and talks about it often. I do my best to reassure him but still I am angered that it happened at all. The worst part, I realized after Finnegan's many tellings of this story, was not that his grandfather had smacked him but that when Finnegan asked him to stop and cried a bit, his Grampy started to laugh. This angers me too—the assumption that crying or vulnerability is not to be respected or met with understanding or empathy. Grampy said, "Are you crying? Why are you crying?" instead of addressing what the pain was. Just recently Finnegan told me, "They try to be nice, but Grammy is cranky and Grampy is grouchy." I'm not even sure that he knows what these words mean, but he seems to already understand more than they do.

Again it happened, and I blamed myself. My parents were visiting. My father was outside while Finnegan was playing in the yard, and I was doing laundry in the basement. When Finnegan went to get his sister out of the car, he was picked up and thrown to the ground. Finnegan cried and told me he was very upset, and I told Finnegan that Grampy is no longer invited to come to our house.

Drunkenness and violence are no more necessary forms of masculinity than any other ones. For now, I will make every effort to separate him from forms of manhood that frightened me as a child to protect my beautiful, masculine son from all of this.

16.
I Was Ward Cleaver

An Apologia

JOHANNA WAGNER

As a lesbian parent, "father," "co-mother," or whatever official documents are calling me these days, I have found the world of parenting much more difficult because I am a feminist. I arrived late to motherhood because I never actually dreamed of having children. I certainly wasn't interested in doing the childbearing, and never assumed I'd end up with a partner who was. Most of my American friends of the same age were likeminded; none of us were particularly interested in having children. It certainly was never a topic of conversation. But then I moved to Europe and met a younger woman. I met my partner in Belgium and found that there are women who don't struggle with their sexualities, whose societies take in stride their individual rights and their rights to have families.[1] There are no arguments in newspapers about whether or not same-sex partners should have children; there are no politicians (or county clerks for that matter) grandstanding about a religious right to keep rights from queers.[2] There are no public suggestions about whether or not to kill the gays.[3] These arguments do not exist for my partner. As a young woman in a more progressive society, her desire to procreate was not a fraught political space; therefore, her only real concern was having children later than she had hoped.

Since my decision not to give birth was based wholly on my own body, when my partner expressed her desire to have children, I had no argument against it. And this is where my troubles began.

In graduate school I firmly embraced feminism and have since become a scholar of literature informed by feminist gender theories. I have read the waves of feminism. I have been enlightened by Wollstonecraft, Mill, Gilman, and Woolf; radicalized by Firestone, Lorde, Anzaldua, Ellman, and hooks; and fortified by Butler, Wittig, Kristeva, Sedgwick, and Irigaray. Much of this reading led to a pensiveness about relationships, especially the ways in which to negotiate honest and equal domestic work. One can imagine, then, my mortification when after the birth of our first child, I came home from work one day and realized that I was Ward Cleaver![4]

Okay, let's get one thing straight: Ward Cleaver was *way* before my time, but he encapsulated the figure of "The Father," and all that was wrapped up in that 1950s-separate-spheres-father-knows-best mentality. For younger audiences, they could use Al Bundy and his almost identical contemporary, Jay Pritchett, sans the blatant misogyny.[5] The sexism of the 1950s might have been blatant, but it was infused with benevolence: a kinder blatancy, if you will. Think, Homer Simpson, for example, minus the silliness.[6] Anyway, the point is that I carelessly observed every chauvinistic impression specifically about domestic roles that I had ever encountered, but to my embarrassment and humiliation, I not only observed them but *absorbed* them. I was now the chauvinist!

Now, let me explain how all of this came about. A feminist, as you know, intellectually explores and actively questions conceptual commonplaces regarding gender. It's what we do. Well, although I had been surrounded by children in my life, I knew early on that I was not a "mother-woman" as such women are named by Kate Chopin.[7] Knowing my body would never bear children, consequently, made the subject of becoming a mother seem moot at a very young age. I never gave it a second thought. Unsurprisingly, then, this lack of thought prevented me from discerning what kind of unidentified ideologies I held about childcaring. I knew what I thought about *childbearing*—it was not for me, but I didn't much care what other people chose to do with their bodies (yes, ok, excellent feminist principles working here). So, what I thought—or in truth did not think—about *childcaring*, well, that turned out to be the problem. In retrospect, that was my ultimate intellectual blind spot: in failing to think something through, we rely instead on natural reactions. This means I automatically operated through an uncontested ideology, and this ideology was anathema to not only my hard fought but my hard *thought* feminism.

It had been established that my partner would bear, breastfeed, and stay home for a time with our child while I continued working on the outside. And it was at this point that I uncovered the distressing ideas I held about motherhood. I found that I did not at all identify as this thing called "mother." On the contrary, as noted above, I wanted very much to fall into the role of a passive "father" from a 1950s television sitcom. I found myself resisting caring for my child when I came home from work. I found myself simply assuming my partner would continue to care to all the needs of our baby even when I was home. I wanted to lie on the couch, put up my feet, and relax at the end of the day. Somewhere in the back of my mind martinis might have even been anticipated.

Sigh.

But my feminist consciousness found my newly discovered chauvinism distasteful and troubling. It wouldn't let me relax into that role. I tried to (god knows I tried!), but it continued to poke at me and to prod at my sense of integrity and fairness.

There was an uncomfortableness that I couldn't shake. Somewhere in my desire to lie down—shoes off, half-napping on the couch—a feeling arose in me that made me truly uneasy with myself. Who was I that I could stand by while my partner worked herself silly taking care of this little creature? What did that mean about me? What did it mean about my deeply held feminist principles? As I struggled with my lackadaisical approach to childcare, I realized that I had internalized not only a particular chauvinism but a heteronormative paradigm of relationships, in which a biological bias was present and thriving. Even though, crucially, I shared that biology.

I saw my partner as the "mom" of our child and placed myself in the category of the "other" parent—some sort of "dad," I suppose. Therefore, for all practical purposes, I had unthinkingly bought into that age-old sexist idea that the bearer of the child naturally must also be the carer of the child. Although feminists have worked tirelessly to break this biological imperative—the obligatory causal connection between bearing and caring for children—I had unwittingly restored its causality: My partner gave birth to our child; thus, it was only right that she also primarily cared for the child.

Let me unpack this a little because as I see it, there were three things going on here: my personal gender identity, gender bias, and heteronormative assumptions about family. Although I identified easily as a "woman," I did not identify as a "mother." I imagine this is because of the baggage placed on "motherhood" and my early and vehement refusal to be forced into this conventional label via childbearing and caring. "Mother" was the embodiment of a femininity that I had rejected, and that was in some way distinct from my own. So, I involuntarily held some kind of bias against "the feminine" relating to children. A further surprise for me was that because of this bias towards this specific femininity, I identified more strongly with a "father" figure inasmuch as I identified with the negative, the opposite, of the "mother"; and in the heteronormative familial paradigm, this is and only has been the "father." Here, I was a woman and my partner a woman, and somehow our gender dynamic changed dramatically with the birth of our child. My partner became more symbolic of the "female" in our relationship, whereas I somehow remained exempt. Complicated things were going on. I was a mother, but I somehow stood outside the idea of the "mother" while identifying strongly with the idea of "woman," but I behaved more as an unfortunate caricature of a "father."[8]

Sigh.

Once I figured out the deep-seated discrepancies at work in my brain, this scraping of feminist principles alongside latent heteronormative ideology, at least I knew why I was struggling so significantly with my role in this new domestic negotiation. It remains a bit shocking how much I must deliberately wrestle with these reflexes, and it is very disappointing how much I seem to have been affected by these specific forms of gender bias, especially as a woman *and* a feminist. But I have now named them and brought these impulses to light. I am no longer puzzled by their elusiveness, nor am I unaware of their antithetical message to my feminist mindfulness. Now, it is just a matter of keeping them in mind and continuing to think them through[9] and get off the couch more often than not.

NOTES

[1]Indeed, Belgium was the second country in the world to legalize same-sex marriage on 1 June 2003. The Netherlands was the first on 1 April 2001.

[2]There have been a number of politicians who have come out against the Obergefell vs Hodges supreme court decision legalizing same sex marriage in June 2015. At the time of this writing, this disagreement was most overtly verbalized by various Republican presidential candidates and most notoriously by the Rowan County Clerk in Kentucky.

[3]This bill is of course in reference to the initiative, the *Sodomite Suppression Act*, aka, the "Shoot the Gays Initiative," a proposition by California attorney Matt McLaughlin that was finally dismissed in June 2015 in that state.

[4]Ward Cleaver was the solid patriarch who acted as the moral center of the family in the sitcom *Leave it to Beaver* (1957-1963).

[5]Al Bundy and Jay Pritchett are father characters in the sitcom Married with Children (1987-1997), and the contemporary mockumentary Modern Family (2009-present) respectively.

[6]Homer Simpson is, of course, the father of the family in the animated sitcom The Simpsons (1989-present).

[7]See Kate Chopin's 1899 novel *The Awakening*. Parsing the various sentiments held in the idea of the "mother-woman" could be a lengthy discussion in itself. Suffice it to say, the selfless and sacrificial aspects of this role in The Awakening awakened much of my own terror about childcare.

[8]I want to make clear that I'm simplifying this very complex argument in order to make some distinct points. I am really not arguing that I or anyone else in this position "feels like a man." Taking this route while discussing lesbians is a tired cliché. I simply use these terms "mom" and "dad" in order to demonstrate how deeply heteronormativity effects us, so much so that a mindful feminist and queer literary critic can be surprised by its subterraneous flow even in her own consciousness.

[9]Nota bene: There is not time here to explicate the following idea, but I put it to you anyway: I wonder if perhaps the language constraint for parents like me, as noted at the outset of this essay in which

names such as "father" or "co-something-or-other," haphazardly bequeathed, act performatively in that they inadvertently assist in the creation of this haphazard, intermediate parent who must find her own way if she is to have an identity in parenting at all.

17.
Gymnastics and Equality

LESLEY BUNNELL

LET'S START with me getting a few things out of the way. I am:

- A black woman
- A single mother of a mixed-race and middle-school-aged daughter
- A feminist
- Part of the working poor
- Being treated for severe depression and anxiety disorders
- A queer person manoeuvring through the world

Now that I've put that all of that out there, I'm going to talk about how I navigate through the world while I raise my daughter and support her through the upper levels of gymnastics.

PART ONE

My daughter first showed an affinity for extreme physicality when she was about a year and a half. To preface, I am an ex-professional modern dancer, and her father was a good athlete and performance artist. She was born a fidgety infant and couldn't even be still during sleep. She would sleep next to me, as a baby and toddler, wiggling, kicking, and punching me. Once she stood and found that she could walk, she practically ran.

During the summer of 2003, she stood on the back of the couch, squealed, and did a back flip, landing on her feet. No one had taught her that. She hadn't even been to a gym. That fall, I enrolled her in a kiddo gymnastics class. She was thrilled during class—bouncing on the trampoline, diving into the ball pit, swinging from a rope, and climbing a mini rock wall, and touching the fish. (There was a rubber salmon at the top of the wall and when the kids touched it, it sang a song and laughed.) The classes were mixed gender, and no one particularly cared about anything beyond herding the kids through their class without hurting themselves or their classmates. After the fall session, one of the instructors pulled me aside and said, "your daughter is very talented. She really is. I hope you'll keep her in these classes."

I smiled and said "thank you" and didn't think much of it, mainly because my daughter was two and lord knows what "talent" means. Sure, she may be good, but they want to keep her in class because they want to keep attendance full and tuition paid. Within the next year, my family packed up our things and moved to a new city, in which we have laid roots and now call home.

I was eager to help her find another place for her to use her body and work out her willies. I found a small space near her preschool and enrolled her, and she stayed there for a year. Towards the end of her stay, she asked to go watch the state championships, where some older girls from her gym were competing. She was agog and thrilled. She was a tiny four-year-old truly seeing what she wanted and could do. I observed the various teams and their coaches and looked to see which coaches seemed centred, down to earth, and kind to their students. I spotted the gym that matched those qualities and sent them an email.

To preface, I knew the horror stories of gymnastics and its brutal training. Or rather, I knew what was in the media. Young women with stunted growth, eating disorders, coaches verbally abusing them, horrific injuries, poor schooling, and shattered self-esteem. As an ex-dancer, I saw what peers went through and suffered. I did not want that for my daughter. But I did not want to discourage her from doing something that she was excited about and enjoyed doing.

The gym I spotted called me back and said, "we're a training gym, and we have a national team that travels across the country throughout the gymnastics season. Bring her in, we'll see how she does and talk about it from there."

She followed the coaches around, beaming. She was so excited to touch and work on the beam, the bars, and the trampoline, and to do basic skills on the floor. After about twenty minutes of being in that enormous space with two total strangers, her main coach walked out and said, "We'll take her. She's great. Let's start in two days."

That was it. Her life and mine were changed forever.

PART TWO

I immediately felt out of place among the "gym moms." They were all very chatty, very invested in their daughters, very middle class or wealthy, and very white. This is nothing new. Since the day that we moved to our new place in a middle-sized capital city—the hub of many private and public universities and specific industries that make A LOT of money for those who run them—we had been on the outside looking in. Starting at this new gym had put a huge strain on our budget, our lives, and our time. I was spending three days a week shuttling my daughter to practice thirty minutes from our home for a two-hour practices. It was a lot for a four-year-old and for me.

Since we did not live nearby, I stayed at the gym and did work or read or ran errands. I would watch practice, but I honestly did not know what I was looking at. My daughter was having a blast and would come out of practice babbling, hungry, and elated. I could not say the same for me. I would be stuck listening to mothers who talked about their enormous homes, their husbands, and their very heteronormative and privileged lives. I had nothing in common with them. If they engaged me, it was simply to talk about our children. Even then, I had nothing to say. I awkwardly nodded and tried to keep up talking about gym and meet fees, who placed first, who should be placing first, who was good in practice but not at competitions, who was naturally talented but lazy, who was a hard worker but not as good, and whose parents were good or bad people. They reminded me of that creepy, overly invested mother from the film *Donnie Darko*, who scolds other mothers for their lack of commitment to the dance troupe Sparkle Motion and for not being "all in." I questioned myself and wondered if I was fucked up for not knowing what skills they were working on in the gym or what the coaches thought of every child, including my child. I also questioned myself about why I did not understand how meets and competitions were run. But then after about six months of tolerating this atmosphere, I stopped caring.

I stopped caring not because I did not love my daughter or want her to do well but because this was not (and has never been) my thing; it was and is hers. I do not have the goal to be a good gymnast, to train well, and to do well at meets, and competitions. My daughter wants those things. My job is to support her and help her achieve those dreams. Furthermore, the gym's social scene contradicted every tenet of my life. I am not an overgrown fifteen-year-old girl, who gossips about other (supposed) adult women and their families, husbands, and which Disney vacation tier they could pay for; about where I got my nails done; or about what suburban, casual dining restaurant experience I most enjoy. This was not and is not a recrimination of other peoples' lives; it was a revelation of how I could not and cannot live my own. I can barely make enough income to pay my monthly bills, which includes rent. I did not and do not care what another woman's husband does at the country club or with his possible mistress. I did not and do not have the capacity or brain space to even keep up with any of it. Moreover, none of this has anything to do with actual feminism, which I stringently follow and try to adhere to. My application of feminism to my life involves supporting other women, supporting the families of mothers, and supporting children in any and all of their pursuits. None of what these mothers did was about supporting their children. It was about these mothers. Whether it was about their unfulfilled dreams, or who knows what else, their behaviour frightened me and is something that I do not want in my life. Moreover, I am a black, single mom, and I was in a situation in which none of my gym cohorts had any understanding of my background or current situation.

PART THREE

Now, almost ten years later, about 99 percent of those moms are gone. Their daughters left the gym to become athletes in other sports, to pursue activities in school, to study dance, or to do other things, and bless them. I hear from other parents at our gym about the families, the mothers. I am friends on Facebook with some of these women. They post about the new kitchens that they are renovating, the underground pools they are installing, the vacations they spend swimming with dolphins. They always have something to tell everyone else, something spectacular and slightly unbelievable. But then again, my world is a world where people can barely make rent or pay their mortgage. They spend days at a time at the SNAP (food stamps) offices. They send group texts to one another asking how to manage the Health Exchange and to find out if they qualify for Obamacare. They look for low-cost or free mental health counsellors and for access to affordable depression medications and community yoga classes. They live quiet, scrappy, and innovative lives.

My daughter? She is doing great. She is still competing in gymnastics. She is on a junior Olympian track and hopes to be a college gymnast. She is thriving in middle school and is still as sparkly eyed and determined as ever. It's inspiring to watch her grow up and find her path. I learn a lot from being her mom, and I love her. As for me? I have lived through breast-cancer surgery and a protracted divorce proceeding that took over four years, and I continued to be underemployed. I am still working, still not making ends meet, and still wondering when my life will blossom. Maybe it won't. Maybe I am just supposed to be on this earth struggling and crying and fighting to stay afloat. But I am still here, still trying to be a contributing member of my community and society, and, foremost, trying to remain hopeful. Being bitter is a poison that infects everyone, and I especially don't want to pass such a sickness to my thoughtful and insightful daughter.

What continues to baffle me is how out of sync the strata of motherhood are. How a tax bracket is not a divisional marker but a lens, and ultimately a barrier, through which one barely sees the world and by which everything is seen (or not) with blinders. It never made much sense to me. I try to put myself on the other side. I try to imagine that with unlimited resources and cash flow I, too, would renovate my home with a chef's kitchen, install a sauna, swim with dolphins in the Bahamas, or cruise around the globe with Mickey Mouse. But I cannot, and not only that, I do not want to. It took a long time to understand and accept that. Maybe that comes with being disenfranchised. When people do not have things, the things that they do want come with a caveat that attaches itself to humanity—it is not just about the consumption or collection of things. My dreams are aspirations for all because equity is what sets free those of us without. Until then, I stay in my lane, work as hard and best as I can, and focus on the future. I laugh in the car, with my daughter, when we hear the latest story about the moms fighting over which spring break vacation is better: Barbados or the Bahamas.

IV.
INTERNATIONAL VOICES AND PERSPECTIVES

18.
The Skies Have Eyes

This angel, a seraph—watercolor paintings for wings.
This belly, my own—moves away from me like a helium balloon.

Movement, ever so slight—to commiserate for an era of discomfort.
Padding the pristine white—I will desecrate this place in time.
Through an endurable tightening. And a stretch.

Small noise. So unbelievably small. A fracas in the dark. Cold. Morning.
Simple songs and metal cups. Swaying and chanting. Globe eyes. Open. Close.

My heedless sense of space. Of self. I am this place and all else guests.
The language surrounding—inaudible.
A juxtaposition between laughter. Chit-chat. Agony. Pressure.

This opening is killer. Closed eyes.
Stand. Bear. Sway. Lacerate. Exist.
A maul—driving down. Driving through.
No matter. This is nirvana.
I am not ostentatious. I take up little space.
I am peevish. Disregarded. In my moment.
Far removed from quilts and the counterpanes.

A remorseless dig. I bow.

A quick snap and my leg is sodden.
My transmutation. I change. I become. I am an animal.
The pain. The forgetting. The unattainable retention of this series of moments.
This urgency. This settling. This ripping. This violence.

Culture and memory and family and forever woven with thread and blood.

Expanding flesh, preparations. A four minute countdown. Three. Two. One.
You. A low rumble of thunder preceding a flash.

In this moment we meet, the zero hour.

In this moment we separate, bronzed as statues who will never be so close again.
No matter my yearning for your rubs and your bounce. Inside.

Now you exist.
We are we.
An empty vessel.

My universe, you become and you join.
To touch you. To separate from you.

Your saliva. Slipping off. Reconnect.
I am rusty at this.
Your quickening. Kicking. Motion from the outer edge.

Awaiting certification. A slip of paper—you are mine.

Outside, snow.
This nature, too harsh for you. For now. So new.
My miracle boy.

Belly lines and wrinkly skin. Commemoration.
I know. I am wise beyond these imperfections.

I will no longer just be.
An inner strength. Resounding.

Holding you. Completeness.
You, to whom I gave life.
You are generations. Fertility incarnate.
Eclipsing the past. In with the new.

I will show you my dreams.
I will show you it all. Every colour.

This breast, my own—warm. Wet.

Your absence, your presence. Your breath on my skin as you sleep.

—Gabrielle McNally

19.
Can Ecofeminism Save the World?

Eco-mommas and Their Quest to Raise Feminist and Environmentally Conscious Children

PAMELA REDELA

IN ORDER TO enter a discussion of eco-mommas and their lifestyle, ecofeminism must first be defined. Karen J. Warren uses the term "ecological feminists" to refer to those who acknowledge the following:

> important connections exist between the treatment of women, people of color, and the underclass on one hand and the treatment of nonhuman nature on the other. Ecological feminists claim that any feminism, environmentalism, or environmental ethic which fails to take these connections seriously is grossly inadequate. (3)

Warren's definition describes well what "eco-momma" embodies. She tends to be a person who values principles of equity and sustainability, and tends to live by those principles through her daily life. My experiences as an aspiring eco-momma are as follows.

I am a middle-class mother in coastal Southern California. My neighbourhood is replete with yoga studios, doulas, support groups for home birthing and home schooling, ecologically minded specialty stores as well as "green" and organic alternatives for most products in every marketplace, including Wal-Mart (not that an eco-momma would EVER shop there!). The cost of living is high, so most households are dual income, but many subscribe to the traditional male breadwinner and female homemaker model. Regardless of the income-generating arrangement, the ideal of "supermom" is definitely a sociocultural norm here but with the added twist of environmental consciousness. An eco-momma recycles like nobody's business, scoffs at those who still say "yes" to plastic at the grocery store, uses only chemical-free cleaning products, and if she is not yet growing her own vegetables, she gets most of her veggies from the local farmer's market.

All of these "go-green" efforts are laudable and certainly abide by the "eco" side of ecofeminism. Buying plant-based cleaners keeps sulfites and other harmful chemicals out of drain water and the ocean. Parents feel free to let their children help on cleaning day without worry. We've all had those moments when an older sibling decides that a younger sibling is dirty and needs a full-body spray down with glass cleaner! Recycling—or better yet choosing reusable containers and bags instead of disposable plastic water bottles and Ziploc bags—can make a big difference in the amount of trash each household generates. Some eco-mommas go as far as bringing their own containers for leftovers when eating out to avoid the dreaded Styrofoam to-go box. Buying organically grown vegetables from a local farm supports the famous "act local-think global" meme of environmental activism and encourages healthy eating habits and sustainable agriculture.

Ecologically minded families are also finding creative ways to grow fresh food in the cramped spaces of apartment and townhome living. Those with even a modest plot of land are creating their own mini ecosystems by composting for rich garden soil, collecting rain water, and diverting grey water to irrigate those gardens while raising chickens for eggs and natural fertilizer. These parents (mostly moms) are also found in the prolific garden movement happening in elementary schools in this area. Some schools are producing enough vegetables to hold farmers markets as fundraisers and "green teams" are popping up in many schools. Spawned by eco-mommas and other volunteers, these initiatives are aimed at reducing the amount of trash generated by lunch programs and classroom parties as well as creating energy saving measures, such as the use of skylights in new construction projects and solar panel covered carports complete with electric vehicle parking spots.

These efforts support what Vandana Shiva and Maria Mies define as "the subsistence perspective," to which eco-mommas subscribe in many ways:

> Modern chemistry, household technology, and pharmacy were proclaimed as women's saviours, because they would 'emancipate' them from household drudgery. Today we realize that much environmental pollution and destruction is causally linked to modern household technology. Therefore, can the concept of emancipation be compatible with a concept of preserving the earth as our life base? (7)

"Going green" often includes doing away with the microwave and foregoing any and all plastic products, including children's toys. Although all of these efforts are to be applauded and continued, a critical feminist eye into the "who" and "where" of all this activity is necessary. A look into the ramifications of subscribing to a competitive style of motherhood, which the concept of eco-momma purports to avoid but is surely guilty of, is revealing a slippery slope on which many women are perched. As such, Shiva and Mies's question as to whether ecofeminism can save the planet and humanity is important to consider. There is a real possibility of this phenomenon becoming yet another patriarchal trap, which sets women and ecologically minded activists up for failure and keeps gender hierarchy and predatory capitalism in place.

Maintaining what I call "feminist vigilance" offers a cautionary tale on the eco-momma phenomenon, yet it maintains hope that eco-momism and its accompanying social and cultural changes do not become a passing fad. Feminist vigilance includes questioning, investigation, and self-evaluation. Are the ever-increasing standards of "good mothering" creating a new generation of green angels in the house or can becoming an eco-mamma—a green goddess—be considered a feminist act?

Women advocating from the position of mother to effect change is still not widely accepted as "real" feminism, and there is good reason to think critically in this regard. Yes, growing one's own vegetables or purchasing from a local farmer's market chips away at the demand for corporate food supply, and proudly claiming the homemaker label can be a radical slap in the face of liberal feminist ideals. The tendency to overvalue career goals and downgrade the eco-momma's obsession with home life is a definite point of feminist vigilance. One can be an eco-momma and hold a job, but part of the point is that subscribing to capitalist ideals of "success" is not central to her existence; this is perhaps a page of the eco-momma handbook that liberal feminists may want to read.

Feminist vigilance, thus, pushes us to take things a step further to examine the eco-momma's relationship with patriarchy and capitalism. Whether she holds a job outside the home or not, lives with abundant financial means, or relies on coupons to facilitate a stay-at-home or part-time employed parent arrangement, what does the division of household labour look like in her home? How about the gender role socialization of the children? Where does the main income that supports this lifestyle come from? If an eco-momma's partner is working for DuPont or a transnational export-manufacturing firm, does her activism go down the drain along with the chemical run-off of maquiladora worker exploitation?

To this point, an eco-momma would respond by saying that she is always mindful of a comprehensive worldview. Rosemary Radford Ruether summarizes this point nicely when she writes:

> In ecofeminist culture and ethic, mutual interdependency replaces the hierarchies of domination as the model of relationship between men and women, between human groups, and between humans and other beings. All racist, sexist, classist, cultural, and anthropocentric assumptions of the superiority of whites over blacks, males over females, managers over workers, humans over animals and plants, must be discarded. In a real sense, the so-called superior pole in each relation is actually the more dependent side of the relationship. (21)

One way that the eco-mommas I know attempt to avoid these pitfalls is to ensure the active involvement of their partners (male or female) in the day-to-day parenting. In heterosexual partnerships, dad does as much childcare, laundry, dishes, grocery shopping and household upkeep as mom does after work and on weekends. To be sure, however, mom is ultimately "in charge" in the sense that she manages and maintains the grocery lists, school paperwork, and children's social and sports schedules at the same time that she ensures equal participation of kids and partners in chores.

Through this line of thought, it can be seen that the dependence on mother that eco-momma fosters in her family can be a transformative force. It can force a renewed look at the value and purpose of care work in a society that places production and consumption on a higher plane than reproduction and sustainability. If eco-mommas are able to maintain the momentum of the movement, to keep a focused feminist vigilance, and to take to heart Ruether's assertion that "there must be a conversion of men to the work of women, along with the conversion of male consciousness to the earth," there may well be concrete change in the next generation.

A CASE IN POINT

A large part of an eco-momma's identity is her style of mothering, and most eco-mommas subscribe to what has become known as "attachment parenting." This parenting style erupted onto the American national scene on May 21, 2012, when *Time* magazine ran a cover with the phrase "Are You Mom Enough?" emblazoned in red alongside a picture of a hip, beautiful blonde breastfeeding her three-year-old son. To add to the shock value of the image, the child is standing on a small chair instead of being cradled in mom's lap. The article discusses the phenomenon of attachment parenting, and it sparked a new battle in the mommy wars around not only the cover photo but also the standards and practices in contemporary U.S. mothering (Pickert).

Of the controversy surrounding the image, *The Society Pages* contributor Elline Lipkin writes, "The responses, though, were mostly negative. In a TODAY.com poll about the image, more than 131,000 people weighed in; 73% saying they would have preferred not to see the image." (Lipkin). Although the content of the article focuses the benefits and challenges of attachment parenting, the general public has focused on the breast as pornographic and has shown its ignorance: the commenters have not done their homework regarding the woman in the photograph or the supposed "founders" of the movement. (Attachment parenting is based on the teachings of a man who was inspired by observations made of poverty stricken indigenous women in Venezuela by a childless woman; these details escape virtually everyone's "analysis" in the buzz surrounding the story.)

Attachment parenting involves intense bonding with an infant that includes co-sleeping and "wearing" the baby through the use of slings. Prolonged breastfeeding is also part of this parenting style, which creates a default dependence on the mother's body as the sole source of care for the infant, but this can certainly be mitigated through the use of breast pumps to extract milk that the dad or partner can feed to baby. I certainly see many men "wearing" their babies these days!

The woman on the *Time* cover is Jamie Lynne Grumet. She is the author of two mommy blogs. *I Am Not the Babysitter,* which focuses the trials and triumphs of her transracial family, and *Mommy Hates Chemicals,* which reviews chemical-free beauty and cleaning products. She is also the founder of the Fayye Foundation, which "was created to aid the orphan crisis [in Ethiopia] by addressing the health, education, and vocational goals of women and mothers." Grumet, her husband, and their biological child are white, and their adopted son is Ethiopian. Although the antichemical blog is cheeky and laden with class privilege (as are nearly all of the mommy blogs out there, eco or not) and the foundation has noble intentions, many would criticize it for subscribing to the "great white hope" meme. I, however, choose to see this case as a move in the right direction. Although it is important to contemplate the role of burgeoning eco-mommas into the blogosphere and the public arena, do we instantly write off their efforts as egotistical competitiveness in the ongoing "mommy wars"? Can't they be seen as an ecofeminist stepping stone into the recognition and use of white, middle-class privilege for progressive social justice aims? Since most of the eco-mommas' parenting advice involves a reduction in consumer spending along with a search for good quality and reasonably priced goods, she is rebelling against the consumerist model. A further step in the right direction would be for her to spread her knowledge and expertise through community education projects, such as free or low-cost gardening or household management workshops at local recreation centres and community colleges.

In support of this stepping-stone idea, Greta Gaard states that "when ecofeminists speak of the interconnectedness of all natural life, they can be understood to be making a political and a spiritual statement simultaneously. The only thing left is for us to realize that" (309). In this sense, the philosophical and emotive "moms can save the Earth" motif that permeates twenty-first-century eco-mommas' everyday mothering and parenting practices does subscribe to an ecofeminist ethic.

CONCLUSION

In contemplating the life of an eco-momma, the issue that remains is the well-known pitfalls of women's acceptance of standards placed on "good" motherhood. The bar is ever rising, and though a great many women *can* handle it all, as the Jamie Lynne Grumets of the world are showing us, does not mean that they *should*. As pondered at the outset, is "buying into" the eco-momma identity setting women up for failure? Not only is an eco-momma taking on the intensive mothering style of attachment parenting, she is now going to save the entire planet from environmental destruction. It is a daunting task to take on between making the organic squash puree for her baby, maintaining a chemical free home, managing every minute and detail of her children's social and academic lives, and looking "hot" while doing it. I leave that question for you to decide. I've got to pick up the kids from school and run out to the farmers market for my veggies....

WORKS CITED

Gaard, Greta. "Ecofeminism and Native American Cultures: Pushing the Limits of Cultural Imperialism?" Ecofeminism: Women, Animals, Nature, edited by Greta Gaard, Temple University Press, 1993, pp. 300-309.

Grumet, Jamie Lynne. "FAYYE Foundation." I Am Not the Babysitter, I Am Not the Babysitter, 20 Nov. 2012, www.iamnotthebabysitter.com/the-fayye-foundation/. Accessed 26 Sept. 2016.

Lipkin, Elline. "Controversy RE: Time's 'Are You Mom Enough' Cover." The Society Pages, W.W. Norton & Company, 30 May 2012, thesocietypages.org/socimages/2012/05/30/controversy-

over-times-are-you-mom-enough-cover/. Accessed 26 Sept. 2016.
Mies, Maria and Vandana Shiva. Ecofeminism. Zed Books, 1993.
Pickert, Kate. "The Man Who Remade Motherhood." *Time*, Time Inc., 21 May 2012, time.com/606/the-man-who-remade-motherhood/. Accessed 26 Sept. 2016.
Ruether, Rosemary Radford. "Ecofeminism: Symbolic and Social Connections of the Oppression of Women and the Domination of Nature." *Ecofeminism and the Sacred*, edited by Carol J. Adams, Continuum, 1993, pp. 11-21.
Warren, Karen J. *Ecofeminism: Women, Culture, Nature*. Indiana University Press, 1997.

20. Feminist Parenting Strategies in Pakistan

ANWAR SHAHEEN

PAKISTAN IS A patriarchal, pronatalist, and multiethnic society transitioning from traditional to modern. Even as traditional family sizes decrease, motherhood continues to enjoy cultural and religious glorification. Much of parenting's value is derived from the perspective of the dominant religion of Pakistanis, Islam, which promises parents rewards in the hereafter. This reward is much greater for mothers than for fathers. The cultural notion of mother's greatness, however, is paradoxically subdued by patriarchy, which confers more social power on men, who ultimately dominate decision making, whereas women largely focus on procreation and nurturing. In this context, feminist parenting becomes an intriguing question both for practice and for research.

This chapter explores the unique ethnic mosaic of Pakistan and presents a variety of cultural notions that are unevenly experiencing change because of variegated development in different regions and among different ethnic groups, classes, and faith groups, which has resulted in great diversity. For instance, cultural attitudes approving of high standards for education and jobs for women exist alongside those that largely deny them any choice in their marriage. Sons and daughters are given unequal freedoms. Frequently, but not always, less is given to daughters. Depending on the class, culture, and intellectual level of the parents, the career and achievement aspirations for girls may override all other considerations. Such a heightened desire to give one's daughter a great education could be attributed to a feminist style of parenting, her mother's own career and educational experience, or the personality type of the child. Interestingly, some highly educated and professionally trained women who spend considerable family and government resources on their education stay home after marriage and do not show any urge for adopting a profession or becoming economically independent. They mostly remain submissive and enjoy it, too. Good education is used for homemaking and childrearing.

Cultural attitudes towards parenting are also affected by where a family lives. There are urban-rural differences that are noticeable, particularly when it comes to allowing the children of both sexes control over their lives and expressions of their own feelings and gender identity, and when it comes to showing tolerance, humanism, and critical thinking about patriarchal contents of the religion.

SOCIOHISTORICAL CONTEXT

Pakistan has inherited mixed traditions of respecting and caring for women in various capacities: mothers, wives, daughters, and sisters. Strangely, young men are taught to show greater kindness for women in blood relations than for their own wives. Marriages are arranged to ensure that wives are younger, less educated or earn less than husbands, so the balance remains in men's favour. Men, as a result, get an upper hand in marriage, whereas women struggle to assert their point of view until they get established through motherhood, which means that mothers of multiple children, preferably sons, become increasingly important with time. Wives feel empowered in the marital home and among the in-laws only on the basis of successful motherhood; all other qualities become secondary.

Women and men can raise their children from feminist perspectives, in as much as they can resist pressures from society. Nonetheless, feminist views and feminist parenting are becoming incrementally popular. Intergenerational difference is clearly visible. The older generations, though not embracing the core ideas of feminism, have been practicing "feminist-like" parenting, which is guided by their belief in human dignity and development as well as by their aspirations for their children's achievements. To the majority of families, feminism is still a "fashion" popular among educated and Westernized women and elite groups who want to "corrupt" the rest of the society by pitting all women against all men and teaching women to abandon motherhood and household roles. After a decades-long feminist movement, Pakistanis who adhere to feminism are mostly educated, aware of world affairs, and have a humanistic inclination. Interestingly, religiosity plays here a double role: both feminists and antifeminists find suitable material for their conviction in popular religious instructions; hence, it complicates the picture.

The feminist movement and activities in Pakistan have gone through somersaults during the past seven decades, from secular to socialist, then Islamic, and now a "twin-pillared feminism," which draws guidance from both secular and Islamic sources. The number of people using religious teachings as a source of inspiration and reliance for feminist messages has been growing strong—especially after 1977, with the global rise in militarism, religious fundamentalism, and extremism. In the 1980s, a strong secular and progressive feminist movement emerged in retaliation to state oppression on women. A problem then arose during the 1980s and 1990s, according to Afiya Zia, because of ambivalence about personal and religious identity of the activists. "Patriarchal fundamentalism" of the 1980s had to confront "an equally patriarchal Islamic discourse" from within the feminist movement. Zia asserts that 1980s was the time when the state in Pakistan and a section of feminists found Islam to be a tool against the onslaught of Western liberal feminism as well as communism. The consequent new religious movements grew stronger, "took on a pro-active, socio-political agenda," and became the most serious political challenge to the state (Zia 33). Their strategies of accommodating religious perspectives allowed those feminists credential who worked within an Islamic discourse, hence creating a "neo-Islamic political feminism" (Zia 33). The perceived US sponsored, Western, imperialist feminist theory has been molded so successfully that now the faith-based politics has become only framework to analyze the women's movement in Pakistan. This new kind of feminism has provided new ways of empowering women through organizational activities, advocating gender equality and pursuing justice (Zia 33). With such enhanced popularity, "there is the very [high] possibility of the fruition of such a new, radicalized, religio-political feminism dominating Pakistan's political future" (Zia 45). No doubt, the movement has now begun to hate modern technologies for their perceived involvement in the continuation of Western colonialism and imperialism (Imran). Moreover, in the post-9/11 years, two distinct contradictory positions and identities have become available to Pakistani women: "modern, liberal woman" or "Taliban-ized, regressive, conservative one," which also represent two streams in politics (Zia 31). The society is also fragmented on these lines. The same confounding reality has made Bina Shah argue that neither laws nor social codes and religious mores can guarantee Pakistani women a secure place as equal citizens to men. As all socioeconomic classes are entrapped in this 'confusion', one can imagine the grey shades in inspiration for feminist parenting.

An interesting aspect of feminist parenting can be seen in the manuals and guidebooks written by Islamist scholars for Muslim parents, which contain mostly the essentials included in feminist parenting theory discussed in the following section. This is not unusual, as religious or moral codes from different societies contain basic moral lessons, which partially concord to the feminist principles—gender equality, equity, human dignity, nondiscrimination, participation of fathers in parenting, giving freedom of choice to children, teaching tolerance, respecting others' personal freedom, boldness to challenge injustice, and the portrayal of women and men in a dignified manner. These and similar instructions, if followed honestly, can help develop balanced personalities who would be more egalitarian and open to change the traditional conservative gender stereotypes. Feminism is no new "religion"; rather it draws on the high moral values that humanity has not yet put into practice.

THEORY

This chapter draws on a liberal-feminist framework of equal opportunity and personal and political autonomy, and it attempts to examine current parental views on childrearing with feminist values. Mostly, the patriarchal nature of traditions, cultural practices, and the institution of parenthood operate in such a way that a female's entitlement to autonomy enabling conditions is reduced, resulting in an autonomy deficit. On the other hand, autonomy can be enhanced through consciously adopting feminist parenting practices. One can see that from the day of birth, patriarchal moralistic notions start governing parenting. Many choices are denied to girls under the same morality notions. Patriarchal paternalistic attitudes confine a women's right to choose. Gender stereotyping and discrimination regarding access to mobility, education, and employment have patriarchal ideology at their roots. If girls are not allowed to decide their own preferences or to explore new avenues in life, or if they experience conditions of poverty or face a higher risk of gender-based violence, then concepts of liberty and equality disappear. Parenting plays a great role in determining a child's level of social competence, psychological development, and success in academe and careers. Parental practices, behaviours, and strategies shape a child's personality according to the parent's preferences and cultural dictates.

The concept of feminist parenting can best be understood in the social conditions that gave rise to new feminism in the West. Feminist parenting was meant to change basic values and norms and to challenge the standards defining appropriate behaviour for both genders. Its major goal "was to give women as many privileges as men, while the major goal of liberation [was] the elimination of social, cultural and psychological barriers in the way of both men and women's realization" (Walters 56). So raising children in a feminist way meant teaching the feminist lesson from the very first stage of an individual's life.

Among the various styles of parenting identified by analysts, this study uses the concept of "authoritative parenting style" described by Diana Baumrind, as she focuses on the elements of responsiveness or unresponsiveness and demanding or undemanding. Her typology explains three parenting styles, but authoritative parenting is thought to be most suitable for nurturing feminist personalities of children; other styles go against the spirit of feminism. Authoritative parenting is highly demanding but highly responsive, too. Such parents try to know their children's feelings and then try to manage them. They do not often punish children but rather help them solve problems. They develop independence among children but try to regulate it as well. They communicate verbally, show warmth, and allow their children the freedom to experience life independently. They believe in positive reinforcement and mutually satisfying interaction, striking a balance between demand and response. As such parents discipline and punish with reason and encourage the right actions, this parenting style usually nurtures children to become self-confident, self-reliant, mature, generous, and responsible according to their age.

Sex role socialization is performed through two interdependent and complementary mechanisms, described by Shirley Weitz as differential treatment and identification; the latter being more overarching and effective (60-67). The standards of emotionality, reasoning, favouring, and punishing are examples of different expectations from boys and girls. This socialization differential has two dimensions: the parents' own sex-role concepts and the child's temperament and behaviour, which trigger the parents' response, both influencing each other in a complex way. Weitz holds that "a truly sex-blind socialization is an impossibility" (Weitz 67). Regarding identification, the models presented by parents are reinforced by other cultural models, such as the media, schools, and similar sources, but parents have been assigned the central role in the theories explaining socialization because of their emotional importance and continued presence. However, parents' attitudes are that of "compromise between the deeply ingrained patterns of the parent's own childhoods and sex roles identities and the pressures of the contemporary world" to change sex role (Weitz 83). Campbell Leaper has also explained early gender socialization and has confirmed that parents have a great influence on gender role socialization and if fathers are involved in housework and childcare, gender stereotyping is discouraged among such children. Similarly, children of working mothers have less gender stereotypical attitudes about the world and their own choices, even though the social environment tries to reinforce the same stereotypes. In short, androgynous parents raise children who become androgynous in their views about careers, and, hence, they can select careers of their own choice, resulting in more enjoyment and fulfillment.

As discussed by Janet Chafetz, feminist parenting is a process of changing traditional sex role stereotypes, which leads to normative changes that favour feminist thinking. What Chafetz feared about the feminist movement of the mid-1970s in the West was that "certain concessions" would be extracted from the contemporary upsurge in the feminist movement, without affecting any fundamental changes in "the sex role status quo" (Chafetz 217). The same is also observable in Pakistan in 2016, as few good laws for women's protection have been framed in recent years. The feminist movement in Pakistan does not take up the task of altering the premises underlying sex role stereotypes. The value and normative structures rest on the basis of social consciousness and on the level of challenges perceived and responded by the legislators, policymakers, educators, opinion leaders, and media managers. Challenging practices gradually take root. Although women still need to resort to legal battles in legislatures for more favourable laws, the task of feminists is to transform each and every parent's mind; a gigantic task, indeed. They must believe that what they do "with great effort and psychological cost to overcome sex role stereotypes will become ... children's habitual responses," which would then create new values, norms and, therefore, new institutions (Chafetz 221).

METHODOLOGY

A survey was conducted with forty-four people, including nineteen mothers, twenty-two fathers, and three nonmothers. A questionnaire was designed to elicit the following information: demographic data about the family, the aspirations of the sons and daughters, concepts of feminism, concepts of femininity and masculinity, impact of nurturing, the question of equal freedoms to son and daughter, and practices used to teach concepts of gender equality to children. In addition to the first sixteen structured questions, a matrix of forty questions was devised to measure feminist parenting practices for sons and daughters. Data was analyzed by simple quantitative and qualitative methods, since the subject largely depended on the perception of the respondents. Detailed discussions with nonsample parents and the researcher's own observation also proved insightful.

FINDINGS

Ethnic and Demographic Profile:

Ethnic and sectarian diversity was maintained in sampling, which included sixteen Mohajirs, seven Sindhis, six Punjabis, five Pakhtuns, two Baluchs, three Brahuis, all belonging to major sects, one Gujarati Shia, and four Ismailis. In the twenty-two sampled fathers, their ages varied: one was under thirty-six years of age; six were between thirty-six and forty-five years of age; ten were between forty-six and fifty-five years of age; four were between fifty-six and sixty-five years of age; and three—with the ages of seventy-four, eighty-five, and eighty-nine—were above this final age bracket. Relatively older fathers were selected because they had comparatively longer parenting experience than young fathers. Fathers' education levels varied: one had less than tenth grade; three had matriculate (ten schooling years) level; five had a BA; eight had a MA; four had beyond a MA; one had a degree in engineering; one had a degree in law; one had a BEd (bachelors of education); and one had an EdM (masters of education). The sampled fathers had the following occupations: teachers (twelve), civil servants (three), doctor (one), businessperson (one), journalist (one), airline manager (one), electrical engineer (one), building contractor (one), and factory worker (one). The ages of the sampled mothers also varied: four were between twenty-six and thirty-five years of age; eight were between thirty-six and forty-five years of age; eight were between forty-six and fifty-five years of age; and two were between fifty six and sixty five years of age. The education levels of the sampled mothers also varied: one had primary education; one had up to secondary level one had higher secondary; three had a BA; six had a MA; and nine had above a MA.

In the sample, there were twenty-eight (60 percent) nuclear families and sixteen (40 percent) joint families. The number of children each family had varied: fourteen families had one or two children; nineteen families had three or four children; five families had five children; and three families had seven children. There were three nonmothers in the sample: two nonmothers were raising their nieces and nephews as devotedly as mothers, and one nonmother was raising her four sisters. Since the responsibilities are the same, this category was included.

FEMINIST PARENTING PRACTICES

Table One: Conception of Feminism and Practices of Feminist Parenting[1]

(Fathers n=22, Mothers n= 22)

Theme-Question	Response Categories			
	Yes	No	Perhaps	
Are you feminist? Male Female	15 9	2 3	5 10	
Do you believe in male-female equality? Male Female	17 16	3 6	2 0	
Are women equal to men physically? Male Female	5 2	9 14	8 6	
Are women equal to men psychologically? Male Female	14 13	3 5	5 4	
Are women equal to men intellectually? Male Female	15 22	6 0	1 0	
Are women equal to men spiritually? Male Female	10 17	2 3	10 2	
Do parents make boys-girls strong or weak through nurturing? Male Female	Yes 12 19	No 1 1	Perhaps 9 2	

Did you raise your children along gender equality lines?	Very Much	Much	Somewhat	No
Male	12	3	4	3
Female	11	9	2	0
Do you approve the following practices?	Very Much	Much	Somewhat	No
Adorning girls like pretty dolls				
Male	1	4	11	6
Female	2	3	9	8
Dressing boys in simple masculine style				
Male	8	6	8	0
Female	7	5	3	7
Forbidding boys liking red or pink dresses				1
Male	5	5	6	3
Female	1	2	6	7
Disallowing boys to have girls-like makeup or have their appearance				
Male	4	4	5	9
Female	2	2	7	11
Forbidding boys playing with dolls				
Male	13	3	6	0
Female	10	4	6	2
Forbidding boys wearing bangles				
Male	6	3	4	7
Female	6	3	3	10
Disallowing girls being sporty like boys				
Male	13	2	4	3
Female	11	5	1	5
Disallowing girls adopting boyish hobbies				
Male	7	2	5	8
Female	3	1	7	11
Giving girls confidence of outdoor tasks				
Male	5	5	10	2
Female	16	2	4	0

Allowing girls ride bicycle or motorbike Male Female	 8 11	 1 1	 4 6	 9 4
Who will decide matters for children? (multiple answers)	Mother	Father	Children themselves	
Wearing dress of own choice Male Female	 13 19	 17 9	 6 3	
Choosing toys Male Female	 12 14	 19 10	 8 8	
Choosing schools Male Female	 13 18	 17 12	 9 8	
Choosing hobbies Male Female	 16 17	 16 11	 12 12	
Choosing subjects or field of study Male Female	 11 7	 19 10	 14 14	
Choosing friends Male Female	 11 15	 16 10	 7 6	
Going out independently Male Female	 8 14	 19 12	 8 5	
Using social media Male Female	 8 15	 19 10	 7 5	
Watching TV program Male Female	 9 13	 18 10	 7 6	
Choosing own gender identity Male Female	 8 13	 13 10	 5 3	
Do you mention or describe a mother's role with pride to children? Male Female	Yes 13 16	No 2 1	Somewhat 7 5	

Do you tell boys to respect women not only as women but also as humans with equal respect Male Female	Yes 13 19	No 3 0	Somewhat 6 3	
Do you let your children criticize you openly? Male Female	Yes 9 14	No 0 1	Somewhat 12 6	Children do not criticize 1 1
Telling children that women are raised as weak beings in patriarchal society so children should resist this attitude Male Female	Yes 6 9	No 3 3	Somewhat 9 9	Women are not made weak 4 1
Do you tell children about harm done to women in patriarchal culture? Male Female	Yes 5 15	No 4 3	Somewhat 11 3	It's hard to explain 2 1

Table Two: Comparison of Parenting Practices and Behaviours Adopted for Sons and Daughters Segregated by Gender of Sample Parents (Fathers n= 22, Mothers n= 22)

Practices and Behaviours Adopted for Parenting	**Father's Response about Using It**		**Mother's Response about Using It**	
	Son	**Daughter**	**Son**	**Daughter**
Psychological violence, threats, abuse, insults	7	4	11	10
Physical violence or hitting with a stick or some object	12	5	16	10
Touching child's body despite his or her disliking	7	6	8	10
Teaching children age-appropriate responsibility about their genitals	12	12	20	19

Strict training of modesty and covering of private parts	15	10	13	18
Disallowing controlling or dominating others	18	19	20	19
Disallowing derogatory remarks about other genders	16	19	17	22
Disallowing derogatory remarks about other sects	16	16	17	20
Disallowing derogatory remarks about other religions	15	16	18	20
Disallowing derogatory remarks about other ethnicities	16	17	18	20
Encouraging the breaking of stereotypical gender and sex roles among children	9	11	16	16
Teaching children that men's dominance is not natural but a social creation	10	13	13	13
Teaching children that fathers can be nurturing	16	18	18	21
Teaching children that mothers can be breadwinners	15	19	18	19
Teaching children self-respect and the love of one's personality	19	21	21	22
Inculcating sympathy and respect for others among children	18	20	19	22
Teaching ways to stop others violating (children's) own body	16	17	19	21
Parents expressing their emotions before children	16	20	19	21
Parents apologizing for their own faults and giving explanations	14	18	19	20

Encouraging children to express themselves emotionally	18	20	19	22
Teaching children to protest the wrongful actions of others	15	17	16	22
Teaching children ways to be flexible and resilient in crisis situations	19	21	20	21
Encouraging children to draw happiness through own initiative	18	20	19	20
Encouraging children to criticize what they feel wrong	15	18	18	20
Familiarizing children with diverse people, ideas, and cultures	14	17	16	18
Scolding boys for not adopting masculine attitudes	12	NA	12	NA
Disapproving girls for adopting masculine attitudes	NA	13	NA	15
Teaching children life skills for self-sufficiency	18	18	18	21
Teaching children to control their temper and telling them the best way to express anger	17	18	18	21
Telling children that God is neither male nor female	11	14	18	19
Teaching children to criticize the hurtful comments about the female body	10	11	13	16
Condemning derogatory media portrayal of women	15	13	17	17
Teaching children how to ensure justice in all walks of life	16	17	18	21
Telling children to support gender equality in all aspects	14	15	14	16

Discouraging masculine portrayal of women in media	5	5	9	15
Allowing children protest unjust adult control	6	8	11	13
Discussing openly all topics among all family members	12	11	12	15
Explaining to children reasons if parents decide against their wishes	14	19	18	21
Giving children age-appropriate home responsibility	16	19	19	22
Telling stories of great women	14	18	15	18
Column Total	494	778	553	656
Average response for 40 categories	22.5 (56.25%)	35.4 (88.5%)	25.1 (62.75%)	29.8 (74.5%)

Table two shows a comparison of responses of fathers and mothers to elaborate difference between practices and behaviours of two parents. One practice adopted by mother or father for son and/or daughter is reported under four headings. This can show which parent is stricter to which child. The average counted in the last row shows degree of adoption of a particular practice since only 'yes' response is presented in the table. Interpretation of the results is given below the table.

A simple statistical calculation of addition and averages in table two reveals that on the whole, the sample mothers' and nonmothers' score on items in conformity with the principles of feminist parenting (given in rows) is higher than the sample fathers. Both sample parents behaved in a feminist way, but fathers scored higher than mothers (total score being 1,272 and 1,209 respectively). Boys were treated more strictly by their fathers than by their mothers (score 494 and 553 respectively), whereas fathers treated their daughters more gently than mothers (score being 778 and 656 respectively). Boys were raised much less than girls on feminist lines (score 1,052 and 1,434 respectively). In a nutshell, mothers usually took more responsibility for teaching and disciplining their daughters; fathers tended to focus more on their sons. Mothers passed on the tradition of feminist motherhood more to daughters than to boys (score 656 and 553 respectively, and mothers are more egalitarian than fathers). However, women were more permissive in allowing children to break gender stereotypes by allowing them choices in plays, appearance, mobility, and so forth.

Fathers in the study allowed their daughters less freedom in outdoor activities and in the public sphere; mothers were more convinced of the importance of this practice than fathers. Fathers preferred to keep the public space for men. Qualitative answers showed that men gave the appearance of being more feminist in their claims and score, whereas women tended to be more feminist in their actual parenting practices.

ANALYSIS

Since the principles of gender relations are explained in Islamic religious texts, those who follow them can be labeled as "religious" and the rest as "secular." The sample parents had explained their concepts about being a feminist from both religious and secular viewpoints. The concept of "being a feminist" expressed by respondents having religious inclination was "giving women all rights granted within the limits of Islam." Those having secular inclinations described it as the following: "equal rights for women and men"; "total equality"; and "looking at women's issues not from gender but a human point of view." Other views alluded to these additional areas: "significance of male-female relations"; "recognizing women's contribution"; "giving women opportunity to develop and to practice their own ideas"; "equal participation in decision making"; "respect to women regardless of their relation or position"; and "striving for women's rights even if it tramples on men's rights." To facilitate those who did not know the word "feminism,"[2] an additional question was posed about their views on the equality of men and women. Interestingly, this question got more "yes" responses than from the previous question, perhaps showing respondents' aversion to the word "feminism" or their lack of awareness of the term. The belief about different aspects of gender equality varied. Explaining the perceived inequality, one man responded: "nowadays women are not oppressed, as now men are listening to them."

Now the media presents a world of knowledge to young minds. Open-minded parents feel free to discuss the topics of gender differences and equality with their children and to guide them accordingly. The children from more traditional families get such information mostly from their peer group.

DISCUSSION

This chapter focuses on four concepts: equal opportunity and autonomy, gender stereotyping, gender role socialization, and feminist parenting. In Pakistan, the concept of feminism has earned more ambivalence than popularity because the region has a deeply embedded history of patriarchal, feudal, and tribal culture. These cultures traditionally give more authority to males, and they hold a higher regard for the masculine and an accommodative and compensating attitude towards the feminine. To ensure its continuity down the generations, parenting norms predominantly reflect this patriarchal pattern.

The participants' comments regarding their concepts of feminism show how feminism is an alien, confused, and disregarded ideology for a large number of educated people. Yet much of what feminists refer to by "feminism" has been used in the parenting style of a significant number of families. But the practices of equality are not recognized or accepted as being "feminist." It is not a mainstream topic and is understood among only a small population—mostly urban, well-educated, and socially conscious people. Most local languages do not have a comparable translation for feminism. The few parents who declare themselves as feminist were largely those who were familiar with the concept and were currently practicing it. When parents were asked about believing in male-female equality, the response was clearer and more definite: a higher level of gender equality is neither conceived nor practiced. Belief in inequality is largely due to the more physical strength of males, the more emotional and expressive nature of females, and a conviction that women were not sent as prophets and are, hence, spiritually inferior. The rise of religious extremism and the conflict among Taliban Islam, prophetic Islam, and modernist Islam have made people more sensitized to the brand of Islam that they find suitable. This imbroglio has contributed to obscurantism and an antipathy about women's existence as well.

Pakistan's society seems obsessed with safeguarding the "honour' of the family, and the idea that the violation of women's chastity violates such honour is at the root of denying equal opportunities to daughters. The traditional concept of femininity prescribes raising women as kind, nurturing, altruistic, motherly, submissive, and caring. So daughters are strictly taught how to perfectly perform the adult roles of wives and mother. Socialization to established gender roles is a priority. Femininity implies weakness, submissiveness, and less competence; thus, nurturing feminine qualities among boys is discouraged. Although a growing number of parents are now allowing their daughters to become confident in public (i.e., male-dominated) space, they are not encouraged to adopt a boyish appearance, or boyish hobbies and sports, lest they appear masculine. This, however, is a less dreaded idea than of boys becoming feminine, as that would invite more criticism and a fear that boys will fail to become perfect men who are breadwinners and protectors of their family. All such findings show that feminism is a "fashion and luxury" and is practiced with confidence among only a minuscule section of Pakistani parents.

One is astonished, however, to find bold examples of men and women following feminist styles of parenting, even a century ago. The changing culture of parenting is encouraging. For instance, the mother of a Mohajir father, Iqbal (included in sample), was born in 1900. She was educated at home by some family men and grew up a true feminist, who respected difference. She raised her only son, Iqbal, to become a devoted social worker, human rights defender, and a trade unionist leader. As Iqbal said: "I got inspiration from my father's social work, who, a government servant devotedly served the community free of cost as *hakim* [indigenous healer]." Iqbal raised his two daughters and one son from a feminist perspective. The credit for this goes equally to his wife—a qualified physician and a self-made woman from lower-middle-class origins. Both parents, now in their eighties, proudly claimed that they maintained gender equality in all aspects of their parenting. Another Punjabi feminist mother, born around 1900 and who was just Quran literate, raised her four sons and only daughter also along feminist lines. Her sons followed a similar pattern; one of them is now eighty years old and has encouraged his daughters' personal development and freedom. It can be concluded that a feminist mother can raise a feminist son, but feminist parents can raise a generation of feminists. Examples of feminist fathers raising feminist daughters are abundant if one looks into the history of today's prominent women and two previous generations of Pakistanis.

Women in a patriarchal society are inclined to become feminist as a reaction as well. Feminist mothers had to assert their point of view when the fathers were not feminist; this was true in the majority of sample cases. Even the more liberal fathers did not allow their sons to become "girlish" to prevent them from being mocked in society or from becoming soft, too kind, and, most importantly, less competitive in their adult life. Conversely, girls were allowed significantly more boy-like freedom unless it endangered their chastity. So the limits and parameters of feminist parenting are clearly set out.

Other aspects of feminist parenting are related to ensuring love, care, security, comfortable marital life, and an ideal parental performance of the sons and daughters. There were sample families who cared and loved their daughters more than their sons, gave stricter punishments to boys than to girls, and who felt more aggrieved about a daughter's troubles than a son's. These families did not simply feel that their daughter was weaker, but they worried that she would become entrapped in a patriarchal system when she entered her marital home, where they could no longer protect her. Thus, feminist parents try to prepare and empower their daughters against these odds through giving them a good education and allowing them to have a career and to have a means for economic security prior to marriage. Such parents often continue to support their married daughters financially, psychologically, and practically, and this moral backing helps their daughters through hard times. Discrimination and injustice done to girls in the provision of education, freedom of choice, mobility, control over income and assets and so forth cannot be justified in any way, yet the natal family cares for them forever; thus, a "less feministic, more caring" pattern is prevalent in the majority of families across all ethnic groups. The ethnic groups are not monolithic entities, as concepts and practices of parenting within the group vary largely. The caring pattern has no conflict with religious teaching, whatsoever. So the Western concept and theories of feminist parenting need to be extended beyond a young age when applied to Eastern and Muslim societies, including Pakistan.

Sex role socialization is not showing any significant change in Pakistan. Participants in this study expressed the common fear that equalizing sex roles would result in males becoming more sensual and emotional and females becoming more rational, psychologically, and intellectually confident and competent. As parents' own insecurities also influence their parenting behaviour, they want to raise adults who fit social standards.

Ethnic differences interplay with class, urban environment, level of education of both parents, and the family culture. In the sample, for example, there is a highly educated Mohajir father with three elder sons. He was very protective and restrictive for his talented and only daughter, who is the youngest. He could afford it because the elder brothers could take good care of the sister. Their mother, a housewife, was moderately educated. Yet in another Mohajir family with highly educated parents, the mother was a full-time housewife, the children were raised on exemplary feminist principles, and the daughter was more pampered, outgoing, and liberal than her brothers. Thus, it is difficult to generalize about income, education, and feminist parenting from the sample. A highly religious Pakhtun father from the lower middle class in Swat, himself poorly educated, gave thorough religious and formal education to both his boys and girls, kept girls in purdah, avoided mixing with other people because of poverty, but let the daughters open a religious school at home where they could teach children to make an income. The daughters were allowed to interact with students' parents as well. The father believed in a simple life, strong but decent Pakhtun personality of boys, girls' sports only within the four walls of home and school, strict moral training, preserving traditional gender stereotypes, and limited communication within the family. During the interview, the daughters shared stories of women as written in the Holy Quran, and explained the concept of God being neither male nor female with the help of translation of *Sura Ikhlas* (*Al-Quran*, chapter 112).

The effects of cultural environment are seen in the responses of Punjabi, Pakhtun, and Mohajir parents who opined that children learn about their gender identity from the environment and that parents do not have to assert it. When young, boys can wear pink and red, but in adulthood that is discouraged. With changing fashion, however, most feminine colours are now seen as changing their characters. Adorning baby girls like dolls was appreciated by both parents in the sample but in a small number. In fact boys' dress was more important for the parents because a male child is more important in the culture, as one Punjabi mother said: "You know what people will say if I dress my only son as a girl, that 'you have got just one son and even then you dress him as girls." One father, who was a professor, seriously objected to his son wearing red trousers, equating it with indecency and dressing like transgender persons. Girls wearing boys-style clothing was less objected to. The rule is the following: masculinity cannot be diminished or degraded by eclipsing its elements; femininity can be upgraded by adding masculine characters. Social dictates largely determine dressing norms, and people of different classes have different environments, so they may have different levels of responsiveness to their normative environments. There are subcultures within the class subcultures, and gender-regulating norms also have ethnic subcultures, too.

There are urban-rural differences as well. Urban families are under less social pressure than the rural families. Cities have complex social structures; hence, more ethnic, cultural and ideological diversity is observable. For one, the Karachi metropolis has immense diversity and presents a continuum of models; people go there and learn more openness regarding gender ideology. Feminism is a state of mind and a way of life, and feminist parenting is an ideology and a mission thereof; thus, it has multiple dimensions, and all parents score differently on its scale, even those living in the same community.

Sample parents having sons only showed strict stereotyping, whereas sample parents of daughters only were more lenient. Gender typing of such children is thus changed as compared to families with both boys and girls. In sons-only families, the sons sometimes do household chores as well. The family with only daughters is more insecure and tries to keep a closer watch on the girls. In less common cases, such daughters are allowed more mobility and outdoor confidence, too.

A key finding of my study is the difference between male and female adults in their conviction and practice of feminist parenting. More men said that they were feminists, but their responses to the following questions erased this claim. Women were less certain about their feminist identities. However, more women than men believed in the psychological and intellectual equality between men and women. Women in the data were more realistic, as they believed that they are not equal physically, whereas men denied women's intellectual equality because to do otherwise would challenge their superiority on a more subtle level. The explanations given demonstrate how women still tend to believe that men have greater muscular strength and that women are more emotional in the time of crises.

In this sample, the women identified more with the role of nurturer in sex role socialization. With regards to gender role creation, the data revealed that women were more liberal. Men and women showed no significant difference in adorning baby girls like dolls, but men were more in favour of making boys appear strong and masculine through their clothing. Men also forbade more their sons to wear red or pink colours, to dress up like girls, or to play with dolls. Disallowing boys to wear bangles was strongly endorsed by men and women equally; in fact, this entails a strong cultural belief and has no relation with religion. Women and mothers were more willing to let girls play boyish games or have boyish hobbies, to ride bicycles or motorbikes, and to encourage them to perform jobs in the public sphere. Thus, they nurtured androgynous personalities more avidly.

Children in the study were given considerable opportunities for choosing their subjects of study, their hobbies, and their friends. Parental instruction guided these decisions. Clothing was largely selected by mothers and toys by fathers; single mothers (in cases where the husband died, deserted, or divorced), of course, had free choice. Fathers were generally reported as having more influence over all issues. However, mothers explained that their children are in their custody more frequently than they are with their fathers, which allows mothers an advantage in parenting them on a daily basis. Conversely, during interviews, fathers forcefully declared that they are in control and mothers are less powerful regarding parenting. This also shows fathers' inclination to dominate. Mothers told their boys to respect women as human beings. Fathers were more permissive in letting children criticize their parents. Mothers were more active in sensitizing their children about maltreatment meted out to women. Educating children about the role that a patriarchal society plays in presenting women as weak persons, and the subsequent teaching of children to resist such a system, was overwhelmingly a concern of women in this study; men mostly shrugged it off.

The use of psychological and physical violence methods is reported in table two. More corporal punishment was performed on sons. Their mothers more frequently delivered these punishments. In fact, women in the study generally touched children's bodies more frequently, as they were responsible for teaching age-appropriate self-care of a child's body and private parts. Modesty lessons were given more to girls by mothers and more to sons by fathers. Both children were almost equally taught by both parents not to dominate others or to pass derogatory remarks on the other gender, sects, religions, and ethnicities.

A number of feminist qualities were taught almost equally by both parents and to both sons and daughters, such as the following: breaking gender stereotyping, showing fathers in nurturing roles and mothers in breadwinning roles, resisting unjust behaviour, having temper control, and striving for justice and gender equality. Mothers and fathers equally encouraged tolerance for diverse ideas and cultures. Similarly, the children were equally taught about self-respect, self-sufficiency, to show respect and sympathy to others, to show flexibility and resiliency in crises, to be content and happy, and to stop someone from violating their body's integrity. Apart from these practices of feminist parenting, a majority of the sample parents also claimed that they apologized for their own faults, listened to children's expression of emotions, expressed their own emotions, and explained things to children when they made a decision that went against the children's wishes.

Excessive adult control over children was the least reported aspect of feminist parenting. Interestingly, mothers were allowed greater control than fathers. Perhaps, parents wanted to keep their upper hand, and not much egalitarianism was encouraged—although discussing all topics openly among family members was reported, according to children's age. In order to foster a specific feminist behaviour, children were equally told stories of great women, and, likewise, children were prohibited from being exposed to media derogatory (and masculine) portrayals of women. The children were also taught ways to respond to bad remarks about the female body and that, above all else, God has no gender—an Islamic concept. The local languages in Pakistan have no such grammatical structure, however, so God is talked about as having a masculine gender.

A future study could be designed to compare men's attitudes towards daughters and wives, since it appears that most "feminist" men have double standards for their daughters and wives. This aspect needs to be analyzed in a scientific way. Today, in many families, the father's role in parenting is minimal. However, in Pakistan, historically, periods of feminist progress have emerged from families whose brothers and husbands encouraged their female relatives to seek the public domain and to act as leaders for the feminist movement. Old social dictates were silenced by these parenting pioneers.

CONCLUSION

Pakistani parents vary in their performance of feminist parenting due to variation in their characteristics—sociocultural, ethnic, ideological, psychological, and economic. All these factors combine in a complicated fashion to define the process of parenting that differentiates between girls and boys. Even if parents consciously try to be just and fair to both daughters and sons, the net effect of environmental factors puts girls at the risk of discrimination. The authoritative parenting style, at times, may become even worse. Family life cycle phases and financial or career pressures may affect parents' level of fairness and responsiveness to their children. The Pakistani families in general do not live in isolation, so all other socializing agents contribute to shaping children's personalities, and parents feel helpless at times. Because of traditional orientation and religious instructions and despite ethnic, class, and sexual differences, parents still command and control. Even the modern communication technologies and a more liberal socialization have not completely overpowered and undermined the status of parents.

The ideal cultural dictates regarding parenting—as prescribed by Islam (basic texts or Holy Prophet's life) or by feminism (liberal in this study)—cannot be seen translated into practice fully in Pakistan. It may be an unrealistic expectation, too, yet the fact cannot give full legitimacy to the real culture. There are conceivable differences between Islam and the Western concept of feminism, hence the clash about feminist parenting. The findings of this study confirm this. Aversion to feminism is clearly visible in the survey data. Speaking feminist principles in indigenous language invites more acceptances. The extent of prevalence and permeation of Islamic feminism must be acknowledged. A partial application of Western feminism in parenting in Pakistan is, therefore, explained in the above paragraphs. Since Western feminism also embodies messages of tolerance for difference, its contents should not be expected to be applied across the world as such. Insistence on this would be tantamount to the West applying hegemonic force to non-Western societies, which are moving at their own pace, have their own moral codes, and have their own balancing mechanisms between the temporal and the spiritual. Feminist parenting, undoubtedly, may be taken as a negotiating link in this scenario.

NOTES

[1]The questionnaire was prepared in Urdu, the national language, and was used by trained observers, at least graduates, well-versed

in local languages. The author translated the information in Urdu version into English.

[2]The question was: 'What do you mean by feminism?' Those who were literate and well educated were expected to know about the word "feminism," as it is used in Urdu as well.

WORKS CITED

Baumrind, Diana. "Child Care Practices Anteceding Three Patterns of Preschool Behavior." *Genetic Psychology Monographs*, vol. 75, no.1, 1967, pp. 43-88.

Bina, Shah. "The Fate of Feminism in Pakistan." *The New York Times*, The New York Times Company, 21 Aug. 2014, www.nytimes.com/2014/08/21/opinion/bina-shah-the-fate-of-feminism-in-pakistan.html?_r=0. Accessed 29 Sept. 2016.

Chafetz, Janet Salzman. *Masculine/Feminine or Human? An Overview of the Sociology of Sex Roles*. F.E. Peacock, 1974.

Imran, Myra. "Dynamics of Feminism in Pakistan Highlighted." *The News International*, www.thenews.com.pk/Todays-News-6-58705-Dynamics-of-feminism-in-Pakistan-highlighted. Accessed 18 Oct. 2016.

Leaper, Campbell. "Parents' Socialization of Gender in Children." *Child Encyclopedia on Early Childhood Development*, CEECD, Aug, 2014, www.child-encyclopedia.com/gender-early-socialization/according-experts/parents-socialization-gender-children. Accessed 29 Sept. 2016.

The Qur'an. Translated by Tarif Khalidi, Viking, 2008. Print.

Walters, Margaret. *Feminism A Very Short Introduction*. Oxford University Press, 2005.

Weitz, Shirley. *Sex Roles Biological, Psychological and Social Foundations*. Oxford University Press, 1977.

Zia, Afiya, Shehrbano. "The Reinvention of Feminism in Pakistan." *Feminist Review*, vol. 91, no. 1, 2009, pp. 29-46.

21. The Stories and Resiliency of Aboriginal Single Mothers in University

MARLENE POMRENKE

Every story has an end, but in life every ending is just a new beginning.

—*Uptown Girls*

THE GOAL OF this chapter is to examine parenting from the perspective of single Aboriginal mothers and to explain how feminist parenting philosophy is used by these mothers during times of transition and change. Using a research study as a framework to examine the resilience of Aboriginal single mothers attending postsecondary institutions, this chapter provides information on how parenting can be both a motivating factor and a challenge to those mothers who seek a way to push back from their societal margins. Many single mothers struggle with either the social norms of marriage or not having partners to help with their children. The challenges from societal expectations, in conjunction with the day-to-day work of providing both financial security and physical care to the family, are often enormous. When mothers take on additional challenges—such as pursuing a university degree, often with little financial and emotional support—the results can be either catastrophic or rewarding.

This chapter provides insight into how a sample of single Aboriginal mothers copes successfully with the academic demands of university while dealing with racism, poverty, and childcare issues. These women were challenged to find new and innovative ways to parent their children amid trauma and adversity. As they moved into new urban centres to begin their university studies, many of these women found their way by relying on the assistance of other similarly marginalized students. Some formed self-help groups, whereas others found existing resources to help with childcare, learning methods, or financial struggles. Some had family or friends that were able to provide either instrumental or emotional support at particularly challenging times in the academic year. A few mothers used their cultural teachings as a way to gain support and guidance. Others had not even begun to understand the significance of their culture until they began their postsecondary studies.

In writing and completing research in this area, I need to point out that I am not of Aboriginal descent. Therefore, I do not have an insider's viewpoint, nor can I fully understand the complex issues of colonialism, racism, and trauma, which are often experienced by this culture and their ongoing challenges in Canada. As Michelle Pidgeon and Donna Cox suggest, "researchers must be sensitive to their own approach to ensure that inherent assumptions and guiding principles of research methodology do not increase the divide of understanding and learning from Aboriginal peoples to address collectively Aboriginal concerns and issues" (97). However, I do have these women's voices, as heard through my research, along with their permission to use their experiences as a way of helping others to create easier paths in the future. It is a privilege to hold their trust, and I share the hope that their words and experiences will guide others through similar life circumstances.

Of note, these women's drive to succeed was often attributed to their being mothers. They wanted a better life for their children. They also wanted to be good role models and teachers. However, in order to succeed, these women needed to understand the societal constraints of their situation. This knowledge became the first step to a greater awareness of their needs. This, in turn, gave them the strength to explore alternative coping strategies as they moved forward in their academic and parental journeys.

STORYTELLING

What are the barriers to Aboriginal single mothers obtaining a university education? How can these barriers be overcome? How do factors such as gender, culture, and single parenthood affect one's decision to obtain a postsecondary education? How do students cope with the combined demands of parenting, university studies, and employment? These are some of the questions that I asked the young mothers in my research study. I found answers by listening to their stories. In my clinical practice with university students, I use narrative therapy as a way of helping students to understand issues of social justice, power, privilege, race, class, gender, sexuality, age, and ability (Epston and White; Freedman and Combs; Madigan). It is a way of listening to individual stories, of both deconstructing and reconstructing that information, and then putting the information into a context outside of the individual. It helps me, as a therapist, to understand the systemic barriers and demands that often contribute to feelings of helplessness and despair. It is the first step to finding alternative ways of interpreting stories. As Madigan suggests, reauthoring conversations invigorates people's efforts to understand what is happening in their lives. The idea of hearing stories, both in a therapeutic context and through the collection of information in research, allows us to understand the history, cultural implications, and background of those we meet. Freeman suggests that storytelling can be important as an antioppressive practice among Aboriginal cultures as it offers people affirmation, connection, and cultural grounding. It also gives the listener a way of understanding the challenges within the framework offered through the story. This study fits with Freeman's antioppressive framework, as it uses a case study approach (Stake) alongside the telling of stories with the purpose of examining their context, connection, and cultural grounding.

I used this qualitative research approach to study a collective of single Aboriginal mothers in Manitoba who had made the decision to become university students. From a semistructured interview guide, the twenty participants told their stories within the framework of their challenges, their cultural views, their unique needs as single Aboriginal mothers, and their journeys into the world of postsecondary studies.

BEGINNINGS

There were various paths that led to these women to begin their postsecondary studies. They each encountered challenges but found ways around those obstacles. Oftentimes, they used the challenges to motivate themselves. Below are some of their stories. One mother stated:

> I went back to school to get my grade twelve. I had my girl who was about three at the time so I started school in September. In October, I found out that I was pregnant with my son, and it was a good kick in the butt for me to finish school because I didn't want to sit around and do nothing. I wanted to be a good example for my children. And I debated getting a job at McDonald's or something but I felt that I was better than that and decided to pursue postsecondary education.

Another mother's story is quite different, but she still talks about how being a mother influenced her decision to enter into postsecondary studies:

> I had always decided that I was going to university because both my parents went. I was going to start university, and, funny enough, I got a letter of acceptance the same day I found out I was pregnant. Being a mom was something I always wanted so I thought university could wait. As my son got older, I talked to him about what is best for our family and best for me. My son is very ambitious, and he wants a university education. So he was always bugging me and bugging me to go back to school. So I thought, okay, now is the time to do it.

One mother also spoke about her son's influence on her decision to attend university:

> I know he is little, but I want to be a good role model for him, and I want him to see that I am trying and what he has in the future is because mommy went to school, mommy worked hard, and I want him to be the same way. I don't want him to drop out of high school. I want him to attend

> university, too. So, I guess, he is kind of the reason why I came back to school; it's all for him.

The following story gives us a glimpse of how feminist thinking (i.e., questioning issues connected to gender) helped frame this mother's decision to enter into university:

> I was the first one in my family to go to university. I had always heard I was pretty, but never that I should go to university. I never really was told that I could be anything else but be good looking. I had always had this feeling deep inside of me that I knew I was meant to be bigger than a sandwich maker at Subway or a factory worker. I knew that the only way I could survive and provide for my children was to secure myself through an education. It wasn't until I actually took a feminist perspective class in school, and it helped me understand why I was the only woman in my family to try to go to university. Just seeing it from a historical perspective really allowed me to keep pushing.

In her book *A Recognition of Being*, Kim Anderson calls on Aboriginal women to resist, reclaim, construct, and act as a process of self-definition (16). She suggests that doing so provides a way of creating a positive self-image as well as a positive Aboriginal female identity. The above stories provide some understanding of how these women use their university attendance as a means to construct their identities. For example, the mother in the previous story found the strength to resist a predetermined, low-paying, and nonchallenging job. She felt that she needed to find a way to reconstruct her identity, both as a caretaker and parent and as an Aboriginal woman. Another participant added the following: "I found an appreciation and renewed energy from going to university. I enjoy working for the future because I want to provide for my babies and show them a different way of seeing our culture."

GENDER ISSUES

Although much of the information gained through these stories can be viewed through a feminist lens, some of the women took time to discuss how gender issues were part of the impetus to consider a postsecondary education. One woman stated:

> I don't want to struggle; I don't want to be working at a full-time job at a low paying job, making less than many men I see there, going from job to job because I have done that for the past seven years. I want to be able to provide for my family. I would like to do it like my mom because she did everything on her own. I always knew going back to school was the way to do it. I guess it's good because my son made me realize, okay, you need to go back to school.

Another woman felt that the teachings of being socialized as a female helped her: "I think my gender actually helped me because being a woman I had learned earlier in life how to seek help. My understanding of how the world works helped me find resources when I began university."

CHILDCARE

Each of these mothers had the primary caretaking responsibilities for their children. A few mothers received minimal help from the children's fathers, whereas others received none. Caretaking was often a struggle financially and emotionally. Here is one woman's story:

> Their father used to be around, but I felt like I was doing most of the work. Currently, we are not supposed to have any contact with each other because of a charge I made three years ago, but within those three years, we had another baby and I don't know, I tried, but I felt like I was taking care of another child because I took care of him too. I felt like I was supporting him ever since we first met ... he was just a playmate for my three boys—five, four, and two. Financially he told me he couldn't provide for me, and he also told me he couldn't help me out with staying home and looking after the boys.

Arranging childcare was one of the biggest challenges for these mothers. In addition to providing the day-to-day care of their family, they had to be extremely strategic about planning care for their children while they studied or attended classes. Many of these women were originally from rural Manitoba or another province. They found it particularly difficult to find daycare within their unfamiliar urban neighbourhoods. The following stories give us a glimpse of some of their strategies:

> My son is at daycare ... I drop him off in the late morning so I can study before my class. My son's grandmother will pick him up right after she is finished work at 3:30 p.m. and keeps him if I have an evening class. If she is not available on that evening I have to miss that class. He does not like being without me for that long, so it is hard on him and me.

> I am pretty independent, but sometimes I feel like I can't do it all ... I ask my brothers for help to watch the kids if they have the time, because sometimes I need to stay longer at school to work but the children have to be picked up from daycare.

> My baby daughter is in daycare during the day, but in the evenings I don't have anybody but myself, so whatever study time I have is very limited and whatever school activities I get involved in have to be during the day.

> I am very methodical and organized, and I am not very spontaneous so when I seriously started thinking about going back to school, I did a lot of research. A woman in my community helped me. She literally got university guides and taught and supported me so much ... she said I need to find a daycare and in my mind I knew I wouldn't attempt anything until my son was three because I know what I can and cannot do. I set it up when I knew I was receiving my Status and our community is so accepting and loving and open. When my family became Status, they just embraced us and supported me through my degree.

Although their children were motivating factors in obtaining their degrees, this mother discussed the competitiveness of the university system. As a single parent, she was not able to do as much work as a childless student. This, from her perspective, meant that she was not performing as well as the other students who lived without the same responsibilities. She explained it in the following way: "Sometimes I get envious when I see students that have no children. They can stay on campus and study and bring in the A's. I can't do this because I have to put my sons' needs first. It would be great if the university system could reflect what is happening in the world."

CULTURAL CONTENT

These women had often faced overt or inherent racism growing up and as adults. For some, it affected their ability to learn. One woman commented on this challenge:

> Because you know you are hurt and you are trying to figure out what is wrong. You really don't know when you are a kid, you don't know what racism, prejudice, discrimination, any of that stuff is and why other kids are being mean to you. You don't understand why your mind is mixed up. I dropped out of school when I was in grade nine. I was depressed for a year after that. My mom was really concerned, and it was at the point where because my room was in the basement, I would just come out at night to eat. I got really skinny, and all I would do is read, and then I decided I would go back to high school through distance education. But then my brother died.

Another woman spoke about how her decision to come to university was tied to the challenges of other Aboriginal women: "I noticed that there are many Aboriginal women that don't finish High School. My mom didn't finish it either. I wanted to do more because I wanted a higher education and I didn't just want to work anywhere. I decided to pursue accounting and go to university to find a career in it."

HEALING

The women spoke about the many aspects of healing that pursuing their university degrees provided for them. Some also used Aboriginal ways to help them in this area of their lives. One mother spoke about the difficult relationship between her and her mother and how her postsecondary studies helped to heal that relationship. She stated:

> When I was taking my undergraduate degree, I asked my mom if she could help me with the childcare when she was living in Northern BC at the time. She always wanted to go to college. She was fifty-nine. We had not really healed our relationship from everything in childhood, so I asked her why don't you come and live with me for a couple of years and go back to school and then you and I and my boy will live together. And she said okay; she's spontaneous. So she started looking into getting early childhood education, and she did it while we lived here, and we were able heal together as a family for those two years.

Many of the mothers had to find ways of connecting to others that both gave them strength as well as helped them to complete their studies. One mother described how she created her support network: "I set up my own little support system with my classmates ... there were other Aboriginal women and we all kind of supported each other. Mostly single parents too, so we studied together and figured out when our kids were okay and kind of managed that all together."

Another mother stated that she "had a very close friend who moved from our community to the city for me ... She helped me with my son if my mom was not around ... I trusted the new friends I made and could then ask them for help." One mother felt that having an Aboriginal teacher was extremely important. She said, "the real life experiences that she had, that she lived, that she was actually an Aboriginal Treaty woman that lived on the reserve, and it was just about making the connection that you felt like it applied to your own life." Being in class where the instructors respected Aboriginal teachings was important as seen through the following excerpt:

> In my course on Aboriginal Peoples, I felt I did a lot of healing. I learned about who I was and our professor was very supportive. So the curriculum provided an opportunity for all of us to learn together, because there were non-Aboriginal students too, and our professor managed the interaction very well. She made it into a respectful place for everyone in the class.

This final excerpt provides an understanding of the power of healing within the context of teaching. In her paper "Aboriginal Education and Anti-Racist Education," Verna St. Denis discusses the importance of critical race analysis, as it provides both Aboriginal students as well as the university system with the knowledge and understanding of the effects of colonialism and divisions between Aboriginal communities. She suggests that this knowledge can help to form coalitions and alliances both within and across the university system that can lead to a commitment to antiracist education.

Another woman talked about the importance of being a student and how this had led to her path of healing:

> I value being a student, I appreciate it and although you do learn a lot you can sometimes walk away without certification. I feel a lot of students lose the opportunity to finish their degree when they encounter personal barriers that have kept them behind for a long time in life. It's like the learning starts the brain to reconnect, and we start remembering things or internalizing things from past experiences in life. I know that some others have dropped out because they can't deal with this stuff, because there is no support, or they don't look for the resources they need to help them. But I found a great person to talk to when this happened to me. She is an Elder and she helps with traditional information and teaching that I needed to hear and understand. We just spent time talking. She helped me heal. She is very, very, great.

RESILIENCE

When considering the notion of resilience researchers need to think about strengths and how we move towards adapting despite difficult life situations or transitions. Michael Unger suggests that resilience can be viewed as the capacity of individuals to navigate to resources that sustain wellbeing. The concept is framed within physical and social ecologies as well as within culture. He finds that resilience is enhanced when individuals are able to negotiate with families and communities to use shared resources in culturally meaningful ways.

Although these women's stories highlight the ongoing challenges that these students experience, they also demonstrate the various resources, both internal and external, that help to mitigate these challenges. The following narratives provide more specific strategies for transitioning into postsecondary studies. The information is given through the headings of Internal and External Resources. Internal resources refer to personality characteristics, such as self-control, empowerment, self-concept, or self-efficacy. External resources refer to support systems such as family, peers, classmates, relationships, community or supports within other larger ecological systems (Masten; Miller-Karas). The following excerpts help to understand how these women use personal coping strategies as well as social support networks. It is a way of seeing both what they have included as well as the gaps in their resources. This information can help others incorporate resources into the community as a way of helping to build resilience, both on an individual level and from a systemic perspective.

INTERNAL RESOURCES

Internal resources are individual to each person but are here seen through the ways in which these mothers find the internal motivation and drive to handle challenges and find success. Examples of these are given below.

> I try to keep a journal. I remember going to see a counsellor in high school because I was dealing with a lot of

> problems there, and she suggested I keep a journal and write down everything as a way of letting things go. So I have been keeping a journal for the past ten years, and it has helped a lot.
>
> I'm very, very driven and I am far happier being too busy than not busy enough, but there have been times when I feel like I am going to lose my mind. I mean my daughter is eleven, she has basketball, and there are so many things to do. And when it gets really tense, like in the last exam period because I worked full time through exams, I actually had to force myself to look at twelve-hour chunks of time otherwise I just got so overwhelmed.
>
> When I got pregnant at seventeen everyone said, oh, "you are just going to be a welfare bum, not finish school, stay home and be lazy." I was like, "no, I'm not," and I showed them. It had a lot to do with my son. He is my main goal, and I want to do this [finish university] for him and us.
>
> I kept going because I had a structure, my routine, and staying in place because as soon as I was knocked off balance, it was really difficult to get back on track.
>
> Just knowing that coming to university every day makes me happy because it's like okay, I'm still here and I'm still doing it. Just knowing that I am one step closer helps.

EXTERNAL RESOURCES

As the following examples indicate, these mothers use various and divergent external resources. It often depends on what support systems are available or how easy they may be to access. For example, some mothers might have suffered trauma within their families of origin and cannot go to family members for support. They have to look elsewhere. Others find families or friends to be their main support, which has enabled them to move towards success. The various avenues for support are seen in each of the examples below.

> My family and the few friends I have ... talking with them [gives me support].

> I am in this saving circle program, it's helping me, we have workshops once a week where we learn how to budget, it helps me understand many things and connect with others and it saves me.

> Single moms don't necessarily have the time to research everything and I wasn't on campus enough to chat with other students. I just didn't have the time to do that. So I got the knowledge of resources through the Aboriginal Centre on campus and they are in touch with me about different places to get help, especially financial ones.

> I use my sister as a role model; she is a strong person. She looks Aboriginal, and she embraced it. She understood that our struggles are not our fault and took a leadership role; she joined a young woman's group and became a social advocate. She's a champion.

> At the university, there is a special building that is called Aboriginal House. I can go there on weekends to study. I bring my son, and he has a place to play. It is a safe haven, and we are welcome there.

> At the university I went to, there was this Aboriginal Women's Sports Centre and I met a lot of people there. When I got pregnant while I was in university, I talked to people there and got the help and connections for child care.

At times, these women's internal and external resources or coping strategies come together as way of helping them realize their potential. This is evidenced through the following stories:

> I sought help just before I was going to quit university. I knew I wasn't going to make the deadline so I thought I would just go back home. But first I went to see my instructor. He sat with me for three hours and said, "you are just below the peak of the mountain, and I want to help you get over it." He walked me through it and I need to thank him for that.
>
> I have learned that it is really important to reach out. Not to think you are only one because ... there is always somebody who has come before us, and there is always a way to strategize about how you can do it. You are smarter than you think.

These women have found ways to adapt or cope with this transition in their lives. Resilience literature suggests that individuals who are able to use multiple levels of adaptation while in the midst of transitions or adverse life situations will be the most successful at overcoming adversity. As well, external resources or programs will be most effective when they tap into these powerful adaptation systems (Masten et al). There were many examples of this premise as seen through these stories. However, these women also speak of the need for different types of resources and changes to the system that, in turn, would enable many others to be successful in their postsecondary studies. One woman commented:

> One thing that I have learned since I have been back here in the city is the amount of social issues that exist for our people. Yes, there are a lot of adaptations, and they have community-based programs addressing those specific needs, but they are almost like Band-Aids because they're not really giving any empowerment skills to these people. I would like to see some way of empowering people to recognize their abilities and see that they are worthy.

REFLECTIONS

Putting together this chapter has provided me with a way to have these women's voices heard. These women's words are a reflection of the strength, healing, and resilience that they built during their postsecondary studies. Even before they began their university studies, many needed to overcome fears and other instrumental challenges. I have attempted to show, through the structure of the chapter and through the women's stories, how both listening and reconstructing their stories are instrumental to understanding their feminist parenting. They have used their resources, both internal and external, and their cultural understandings to find ways to cope with a variety of constraints posed by their postsecondary studies.

In my role as a clinician, it is important to understand how society and other structures perpetuate social injustice and gender inequities. This helps in putting a context to the challenges and struggles of those seeking help. Many of these women had to heal from trauma, addictive behaviour, and/or other self-destructive coping strategies before they could pursue postsecondary studies. They found ways to come back from the margins of society and to move towards a new and bright future, both for themselves and for their children. As one woman said, "It's tough but, in the end, it is worthwhile, and will get me what I need and want." Some students were able to build their resilience by finding and using resources that were available. Others built on internal strengths and their inner resources to move forward. The women are role models to their children and to the rest of the community. As an example, one woman, in conjunction with the Elder that works at the university, decided to facilitate a mentor program for single Aboriginal mothers just beginning university. In her role, she talks to others about what is hard about being single mothers in university and helps them to find both inner strengths and external resources.

These women provide inspiration and hope to all who are following in their paths. It was a privilege to be allowed to hear their stories and to find a way to interpret them that reveals the resilience and hope within them. As Donna Baines states, "advocacy, organizing and activism keep us grounded in the real struggles of our communities and provide ethical and humane links between us and our clients" (66). This framework helps me in my clinical work when I spend time with mothers who are challenged because of all the inherent demands on their time. I attempt to frame their challenges within a feminist perspective and how they view themselves as mothers. I also discuss their strengths, how they can build on these strengths, what being in a university setting means to them, and what it may mean for their children. Using this strength-based paradigm allows me to see opportunities, hope, and solutions rather than just pathology and hopelessness. Through this framework and by listening to the stories of those who have travelled this journey, I avoid labelling and can help those with challenges to understand that they can advocate for themselves and their family. It is a beginning to a new story—perhaps an alliance between Aboriginal and non-Aboriginal communities in a common search for answers and change.

I want to end this chapter with some words of wisdom that one of these mothers wanted to share with others following this path:

> Take care of yourselves. Take a day out of the week that you don't have to pressure yourself with either studying or taking care of others. Self-care will save you.

WORKS CITED

Anderson, Kim. *A Recognition of Being: Reconstructing Native Womenhood.* Sumach Press. 2006.

Baines, Donna. "Bridging the Practice-Activism Divide in Mainstream Social Work: Advocacy, Organizing and Social Movements." *Doing Anti-oppressive Practice: Building Transformative Politicized Social Work*, edited by Donna Baines, Fernwood Publishing. 2007, pp. 50-66.

Epston, David and Michael White. *Narrative Means to Therapeutic Ends.* WW. Norton. 1990.

Freedman, Jill, and Gene Combs. "Narrative, Poststructuralism, and Social Justice: Current Practices in Narrative Therapy." *The Counselling Psychologist,* vol. 40, no. 7, 2012, pp. 1033-1060.

Freeman, Bonnie. "Indigenous pathways to anti-oppressive practice." *Doing Anti-oppressive Practice: Building Transformative Politicized Social Work*. Ed. Donna Baines. Halifax: Fernwood Publishing, 2007. 95-110. Print.

Madigan, Stephen. *Narrative Therapy: Theory and Practice.*

American Psychological Association. 2011.
Masten, Ann S. "Ordinary Magic: Resilience Process in Development." *American Psychologist,* vol. 56, vol. 3, 2001, pp. 227-238.
Masten, Ann S, "Resilience in Development Systems: Progress and Promise as the Fourth Wave Rises." *Development and Pyschopathology*, vol. 19, no. 3, 2007, pp. 921-930.
Masten, Ann S., et al. "Resilience in Development." *Oxford Handbook of Positive Psychology*. 2nd ed., edited by C.R. Snyder and Shane J. Lopez, Oxford University Press, 2009, pp. 117-131.
Miller-Karas, Elaine. *Building Resilience to Trauma: The Trauma and Community Resiliency Models.* Routledge. 2015.
Pidgeon, Michelle, and Donna G. Hardy Cox. "Researching with Aboriginal Peoples: Practices and Principles." *Canadian Journal of Native Education*, vol. 26, no. 2, 2002, pp. 96-200.
St. Denis, Verna. "Aboriginal Education and Anti-Racist Education: Building Alliances across Cultural and Racial Identity." *Canadian Journal of Education*, vol. 30, no. 4, 2007, pp. 1068-1092.
Stake, Robert. *Case Study Methods: Design and Methods*. Sage Publication, 2013.
Unger, Michael, "Resilience across Cultures." *British Journal of Social Work*, vol. 38, no. 2, 2008, pp. 218-235.

22.
Lone Motherhood in Poland

IZA DESPERAK

IN POLAND, women are typically expected to be financially independent. Regardless of their relationship status, a woman is responsible for 100 percent of the economic support of their children. As a result, mothers frequently play the role of both parents. A study of single parenting in Poland reveals a model that is somewhat exceptional to other places in the world. Although this model may appear to be feminist in nature, parenting without fathers, in reality, is not necessarily the decision of an empowered, independent woman. Instead, motherhood is a product of a culture that defines women as sole parents and that gives men the option either to play the father's role or to abandon it. This phenomenon is the result of a very particular definition of gender roles, in which femininity is associated with motherhood, yet masculinity has very little association to parenthood.

Fathers abandon their children in many ways: by never marrying the mother, by divorcing her and abandoning his children, or by staying together with his wife and children but not actively parenting. Polish fathers can refuse to provide financial and parental support for the children without facing consequence. It is significant, then, that the Polish term for single mother is "lone mother" (*samotna matka*). It highlights the abandonment of a mother and her children by society, not necessarily her single marital status.

Fully understanding the Polish concept of lone mothehood requires examining its sociocultural and historical foundations. It may be contextualized through three phenomena: Catholicism and patriotism, resulting in the figure of the "Mother Pole"; a Soviet political past; and a neoliberal model of political transition.

CATHOLICISM AND PATRIOTISM: THE EMERGENCE OF THE MOTHER POLE

The Catholic Church and its teachings have been a significant force in shaping female identity in Poland. Devotional practices to honour Mary, the Virgin Mother of God, are very popular, especially among women. Images of Mary, such as the Black Madonna of Częstochowa, are found throughout the country, and there are an estimated seven hundred shrines devoted to Mary. May is traditionally Mary's month, offering pilgrimages, celebrations, and devotions. According to Inga Kuźma, many pregnant women offer prayers to Mary to ease the pains of delivery. Women in the country traditionally pray around the small chapels in the fields, often without the priest.

Polish motherhood has likewise also been shaped by the turbulent events in Poland's political history. As Bozena Tieszen explains:

> The partition of Poland in the eighteenth century and subsequent Polish uprisings against the occupying powers led to the creation of a symbolic self-sacrificing maternal figure of courage and great moral strength, referred to as Mother Poland after a poem by Adam Mickiewicz, "Ode to Mother Poland" [*Oda do Matkipolki*]. (220)

Mother Pole (*Matka Polka*) is a unique Polish definition that encompasses both motherhood and patriotism. Written and published after the fall of the first national uprising against partition (1830-1831), the poem addresses mothers and encourages them to follow the sacrificial example of Our Lady of Sorrows. Mothers are scripted to save Poland by taking responsibility for the patriotic and spiritual education of their children. With the vast support and adoration of political and religious leaders alike, the Mother Pole as the model for the ideal maternal identity endured a hundred years.

The Black Madonna of Częstochoswa (Wikipedia).

Poland, as a state, disappeared in 1772 and only regained independence in 1918. Polish identity, culture, and language survived under the guardianship of the Catholic Church. The Church continued to rely heavily on mothers to teach the Polish language and to pass on Polish culture within the home. Furthermore, mothers were expected to foster a new generation of Polish patriots who would continue to fight for Polish independence.

During the partition of Poland, women often accompanied their husbands during their military missions and in the Far East borderland, women often took part in battles alongside men. Emilia Plater fought in the November 1830 Uprising and received the rank of captain in the Polish insurgent forces, which is portrayed in the poem *Śmierć pułkownika (Death of a Colonel*). During the second uprising in 1863, Maria Piotrowiczowa, who fought while pregnant, died in the battle of Dobra. After this incident, Polish leaders forbade women to fight with the Russians. The role of "patriot soldier" for Polish women was once again replaced by the role of "patriot mother."

Subsequent uprisings during the First and Second World Wars resulted in a renewed appeal for the Mother Pole. These wars saw many men imprisoned, exiled, or killed. The scale of single motherhood became vast, and a culture of mother-widows was the result. In 1945, Poland joined the Eastern Block and the future coalition of counties under the Soviet influence. For some, it meant another foreign occupation, but the Soviet influence also brought the rudiments of a secular state that included civil marriage, divorce, legalized abortion in 1956, and equal rights for children born out of wedlock. During this time, single motherhood lost its taboo, and women could always pretend that their husbands died during the war.

THE RISE AND DECLINE OF THE STATE ALIMONY FUND

Forced, fast industrialization, accompanied by the emancipation of women and scarcity of men, resulted in increased single motherhood. The financial impact of the high rates of single parenthood was rarely investigated, since research on poverty was censored, even in academic publications. Still, the vast number of children not receiving any alimony from their fathers was alarming. The level and scale of poverty experienced by single mothers and their children was significant enough that the state deemed it necessary to intervene.

It was under socialism, in the 1970s, when the problem of absent fathers was discovered in Poland. By 1974, the state decided to address this problem. The solution that the socialist state came up with was to make having a job obligatory and to constitutionally guarantee equality for children born out of wedlock. The state also introduced a special fund to pay alimony to women in advance, and then use the courts, police, and administrators to get the money back from fathers by garnishing their salaries from the state controlled companies that they worked for.

In 1989, the process of democratic transition was started in Central Eastern Europe. It meant a redefinition of gender roles, as Barbara Einhorn observed: "Transformation in East Central Europe is serving to retrench women, displacing them from participation in the labor force and planting them squarely back in the family, their primary sphere of responsibility" (Einhorn 5).

In Poland, the transition to democracy included an introduction to a market economy and a labour market. This shift complicated the state's ability to pressure fathers to have a job and to pay alimony. The Polish citizens then had to find their own work, since their government no longer provided them jobs. Many families faced unemployment. Not surprisingly, this had a impact on the alimony fund. By 1996, employers were no longer required to retrieve alimony money directly from a father's salary. During this time, the Polish alimony fund went into debt. State institutions continued to pay mothers the alimony that fathers did not pay, whereas the state bailiff was no longer able to track fathers in order to get the money back.

By 2000, the alimony fund money had been guaranteed only to families whose monthly income per capita was not bigger than sixty percent of the average salary. Since alimony was welfare for the poorest, thousands of mothers appealed to the courts for alimony that kept up with inflation. For example, alimony of 10,000 zlotys—a figure decided by the court in late 1980s as proper alimony—was still enough to buy two pairs of cheap tennis shoes in the 1990s. However, by 1995, after the devaluation of Polish currency, 10,000 zlotys was not enough to buy a newspaper.

In 2002, the average monthly alimony paid by the fund was 22,489 zlotys, which amounted to 12.7 percent of the average salary at the time. The alimony fund was able to collect 62.8 percent back from fathers in 1980, 67 percent in 1989, and 12.3 percent in 2002. The poor financial efficiency of the Alimony Fund finally caused it to close down on May 1, 2004, the same day that Poland became a member of the European Union.

THE NEOLIBERAL MODEL OF POLITICAL TRANSITION

The financial crisis of the alimony fund was met by neoliberal ideology, which announced that the state was no longer going to be responsible for the debts of irresponsible fathers. Jolanta Banach, the co-minister of work and welfare at the time frankly declared, "the state is not a father" (Kalukin). What is interesting is that the reductions in automatic alimony guaranteed by the state to mothers for children was explained as necessary because women often started new relationships with men who replaced the father. The poorest single mothers who could prove extremely low income were offered a low allowance of 170 zlotys or 40 euros instead.

Today, single mothers are still socially excluded. Right-wing politicians label single-parent families "pathological," and many citizens share this attitude. Public discourse on the topic of alimony has recently created a new trope: the "mother con artist." This is a figure of a mother having children to get some free money from welfare. Poor mothers are presented as parasites on society. This figure promotes the neoliberal virtues of self-sufficiency and non-government support as a model for what is considered a successful life, whereas those, such as single mothers (and their children), who need government assistance are defined as problems. Today, popular and public discourse about single mothers put all the responsibility on them to raise their children without adequate support. Single mothers in Poland are raising their children in poverty and in miserable conditions. The legacy of the Mother Pole has all but disappeared. Today, there is very little social compassion for these mothers and little support from the state.

This decision to close the alimony fund was not accepted by single mothers. As Renata Hryciuk and Elżbieta Korolczuk note, a very marginal and weak movement against closing down alimony fund was formed. The movement had some support from some groups, such as anarcho-feminists in Lublin, Lodz Gender in Lodz, the tabloid *Super Express* and a Catholic prolife organization in Lodz, and later from two political parties: *Prawo i Sprawiedliwość* (Law and Justice) and *Samoobrona* (Self-Defense). The mothers' movement not only organized protests, but they drafted a governmental bill to bring back the alimony fund. The bill project included some significant corrections, such as regionalizing it to make it more efficient.

The mothers' movement managed to gather the 100,000 signatures needed to submit the bill to parliament. It took until 2007 for parliament to accept the bill. The new alimony fund began in 2008 but it did not change much in the everyday life of single mothers. In 2015, only between 8 and 20 percent of alimony decreed by the court was paid (Chełstowska et al.). More than 80 percent of alimony decrees are not effective, and both the social and legal system ignore this problem. Mothers care for children without the financial resources necessary, whereas fathers choose whether or not they wish to participate in the economic and social responsibility of raising a family.

The legal system in Poland supports unequal parenting: fathers can choose to participate, mothers cannot. A questionnaire by the Center of Women's Rights, conducted in 2004, showed that bailiffs, responsible for garnishing alimony from men, often colluded with fathers, helping them to avoid paying. Their friends, relatives, and new partners support fathers who do not pay alimony, as there is no stigma to not paying alimony.

ABSENT FATHERS AND LONE MOTHERS

Iwona Chmura-Rutkowska and Joanna Ostrouch who study middle-class men in midlife have found that they practice a dominating "traditional" conservative family model. Married women, when asked about their self-identity, significantly more often than men, define themselves through parenthood (Titkow et al 166). Elizabeth Dunn—an American anthropologist who has conducted her research in a factory in the region of Rzeszów that had just been privatized and sold to an international company specializing in baby food—shows that female workers strongly self-identified as mothers or mothers-to-be; they, thus, felt quite responsible for the quality of baby food, as if they were preparing it for their own children.

A majority of couples in Poland practice a traditional model of the family. They consider women as the main person responsible for the children and household. The model of male breadwinner, on the other hand, is rarely practiced. Today, there are many families in which men do not contribute financially. Under socialism, the popular solution was for a wife to collect his salary directly from the company that he worked for. Today, obstacles to male family support include unemployment and economic migration by fathers who stop sending money and/or visiting their families.

The modern day Polish adjective "feminist" has a pejorative resonance, and single motherhood remains disassociated from the word. Instead, being a feminist is very much considered to be a free choice that women make. Single mothers are sometimes called "feminist," but it is a sort of an insult. Female judges, working for civil courts, are frequently called feminist because they are considered responsible for everything that is bad in society.

If the Polish model of lone motherhood is unique, it should be described as an anthropological curiosity only. It is so exotic to Western readers that Polish researchers find it difficult to describe it in Western language or explain it to the listeners during international conferences. However, colleagues from Russia and some post-Soviet countries, such as Ukraine, understand it quickly. This similarity of experience may suggest that this model of sole motherhood is a result of a shared experience with Soviet policies. That is why, after several years of neglecting lone motherhood, there is today a renewed social campaign to advocate for alimony pay. This is the first time in years that single mothers are not alone.

NOTES

[1]The author is responsible for all Polish-to-English translations.

WORKS CITED

Center for Women's' Rights. *Alimentare znaczy jeść [Alimentare Means Rating]*. Center for Women's Right, 2004

Chmura-Rutkowska, Iwona, and Joanna Ostrouch. *Mężczyźni na przełęczy życia. Studium socjopedagogiczne [Men in Life Peak. Sociopedagogical Studium]*. Wydawnictwo Impuls, 2007.

Chełstowska, Agata, et al. "Ojcowie mogą, matki muszą. Dlaczego tolerujemy niepłacenie alimentów" ["Fathers Can, Mothers Have To. Why Do We Tolerate Not Paying Alimony?"]. Kultura Liberalna, Kultura Liberalna, 2016, kulturaliberalna.pl/2016/01/04/alimenty-zakowski-wywiad-komentarz/. Accessed 27 Sept. 2016.

Dunn, Elisabeth. *Privatizing Poland: Baby Food, Big Business, and the Remaking of Labor*. Cornell University Press, 2004

Einhorn, Barbara. Cinderella Goes to Market: Citizenship, Gender and Women's Movements in East Central Europe. Verso, 1993.

Hryciuk, Renata Ewa, and Elżbieta Korolczuk. *Pożegnanie z Matką Polką? Dyskursy, praktyki i reprezentacje macierzyństwa we współczesnej Polsce [Farewell to Mother Pole? Discourses, Practices and Representations of Motherhood in Contemporary Poland]*. Warsaw University Press, 2012.

Kalukin, Rafal. "Państwo nie jest ojcem" ["State Is Not a Father"]. Interview with Jolanta Banach. Wysokie Obcasy, supplement to Gazeta Wyborcza, 8 Nov. 2003, p. 44.

Kuźma, Inga B. "Maryja jako prefiguracja kobiety, Wizerunek Maryi w literaturze antropologicznej, Maryja: siostra - przyjaciółka - matka – święta" ["Mary as Prefiguration of a Woman, Mary's Image in Anthropological Writing, Mary: Sister-Friend-Mother-Saint"]. *Współczesna religijność kobiet. Antropologia doświadczenia [Contemporary Religiousness of Women. Anthropology of Experience]*, Seria "Archiwum Etnograficzne," vol. 46, 2008, pp. 301-346.

Tieszen, Bozena. "Matka Polka (Mother Poland) and the Cult of the Virgin Mary." *Language and Religious Identity*, edited by A. Jule, University of Glamorgan Press, 2007, pp. 220-228.

Titkow, Anna, Danuta et al. *Nieodpłatna praca kobiet. Mity realia perspektyw [Unpaid Women's' Work: Myths, Reality, Perspectives]*. Wydawnictwo IFiS PAN, 2004.3

About the Contributors

Elizabeth Ann Bartlett is a professor of women, gender, and sexuality studies at the University of Minnesota Duluth. Her areas of specialization are feminist thought, ecofeminism, spirituality, and motherhood. She is the author of several books and articles, including *Rebellious Feminism: Albert Camus's Ethic of Rebellion and Feminist Thought*. She is the mother of one son.

Jana Bühlmann has written several brief biographies over the past few years in her advocacy work as a bald woman and as a woman thriving with the disease alopecia areata. She has never written a biography for herself as a mother, yet it is the pivot point that has provided her with her own life. Several years ago, she created a photo book of images taken by her and her daughter, and this bit of prose likely best represents who she is in this regard.

Lesley Bunnell lives, works, and writes in Providence, RI. She and her thirteen-year-old daughter share their old, creaky house with a brother and sister cat duo named Mr. Pibb and Rihanna, a one-year-old pit bull rescue named Bernie, and a lots of dust bunnies.

Lynn Comerford is a sociologist and professor of human development and women's studies at California State University, East Bay, where she is director of women's studies. Her areas of specialization are social theory, sociology of the family, and parenting rights. She is the co-parent of one daughter. She can be found on Twitter @lynncomerford.

Iza Desperak works as the chair of sociology of politics and morality at Lodz University. She is a sociologist of gender and deals with reproductive rights (particularly the ban on abortion), and the feminization of poverty. She has also published a book on the gender dimensions of democratic transition in Poland (2013, Lodz University Press).

Shannon Drury is the author of the memoir *The Radical Housewife: Redefining Family Values for the 21st Century*. She writes a column for the Minnesota Women's Press and her writings have appeared on numerous websites and anthologies.

Lucy Hare is a Toronto-based artist who enjoys working in different mediums. She addresses themes of gender, sexuality, and mental health in her work. She explores both figurative and abstract painting styles. She has been a student at OCAD University since September, 2015.

Heather Jackson, a former teen mom, is now a thirty-something single mom of a teen. She is a former site producer of *girl-mom.com*. Currently, she works as a birth doula, case manager of pregnant and parenting teens, bicycle-youth instructor, and community organizer in the Upper Northeast. She recently published a chapter in *The Bakken Goes Boom* regarding maternal and child health issues related to the oil boom in North Dakota (where she grew up). Her writing has also been published on websites—*thepushback.org, hipmama.com, girl-mom.com, muthamagazine.com*—in books (including Demeter Press), and in zines (ramonegirl on etsy). She bikes everywhere, plays guitar in an all-female punk band called Cramptown Mayors, and is an anarchist.

Sara Hardin Keeth is a lecturer at the University of Texas at Dallas. Her current research centres on maternity in Shakespeare's English history plays. In addition to her work on maternity and Shakespeare, Sara writes fiction and nonfiction. She and her husband are the feminist parents of two boys.

Kandee Kosior is a feminist mother with special research interests in women and the law, moral regulation, women's human rights, and motherhood. She has a BFA from the University of Regina, a BA in criminology from University of Toronto and is a graduate of the Women's Human Rights Education Institute, OISE/UT. She is a longstanding member of ARM and MIRCI, where she has guest edited JARM's *Mothers and Daughters* in 2008 and JMI's *Mothering Violence, Militarism, War and Social Justice* in 2010. She is currently on the editorial board for the inaugural issue of the Museum of Motherhood's *Journal of Mother Studies* (JourMS).

Mae is a feminist young woman and student in anthropology and sociology. She hopes to become an activist and advocate for children and young people who have lived with, or are living with, domestic violence. She plans to use her experiences as an adult survivor of domestic violence to raise awareness about the issue.

Gabrielle McNally is an assistant professor of digital cinema at Northern Michigan University. She received her MFA in film and video production at the University of Iowa. Both McNally's scholarly and creative work explores memory, performance, autobiography, and gender with an emphasis in poetic text. Her work has appeared internationally.

Quincie Melville teaches and mentors students in the Women's History Week Program at her school, which empowers them to bring the stories of women's importance in society to younger classmates. She was chosen to be the mother of her son by his birth mother, which she considers her greatest gift in life.

Marilyn Metta is a feminist academic at Curtin University, and a practicing psychotherapist at the West Leederville Counselling Centre, Perth. She's the founder of *Mettamorphosis Inc.* Her research interests are feminist philosophies, life writing, family and domestic violence, Asian-Australian studies, human rights, asylum seekers, and refugee issues.

Rachel O'Donnell is a doctoral candidate in political science at York University, Toronto. Her ongoing work is on feminist critiques of science, colonialism, and biotechnology. She has lived and worked in Latin America, and has previously published on Sor Juana de La Cruz, revolutionary movements, migration, and mothering, as well as a few works of short fiction.

Andrea O'Reilly is professor in the School of Gender, Sexuality and Women's Studies at York University. O'Reilly is founder and director of *The Motherhood Initiative for Research and Community Involvement*, founder and editor-in-chief of the *Journal of the Motherhood*, and founder and editor of Demeter Press. She is co-editor or editor of nineteen books, including most recently *This Is What a Feminist Slut Looks Like: Perspectives on the SlutWalk Movement* (2015); *Mothers, Mothering and Motherhood across Cultural Differences:A Reader* (2014); and *Academic Motherhood in a Post Second Wave Context: Challenges, Strategies, Possibilities* (2012). O'Reilly is author of *Toni Morrison and Motherhood: A Politics of the Heart* (2004), *Rocking the Cradle: Thoughts on Motherhood, Feminism, and the Possibility of Empowered Mothering* (2006), and *Matricentric Feminism: Theory, Activism, and Practice* (2016). She is editor of the first encyclopedia (3 volumes, 705 entries) on motherhood (2010). She is a recipient of the CAUT Sarah Shorten Award for outstanding achievements in the promotion of the advancement of women in Canadian universities and colleges; is twice the recipient of York University's "Professor of the Year Award" for teaching excellence; and in 2014, was the first inductee into the Museum of Motherhood Hall of Fame.

Kate Parsons is professor of philosophy at Webster University, St. Louis, Missouri in the United States. She currently serves as chair of the Philosophy Department and director of the Women and Gender Studies Program. She teaches a range of courses in feminist theory, sustainability studies, and ethics.

Marlene Pomrenke has been on faculty at the University of Manitoba for the past eight years. Her research interests include resilience, parenting, international adoption, and mental health. She enjoys her work with postsecondary students and uses a narrative and feminist lens both in research and clinical work.

Emily Powers is a first year undergraduate student in the Northrop Frye stream of the Vic One program in Victoria College at the University of Toronto. When she is not nose deep reading novels, she enjoys writing, painting, sewing, and exploring Toronto.

Pamela Morgan Redela is lecturer faculty in the Women's Studies Department at California State University, San Marcos. She also teaches Spanish language, literature and culture courses for National University. Her research interests include ecofeminism, women's organizing around femicide in Guatemala, and all aspects of feminism and family life.

Anwar Shaheen is a professor of sociology at Pakistan Study Centre, University of Karachi. With degrees in Pakistan studies (Karachi) and a MA in gender and development (Sussex), she has published three books, twenty-three research articles, and six chapters in refereed volumes. Her special areas of interest are gender, culture, social change, civil society, and displacement.

Cassie Premo Steele is the author of thirteen books, including four poetry books. Her poetry has been nominated three times for the Pushcart Prize, and she was recently a finalist for the 2016 Joy Harjo Poetry Award. She teaches a course combining mindfulness and feminist theory for women academics called The Feminar. More info can be found at www.cassiepremosteele.com.

Johanna Wagner is a visiting associate professor of English Literature at Høgskolen i Østfold in Halden, Norway. Wagner's primary fields of research are modern British and American women's fiction, feminist, gender, lesbian theory, and criticism, with secondary fields of research in narrative, affect theories, and representations of women in visual culture and the gothic.